Heroes and Revolution in Vietnam

Heroes and Revolution in Vietnam

Benoît de Tréglodé

Translated by Claire Duiker

NUS PRESS
SINGAPORE

IRASEC
INSTITUT DE RECHERCHE SUR L'ASIE DU SUD-EST CONTEMPORAINE
RESEARCH INSTITUTE ON CONTEMPORARY SOUTHEAST ASIA

Published by NUS Press in association with IRASEC

Published by:

NUS Press
National University of Singapore
AS3-01-02, 3 Arts Link
Singapore 117569

Fax: (65) 6774-0652
E-mail: nusbooks@nus.edu.sg
Website: http://www.nus.edu.sg/nuspress

ISBN 978-9971-69-554-5 (Paper)

National Library Board, Singapore Cataloguing-in-Publication Data

Tréglodé, Benoît de.
Heroes and revolution in Vietnam / Benoît de Tréglodé; translated by Claire Duiker. – Singapore: NUS Press, c2012.
p. cm.
Includes bibliographical references and index.
ISBN: 978-9971-69-554-5 (pbk.)

1. Heroes – Political aspects – Vietnam (Democratic Republic). 2. Hero worship – Political aspects – Vietnam (Democratic Republic). 3. Patriotism – Vietnam (Democratic Republic). 4. Vietnam (Democratic Republic) – Politics and government. I. Duiker, Claire. II. Title.

DS560.6
959.704331 — dc22 OCN742519245

Cover: Vietnamese propaganda poster in the 1960s (detail).

Typeset by: Scientifik Graphics
Printed by : Mainland Press Pte Ltd

To Emile Brindejonc de Bermingham,
Yves-Marie and Alain Brindejonc de Tréglodé,
who spent time in Vietnam, respectively, from
1859–1861, 1888–1889 and 1953–1954.

Contents

List of Maps and Figures

Archival material is from VNA, Vietnam News Agency; photographs are by the author.

Foreword

The study of the history of Vietnamese communism has declined markedly since the Cold War ended in 1991 and the battles for Vietnam fade ever further into the past. Setting aside the never-ending biographies of Ho Chi Minh,[1] one would be hard pressed to find in 2011 a new history of Vietnamese communism. Scholarly interest has moved on to new topics. This is a natural tendency in any field and a good one at that. However, one unfortunate result in the case of Vietnamese studies is that our understanding of Vietnamese communism, as well as the wars that shaped it, has remained stuck in something of a time warp — a prisoner of the debates dividing scholars of the "Vietnam generation" over the legitimacy of Western intervention in Indochina.

On the one side are those who supported the Democratic Republic of Vietnam's (DRV) struggle for independence against French and American intervention. For these mainly Western-based writers, the communist core of this government and its links to Beijing and Moscow were less important than the fact that Ho and his entourage were the "authentic" nationalists fighting for the just cause of national liberation. It was vain for the French and the United States governments to intervene against the DRV, for it enjoyed the overwhelming support of the Vietnamese people. On the other side are those who downplayed and even denied the DRV's nationalism, focusing instead on its expansionist, totalitarian, and internationalist communist character. Ho was not the "father" of the nation, as the orthodox school would have it, but the Comintern's point man for promoting communism in Southeast Asia. For these revisionists, American intervention to protect Vietnam from communism was thus fully justified. To this day, battles still rage between "orthodox" and "revisionist" scholars who clash

[1] Daniel Hémery, Pierre Brocheux, William Duiker, Sophie Quinn-Judge, and Martin Grossheim have published the most recent biographies of Ho Chi Minh (Brocheux penned two!).

over the meaning of Western involvement in the Vietnam War and the nature of the Vietnamese communist state.[2]

Fortunately, new studies inevitably come along to provide a new take on a seemingly worn-out topics. Anthropologists Heonik Kwon and Shaun Malarney have done just this with their landmark studies of the "war after the war".[3] Each of these authors published theoretically sophisticated and remarkably insightful socio-cultural studies of the "lives of the dead" left behind by the wars and explored contesting village and party-state efforts to console, commemorate, and legitimate. Neither of these young scholars got bogged down in the stale debates of the past. Instead they take our understanding of Vietnamese communism and the wars that drove it to new analytical and theoretical heights. What is more is that they did it based on impressive fieldwork in Vietnam.

French historian, Benoît de Tréglodé, has done something just as important in this path-breaking study of Vietnamese communism, *Heroes and Revolution in Vietnam*.[4] Whereas Heonik Kwon and Shaun Malarney focused on how local communities sought to devise ways to solve major existential questions ignored or manipulated by the Party-State, namely the religious rituals essential to putting to rest the wandering souls of loved ones killed in war, Benoît de Tréglodé focuses instead on how the Party created a pantheon of "new heroes" — among the living and the dead — as part of its wider project to mobilize for war, forge a new bureaucratic elite, and remake the society in the image of the communist creed, between 1948 and 1964. Like his anthropologist colleagues, de Tréglodé's is no *histoire événementielle*. This study is theoretically informed, analytically nuanced, and interdisciplinary in its approach.

---

[2] See Peter Zinoman's insightful, post-revisionist assessments of Mark Moyar's revisionist and Mark Bradley's orthodox accounts of the Vietnam Wars at <http://www.h-net.org/~diplo> [accessed 25/11/11].

[3] Shaun Malarney, *Culture, Ritual and Revolution in Vietnam,* London: Curzon Press, 2003 and Heonik Kwon, *After the Massacre: Commemoration and Consolation in Ha My and My Lai,* Berkeley: University of California Press, 2006.

[4] *Heroes and Revolution in Vietnam* first appeared in French in 2001 (L'Harmattan), the product of Benoît de Tréglodé's doctoral dissertation at the École des Hautes Études en Sciences Sociales in Paris under the direction of Yves Chevrier, specialist of communist China. However, the English-language version here is more than a simple reproduction of the earlier French version. De Tréglodé has updated and revised large parts of the original manuscript. He also incorporated new field research which he conducted since the publication of the French version.

In a fine opening chapter, the author provides an insightful account of "heroism" in Sino-Vietnamese culture and in Vietnam before situating his analysis of the Democratic Republic of Vietnam's attempt to import the "new hero" (*Anh hùng mới*) from the communist world starting from 1948. On the one hand, he analyzes expertly how this model borrowed from the communist world was adjusted to a Vietnamese context. On the other hand, he explains how the Party-State sought to use it into the 1960s to mobilize and transform the society along increasingly communist lines pushed by the communist core. If scores of scholars of earlier generations have focused on "nationalism" and "communism", few if any have truly explored the Party's use of "emulation campaigns", "new heroes", "rectification", and the mobilization of the "heroes". Indeed, heroes, coming from the living and the dead, are at the center of de Tréglodé's story. In so doing, he has opened up a whole new way of studying and understanding communism as a socio-cultural, transformative project. And while it has never been his goal (and he is right in my view), his book helps us move beyond the overused binary debates of the past and rethink Vietnamese communism, and even the wars, in entirely new ways.

It is a fascinating account based like no other account in French and English on primary sources coming from Archives no. III in Hanoi — many have claimed to have used such archival sources; Benoît de Tréglodé actually did it. What makes this book even stronger in methodological terms, again like those penned by Malarney and Kwon, is that de Tréglodé did not remain trapped in the world of the Party-State, holed up in the archives, or a prisoner of trendy discourse and theory. This French scholar got on his motorbike and conducted scores of interviews with local officials, villagers, and with "new heroes" themselves. It is a fascinating read.

We should also thank Claire Duiker for her expert translation of what was a very difficult French text to translate. *Heroes and Revolution in Vietnam* is an outstanding piece of scholarship — original, very well written, impressively researched — and makes a major contribution to Vietnamese, Southeast Asian, communist, war, and memory studies. For me, this book goes right up there next to the ones recently published by Heonik Kwon and Shaun Malarney.

Christopher E. Goscha
Professor of International Relations
Université du Québec à Montréal

Acknowledgements

I would like to pay tribute to the memory of Professor Denys Lombard (1938–1998), without whom this work could never have been done. I remember his invaluable help during my fieldwork in North Vietnam, his unique and fascinating character, his scholarly work, and his passion for Asia. I thank all those who accompanied me during my years on the road. In France: Pierre Brocheux, Yves Chevrier, Jean-Luc Domenach, Alain Forest, Daniel Hémery, and Hugues Tertrais. In Vietnam: while I am not able to cite all of those who encouraged me with their friendship and advice, I would like to mention here Professors Phan Ngọc, Hoàng Cao Cương, Hoàng Văn Hành, and Bùi Đình Thanh, as well as Phan Thế Hồng, Hoàng Nguyên, Mai Nam Thắng, Vũ Thị Minh Thắng, and particularly Lan Anh. I am also indebted to everyone at the École française d'Extrême-Orient (EFEO) in Hanoi and the Institut de Recherche sur l'Asie du Sud-Est contemporaine (IRASEC) in Bangkok. I am also grateful to the Centre for Vietnamese Studies and the Academy of Sciences in Moscow for their welcome and support during my trips to Russia, especially to Vladimir I. Antochtchenko, Anatoli A. Sokolov, and Paul Noujaim; the Collegium Budapest in memory of Diana Masson, Ferenc and Vera Eros; the Nordic Institute of Asian Studies in Copenhagen; the Centre of Asian Studies in Amsterdam (IIAS); the Groupe d'études sur le Viêt Nam contemporain à Sciences Po/FNSP and the Maison des Sciences de l'Homme in Paris. This work owes a lot to the friendship, experience, and deep understanding of the Vietnamese reality of Christopher E. Goscha, Andrew Hardy, John Kleinen, Stein D. Tønnesson, Ben Kerkvliet, Boris Lojkine, Ben Kerkvliet, Jacques Ivanoff, Jérémy Jammes, Pauline de La Grandière, Cécile Le Minh Triêt, Robert Lacombe and Christine Hemmet. My heartfelt thanks go lastly to my editors (and their readers behind-the-scenes), Frédéric Mantienne in Paris and Paul H. Kratoska in Singapore, to Claire Duiker, and Serge François, currently in charge of the training bureau for overseas French at the Ministry of Foreign and European Affairs, without whose help my fieldwork would not have been possible.

Vietnam in 1960

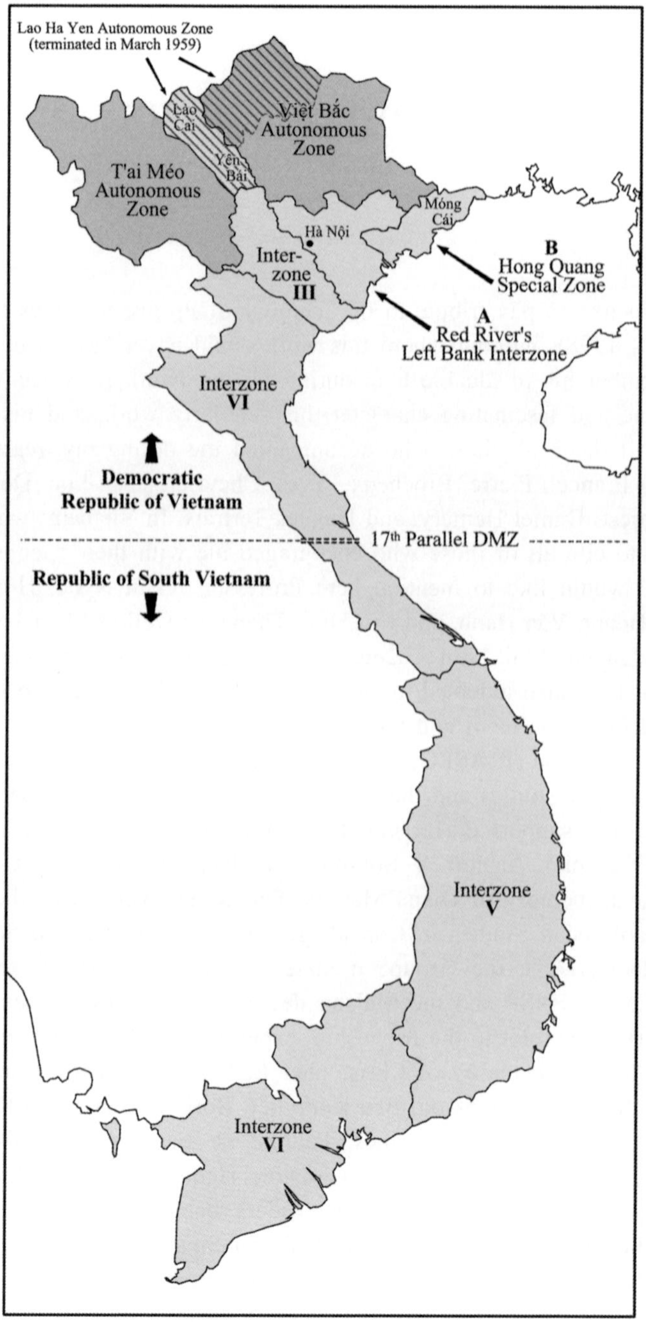

Figure 1. Administrative map of the Democratic Republic of Vietnam

INTRODUCTION

> ... when what we see with our very eyes leads to the wildest rumours, there was no telling what had happened in a place beyond eight layers of white clouds.
>
> Ueda Akinari (1732–1809), *Tales of Moonlight and Rain*

On 2 May 1952, as La Văn Cầu prepared to mount the podium in front of him, he thought about the words Võ Nguyên Giáp had just used to introduce him: "La Văn Cầu is a symbol of the Emulation Movement, an emulation to defeat the enemy and accomplish great deeds."[1] He knew that in a matter of seconds the President would name him the first new hero (*anh hùng mới*) in the history of the Democratic Republic of Vietnam (DRV). He thought about his village, Lũng Đình, in the far reaches of Cao Bằng province, and about the arm he had lost in the carnage of Đông Khê in the fall of 1950. Once just a small ethnic Tày who could barely read and write, he was now a hero of the Vietnamese nation, and government cadres were comparing him to Ly Thường Kiệt (1019–1105), Trần Hưng Đạo (1228–1300), and Phan Đình Phùng (1847–1896).

In the hills of Tuyên Quang province in early May 1952, leaders of the DRV organised a grand celebration to honour the merits and dedication of dozens of emulation fighters (*Chiến sĩ thi đua*). Seven among them — La Văn Cầu (1932), Nguyễn Quốc Trị (1921–1967), Nguyễn Thị Chiên (1930), Trần Đại Nghĩa (1913–1997), Ngô Gia Khảm (1912–1990), Hoàng Hanh (1888–1963), and the martyr Cù Chính Lan — were awarded the title of either "military hero" or "labour hero".[2] From 1948, when the first emulation campaign was launched, to 1964, just before the outbreak of war

[1] Interview with La Văn Cầu, Hero of the Armed Forces (1952), Hanoi.

[2] *Đại hội toàn quốc chiến sĩ thi đua và cán bộ gương mẫu (1–6.5.1952)* (National Conference of Emulation Combatants and Outstanding Cadres, 1–6 May 1952), in AVN3 (National Archives of the Socialist Republic of Vietnam, Centre no. 3), BLD (Archives of the Ministry of Labour), file no. 432, 529 pp.

with the South, DRV leaders (based in the northern region of the Việt Bắc) redefined the notion of patriotic exemplarity. "Vanguard workers" (*Lao động xuất sắc*), "emulation fighters", and "new heroes" made up the ranks of a new "exemplary society" where political virtue served as a principle for mobilising the population. This book examines the productivist and political elite that sprang up, often in great numbers, in the towns and countryside of North Vietnam. Between 1950 and 1964, the DRV elected 148 "new heroes" and nearly 100,000 "emulation fighters".

To understand the implications of this move, one must first forget the names and individual lives of these new social players, and focus instead on the different categories elaborated within the schema of social reconstruction. The Sinologist Susan L. Shirk identifies three types of governance: meritocracy, feudocracy, and virtuocracy, based on Max Weber's three principles of authority.[3] In a virtuocracy, the distribution of titles, certificates, and medals on the basis of virtue plays a key role in the strategisation of power. It is the source of the government's ability to transform the social system and its hold on the people, to increase its legitimacy as well as its political strength. This type of political response is natural in both traditional societies and Confucian cultures. In fact, an "exemplary society" in the sinicised world has always been based on the three pillars of discipline, education, and morality".[4] A revolutionary government that grants rewards and decorations to its model citizens in order to bring about a moral transformation of society can also be called a virtuocracy. The problem is determining whether it is a core phenomenon or a peripheral one within the government's agenda, especially when that agenda encounters historical continuities it cannot break or change completely.

The Democratic Republic of Vietnam was a virtuocratic regime. From its inception in September 1945, leaders based in the Việt Bắc region (north of Hanoi, and the government's base of power until the end of the Franco-Vietminh war in 1954) strove to offer the formerly oppressed classes a place in the new system. It was not just a question of replacing the "old collaborationist regime" with new masters, but an overall rethink of the criteria for reconstructing a political era, or beyond that, a new

[3] Susan L. Shirk. *Competitive Comrades: Career Incentives and Student Strategies in China*. Berkeley: University of California Press, 1982, pp. 9–10.

[4] Børge Bakken. *The Exemplary Society: Human Improvement, Social Control and the Danger of Modernity in China*. Oxford: Oxford University Press, 2000.

social relationship. The egalitarianism of a virtuocracy is meant to negate or redress a past injustice. The model — or modelling — of the "new man" in sinicised societies naturally arose at the junction between the failed compromises of the past and the demand for a new ideal. The guarantors of virtue were entrusted with the responsibility to sculpt and guide the first steps of an exemplary man, and reform society from the inside. The rise to power of any revolutionary group, regardless of its nature and ideological stance, invariably entails an attempt to transform society through the honour and celebration of its outstanding citizens.

My interest in the virtuocratic aspect goes beyond the symbolic level, an aspect already prioritised in Confucian tradition. The importance of heroic exemplarity in the development of Vietnamese communism is also due to the particular social and political context in which this development took place, which was diametrically opposed to the urban and internationalist world envisaged by Marx and actually inhabited by Lenin. In fact, Communist Vietnam is unique in that it was born out of a prolonged civil war instead of social revolution, within an agrarian society that was barely urbanised and strongly Confucian in nature. The context was similar to that of China in the 1930s–1940s with some important differences — Vietnam was under colonial rule prior to the revolution, and the nation underwent a transition that was, in fact, highly structured around heroic symbols. These characteristics have been thoroughly discussed elsewhere, both in their structure and consequences, so I will not deal with them here. My aim, rather, is to show that the establishment of a national model of heroism by the new communist Vietnamese regime arose mainly from its need for legitimacy and identity. This need took two forms, one global and the other domestic. On the international scene, the movement led by Hồ Chí Minh needed internationalist recognition, which had become central to their strategy in the early 1950s. Becoming a part of the international communist world engendered a host of symbols, but this was also shot through with political tension. In no way was the process neutral, be it in the choice of symbols or the affiliation with either Russia or China. On top of this internationalist alignment was superimposed a process of self-identification, involving a legitimising strategy that relied on powerful symbols of Vietnamese nationalism and which had to be implemented within the social reality.

Many people have denied the importance of the new hero in the DRV's identity formation. Since it was basically a foreign concept based on Russian and Chinese internationalism, these heroes were thought of as simply tacked-on compared to the more substantial reality of national heroes from Vietnam's long history. In the 1990s, the government encouraged the return of religious festivals and rituals in an effort to minimise the impact of these new heroes, but the new morality and politics that they represented could not help but enter into dialogue — or at least into contact — with traditional models. The new hero often polarised the debate between those insisting on a clear demarcation between nationalism and communism within DRV ideology, but I prefer to situate the analysis outside of this opposition from the outset. In fact, separating nationalism from communism in developing countries is quite irrelevant. Such a distinction, based on the opposition between culture and ideology, stems more from rhetoric — if not from ideology itself — than from reality. For those in the countryside, the appearance of the new hero in the hills of Tuyên Quang in May 1952 did not seem like a total rupture with their national history. And yet, there was no direct historic progression. As seen from Hanoi, the hero was not the same as the ones already present in the towns and villages around the nation. How can this duality be explained?

The origin of the exemplary man reveals an intentionalist underpinning. While official historiography claims that the new hero was the fruit of a heroic land, I believe, on the contrary, that the heroic figure was born of a political decision with a particular aim — as per Saint Thomas Aquinas, "intention refers to an act of will by which reason ordains something towards its end".[5] Far from denying the historical existence of heroic figures in Vietnam, the intentionalist approach sees communism as a technical problem rather than a philosophical or ethical one. The creation of the new man in the DRV was first a matter of organisational necessity. The main focus was not so much on developing a concept of materialism to influence minds, but on finding ways to organise the material itself. The viability of communism was above all a technical matter. Emulating the new model citizen was not only seen as a communist invention, it also helped to perpetuate a tradition that had relied on heroic tales for centuries to educate the people.

My main focus here is how the social process brought about by the emergence of an elite virtuous class became a motor for social reform. In other words, the new hero and the emulation fighter in North Vietnam were the beginnings of a re-evaluation — if not a recasting — of social

[5] Francisco Suárez (1548–1617). *Disputes Métaphysiques*. French translation of the Latin and annotation by Jean-Paul Coujou. Grenoble: Ed. Jérôme Millon, p. 19.

relationships, not of the group as a whole, as claimed by some in the communist ideological camp. As Andrew G. Walder wrote in the case of China, the establishment of communist regimes in the sinicised world led these countries to an exchange whereby "political loyalty is rewarded systematically with career opportunities, special distributions, and other favours that officials in communist societies are uniquely able to dispense".[6] What Walder called "neo-traditionalism" describes political regimes which set out to recast social relationships around values of loyalty and the political value of "exemplary men".

I do not wish to overstate the role of cultural determinism in the DRV's endogenisation of the new heroic figure, but I return frequently to the question of how the hero was adapted to fit the Vietnamese reality. The new model citizen is not an isolated object. His modernity lies not so much in the simple acceptance of an exogenous model than in the modifications he represents to a transmitted heritage. Accepting the continuity of the heroic figure in Vietnamese society does not necessarily mean opposing the rupture implied by an ideological approach. This sort of dualist vision of history arises when one ignores the facts. In Vietnam, the development of the new society sometimes seemed more like a conservative reaction to the growing influence of Western modernism, first introduced by the French and then by the Americans. While DRV leaders were certainly aware of the changes going on in the world around them, the political rupture of the late 1940s — which engendered a host of thoughts about the new man — sprang more from their desire to re-Asianise their political vision, which had been shaken by the spread of Western modernity since the late nineteenth century.

The question still remains of the new hero's position within the timeline of Vietnamese history. Previously, according to the historian François Furet, "the notion of subaltern classes evoked mainly a sense of quantity and anonymity".[7] But a vast number of these minute lives found an ear, a writer of history, in the State. The real question was not whether the details of a particular hero's life were true or false, nor how he was created by the institutional process. Rather, one should examine how the hero was culturally anchored within Vietnamese society and how official

---

[6] A.G. Walder. *Communist Neo-Traditionalism: Work and Authority in Chinese Industry.* Berkeley: University of California Press, 1988, p. 6.

[7] François Furet. "Pour une définition des classes inférieures à l'époque moderne" (Defining the lower classes in the modern era), *Annales ESC* 18(3), 1963: 459–74.

historiography described the daily lives of these new characters. That is, despite the superficial or stereotypical nature of the life stories of these exemplary men, their heroic feats spread out and resonated throughout the countryside, thus spreading the theatocratic ideal of the new North Vietnamese regime. In so doing, the DRV began to control the rules governing the daily life of the collective. The hero allowed the State to have a better command of the real through an imaginary canvas, one that came naturally from their ancestral past and guided their political reorganisation. Once again, the preponderance of cultural elements was necessary given the still vague notion and quite "modern" sense of the revolutionary phenomenon.

The political functionality of the new hero was an expression of the government's desire for national reunification; by presenting such a seemingly "normal" figure, they maintained the illusion of a State "by and for the people". Historians, however, should not see the sudden appearance of this new figure as simple political manipulation. North Vietnamese leaders wanted to control the real via the imaginary of the heroic myth. For them, the hero was not confined to his immortal existence in the archives, as he was in Maoist China. In communist societies, the heroic dead were usually subsumed as individuals behind the political significance of their lives (see the myth of Lei Feng in the PRC). In Vietnam, however, the exemplary man was put on display in all the normality of his daily life, confirming Montesquieu's notion that "to accomplish great things, one must not be above other men, but with them".[8]

The new exemplary men of the DRV are representatives of the people, of common citizens in a society that revolves around the land and their labour. The institutionalisation of communism destroyed the anonymity of class. The new man in Vietnam had little to do with the reconstruction of lives based on the modern idealities of politics and the city; it was mainly a peasant issue. It was about real lives, with real names, dates, and places. Behind them were "men who lived and died, and suffering, meanness, jealousies and outcries".[9] The words of the exemplary man were written down and transcribed, and though they were sometimes vague or idealised,

---

[8] Cited by Jean-Claude Bonnet in *Naissance du panthéon. Essai sur le culte des grands hommes* (The birth of the Pantheon. Essay on the cult of great men). Paris: Fayard, 1998.

[9] Michel Foucault. "La vie des hommes infâmes" (The lives of infamous men), *Les Cahiers du chemin*, no. 29, 15 January 1977: 12–29. Re-issued in Foucault's *Dits et écrits, 1954–1988*, vol. III. Paris: Gallimard, 1994, p. 239.

or borrowed or even suggested outright by those in power, their simplicity does not hide any falsity, lies, or injustice. They evoke an era in which the utopia of a socialism of resistance blended with memories of a vanished youth, and describe the intersection between the simple lives of selected families with the official granting of honours.

Thomas Carlyle wrote that "History is the essence of innumerable Biographies."[10] Indeed, ruptures, erasures, forgetting, and the intersecting discourses of the new hero led to a reconstruction of the past. At first glance, of course, these brief lives seem fabricated, constructed, or even manipulated, but the simple and sincere way in which they are told gives them a very real sense of truth. Hence, my study is twofold, and deals with the history of the DRV as well as individual biography. Studying the new hero and the emulation fighter is not a means for re-examining the political and social history of the Vietnam, but rather an independent standpoint that can shed some light on the latter from the inside.

As a general rule, the everyday life of the new man in North Vietnam was not a matter of interest except where his productivist and military action could serve as a lesson and example, and the new heroism took root in this dimension of immediacy. The physical anchoring of the new heroic figure is important. Although they were presented as national symbols, the new heroes were actually intended from the beginning (in 1952) to serve as a relay between the centre and the periphery, that is, to consolidate or even create a political space in the literal sense of the term. Once the logic behind the exemplary man took on a geographic dimension, a decentralised approach was needed to understand him. The new hero's message speaks unequivocally of spreading, and thus anchoring, the State discourse within the local. In order to grasp this concept from the outside, we have to listen and observe at ground level, far from the centres of power, to the words and the actions of peasants, workers, low-level government employees, and local factotums, to whom the central government once awarded a certificate of merit, aware that they were shattering forever the ancient order of things.

The new hero thus has to be studied on the provincial level. It is often said that the Việt Minh revolution was a peasant revolution, but recruitment of the movement's top cadres took place mainly in the cities.

---

[10] Thomas Carlyle. "On History", in *Critical and Miscellaneous Essays*, vol. II. London: Chapman & Hall, 1869, p. 255.

The countryside, on the other hand, presented a challenge for the new regime to conquer hearts and minds, but rewarded it in return with a potent political legitimacy. This, however, led to a rupture that threatened the ancient notion of village autonomy for the sake of democratic centralism. One cannot see this as just a local phenomenon defined by local circumstances, nor situate the facts of the hero's life within pure individuality. In this case, the local community no longer represented the isolated and autonomous community so sought after by historians and ethnologists for abstract experimentation. While the ethnologist Claude Lévi-Strauss saw a very restricted study of isolates (villages, neighbourhoods, ethnic groups, etc.) as a way to get back to the authenticity of the Other,[11] understanding the reality of these new honourees required going beyond a monographic or micro-historical approach. The new hero was measured along two axes, in a constant back-and-forth between the local and the national. The new outstanding citizen was established in North Vietnam to help garner internationalist recognition. As a foreign concept, he had to fit into a specific cultural context to establish his legitimacy. He was to become the symbol of identity transformation to the outside world, and the expression of continuity within his own.

The first chapter examines the role of the Vietnamese heroic figure through time (Chapter 1: Heroism in Vietnam), studying how the hero was portrayed in classical Vietnamese historiography, then the rupture brought about by the writings of Phan Bội Châu, the early nineteenth-century freethinker and patriot. These overlapping discourses and the resulting singularity of the new hero revealed just how the official historiography made this new object its own. The launching of the first patriotic emulation campaign in June 1948, and especially the reforms enacted in the first semester of 1950, provide a prism for understanding this phenomenon and the demands placed upon it by outside forces. The new hero was the product of emulation, which announced straightaway his connection to the institutional apparatus of communism (Chapter 2: Patriotic Emulation (1948–1952)). The following chapter takes a closer look at the official historiography itself and tracks the progression of the new figure in order to present a profile of the emulation fighter (Chapter 3: The Emulation Fighter (1950–1964)) and the new hero (Chapter 4: The New Hero (1952–1964)). I noticed that among the common people, discourse about the hero implied the adoption

[11] Claude Lévi-Strauss. *Anthropologie structurale* (Structural Anthropology). Paris: Plon, 1958, p. 400.

of a new civic virtue, which was often more concrete than the actual requirements for receiving the title. It is difficult, however, to understand the value of this mass mobilisation if we know nothing about the daily lives of these outstanding men and women. A large part of this study is thus devoted to their words and deeds, which I then systematically compare with the official government documents that supposedly represent them.

Finally, after examining the origins and the daily life of the new man, I broach another aspect of his integration into North Vietnamese society. Though the new internationalist hero was still a living and active member of his community, I also considered the lives of the heroic dead who, as national martyrs, were seen as cultural doubles of the new patriotic hero (Chapter 5: The Life of the Dead). Beyond the formalist concession to proletarian internationalism, the national martyr also adopted a traditional face to both protect and mobilise the national community. However, after the DRV victory at Điện Biên Phủ (1954), this mechanism took on a more global aspect. Government leaders gained more control over the lives of their honoured dead, which led them to rethink the role of past heroes as well as accord the newly fallen with a veneration more in line with ancestral principles (Chapter 6: The Cult of the New Hero). Chapter 7 then examines the way in which the new heroic figure — now as an object of representation — took part in the reconstruction of a national patriotic imaginary. It is an idealised version of his life that was carried down to the village as a tool of propaganda. Lastly, the new hero was also part of the national discourse, which leads to the question of Vietnam's patriotic pantheon. The veneration of the new hero indirectly gave rise to a network of identity references, thus establishing the blueprint for a new collective memory.

This latter element is part of the complex system governing the right of access within Vietnamese society. The observer's position (age, profession, ethnicity, life story, etc.) determines his access to a certain type of information. What would happen if we change the nature of the person speaking? It is important to keep in mind the space accorded to foreigners in Vietnamese society.

Since 1986, Vietnam has operated on two distinct and carefully controlled levels of openness, one economic and the other political. In keeping with long-standing regional tradition, and in the hopes of legitimising their return to the international scene, Vietnamese leaders have been rather reserved since the mid-1990s about the extent of their involvement in the establishment of global communism from the 1950s onwards. With the policy of openness known as *Đổi Mới*, the official historiography initiated a return to the cultural origins of its political identity. The Socialist Republic of Vietnam liked to call attention to the religious renewal taking place, a timely topic as the regime was turning towards the West.[12] This study thus seeks a balance between these two fundamental tendencies in national historiography. How do we account for a choice that seems to run counter to the most immediate interests of those in power? The new hero continues to tie Vietnam to a past that its present seeks to ignore. On the other hand, directing foreign attention to the return of the rites and customs of their ancient traditions reveals their intention to reassure the West about their political openness. Of course, this orientation still conforms to the tradition of government intervention and implies the use of control tactics. Contemporary foreign scholars in Vietnam must seek official approval, and their jurisdiction and access to the national reality are still carefully controlled. Yet to turn away from the reshaping of the patriotic imaginary in the DRV as a result of intimidation would be to ignore an important part of the remaking of national identity that has been going on for a half a century.

[12] Philip Taylor, ed. *Modernity and Re-enchantment: Religion in Post-Revolutionary Vietnam*. Singapore: ISEAS, 2007; Olga Dror. *Cult, Culture, and Authority: Princess Liêu Hanh in Vietnamese History*. Bangkok: Silkworm Books, 2008; and Pham Quynh Phuong. *Hero and Deity: Tran Hung Dao and the Resurgence of Popular Religion in Vietnam*. Chiang Mai: Mekong Press, 2009.

Chapter 1

Heroism in Vietnam

> But where was the new man? On the third day he suddenly asked his guide this question. 'The new man?' said the guide, somewhat taken aback. 'The people you see all around you — in the café, in the street. They're the new men!' They were strolling along Tirana's main boulevard. Krams felt he'd been had. 'Excuse my frankness,' he said, nodding towards the passers-by, 'but the last thing I'd call these people is the new men! Look at the way they're dressed! Look at the way the boys move, look at the girls' eyes! I don't know how to describe them.' The guide laughed. 'They're just human movements, human looks. Why should they need any other description?'
>
> Ismail Kadare[1]

Communist historiography in Vietnam made Hồ Chí Minh the natural successor of the nation's heroic ancestors.[2] The hero in Vietnamese tradition helped define his era and was integrated into a social order that ensured the harmony of the community, guaranteeing the time-honoured relationship between the citizen and the land of his ancestors. The cult of the tutelary spirit in Vietnam goes back to the thirteenth century and gradually incorporated animist rites and beliefs. The ritual practices that emerged from this spirituality and the relationship to the sacred were

[1] Ismail Kadare. *The Concert*. Translated from the French of Jusuf Vrioni by Barbara Bray. New York: Arcade Publishing, 1994, pp. 173–4.

[2] Võ Nguyên Giáp. *Banner of the People's War.* New York: Praeger, 1970. Le Duẩn, "Revolution is the work of the Masses" (1958), in Trần Văn Đình, ed., *This Nation and Socialism are One.* Chicago: Vanguard Books, 1976. The question has been the subject of a number of studies in recent years, the best of which is Shaun Malarney's *Culture, Ritual and Revolution in Vietnam*. New York: Routledge-Curzon, 2002.

> ... inseparable from the social, economic, historical and political reality of the human community that created them. An examination of these practices thus involves an examination of their context and their relationship with both actual and imagined realities. The nature of these relationships determines the survival strategy of the rituals in one form or another, whether dressed up as myth or taken over by the state, which bedecks them with patriotic elements to transform them into events within the nation's history.[3]

The Vietnamese village was defined by its geographic space, which lay in the hands of protective spirits to whom one owed respect and veneration. The arrival of a new actor on the communal stage had to be accompanied by a cultural framework that was easily understood by everyone. To the outside world, the hero symbolised a transformation of identity, but within the DRV he was to be part of a continuity. The new government sought a rupture between the old and the new for political ends: the taking and managing of power. DRV leaders had no real cultural substitute to offer. In the early 1950s, the new heroic figure gave government leaders a means of penetrating into the traditional core of communal independence. But this did not take into account the mistrust or disinterest of the rural population for foreign concepts.[4]

The Hero in Vietnamese Culture

One of the cultural elements that the Vietnamese took over from China is the belief that "men were born unequal in talent".[5] As a result, the idea of social difference, an individual's place in society, was inherent in the

---

[3] Nguyên Van Ky. "L'évolution des cultes villageois au Vietnam dans leurs rapports avec le macrocosme" (The evolution of village cults in Vietnam as they relate to the macrocosm). Paper presented at the Euroviêt Conference in Amsterdam, July 1997, p. 1.

[4] A report written in 1956 by the people's committee of Hồng Quảng illustrates the problems encountered by cultural teams in spreading the example of these foreign figures: "Workers would much rather see Vietnamese propaganda films than foreign ones. Of the latter, they prefer Chinese or North Korean films since they feel a cultural similarity and a feeling that they don't find with the Soviet ones", in *Báo cáo tình hình nghiên cứu về công tác văn hóa phục vụ công nhân tại Khu Hồng Quảng* (Report on the cultural activities aimed at workers in the zone of Hồng Quảng), in AVN3, BVH, file no. 880, document no. 3/BC, 25 November 1956.

[5] Alexander Woodside. *Vietnam and the Chinese Model.* Cambridge: Harvard University Press, 1971, p. 10.

conception of social order. The three relationships that were essential to eternal socio-political harmony were: the loyalty of the bureaucrat to the emperor, the obedience of a son to his father, and the submission of a wife to her husband. Society was built upon a vertical organisation of social differences via the application of the Confucian hierarchical principles. This principle of submission could be extended to include the submission of the inferior to his superior, ensuring the cohesion of the social whole. Social relationships between community members were hierarchical, and one's responsibilities depended on one's position within the group.

The hierarchisation of the Vietnamese community did not result in inequality, however. All men were not born equal, but this meant that they had different duties as well. A leader's greatest responsibility was to be a model of virtue for his people. It was his duty, for example, to practise the virtues of loyalty, piety, self-sacrifice, etc., in order to instil the values of the community in his inferiors. As one proverb goes, "If leaders are not exemplary before their inferiors, the latter will never have an orderly life." For centuries in Vietnam, rulers paid homage to their exemplary subjects. The hero was a sort of barometer of patriotic virtue, and was connected to his nation by a filial link. The description of a heroic life was less concerned with biographical details then with situating the hero's life at the border between the personal and the collective. The hero's life story was usually generic and impersonal. He represented a certain social order but not the heart of the system. The ruling power came into the picture only when involved in national defence. The hero shared in this legitimacy by playing the role that society expected of him; he offered his body to the abstraction of a political body, and was defined by the fatherland in return. The hero was created by the fatherland and was the best possible servant to his nation, the inferior to a superior being. The public recognised this subjection of the "exemplary man" to the collective. In homage, they agreed to venerate the heroic figure in order to re-establish a parity within the symbolic exchange that underlies the harmony of a Confucian society.

In Vietnamese, the idea of "love for one's country" (*yêu nước* or *ái quốc* in Sino-Vietnamese) blended with the expression of "loyalty" (*trung*), which referred more specifically to the loyalty of an individual to the king, the family, or a relative. The concept of a nation took hold relatively late in Vietnam and went beyond the mere physical space of a territory.[6]

---

[6] Christopher Goscha. *Vietnam or Indochina? Contesting Concepts of Space in Vietnamese Nationalism 1887–1954.* Copenhagen: NIAS Books, 1995.

The land of the ancestors sought a perenniality in the supernatural, where "the miraculous spirit of rivers and mountains" determined the limits of national space.[7] According to Vietnamese mythology, the spirits of the elements gave birth to invincible men and women. The souls of the generations of heroes who lived and died on the land made it a sacred place. For having harboured these heroes, Vietnamese soil was sacred, and its people had been heroic since the dawn of time. Protecting the soul of these mythical heroes linked the Vietnamese people to their land. Leaving home meant breaking the filial bond that tied one to one's heroic ancestors. It was hard to distinguish the national from the individual, the familial, or the communal in the depths of this ancestral patrimony.

The hero was tightly bound by the time and space of this mythological past, and he alone defined the spirit of his age.[8] His fusion with the elements made him the representation of national identity. Legend tells us that the ancestor of the Vietnamese people was the dragon Lạc Long Quân (Hán tự: 雒龍君; literally "Dragon Lord of Lạc", sometimes spelled 駱龍君 or 貉龍君 and also called Hùng Hiền Vương). North Vietnamese communists preferred to invoke the continuity of the "national spirit" rather than the "Vietnamese soul", but the myth of their "4,000-year-old history" made it necessary to incorporate this heroic heritage. The Indochinese Communist Party (ICP) presented itself as the direct descendent of the nation's heroes.[9] The heroic figure distilled the essence of the national character. There was no patriotism without heroes, nor heroes without patriotism. The cult of mythic heroes was a natural part of delimiting the physical boundaries of the nation. They had fought for centuries to defend these tracts of land, which thereby linked them forever to its perenniality.[10] The belief in this fusion between the exemplary man and the physical

---

[7] Phạm Cao Dương. "Comments on the Vietnamese Sense of the Past by John K. Whitmore", *The Việt Nam Forum*, Yale University, no. 1, Winter-Spring 1983: 13.

[8] "Whether mythical or historical, these heroes took on a spiritual power and joined the ranks of the cult figures who used to fill the Vietnamese countryside, and thus helped to define it." J.K. Whitmore, "The Vietnamese Sense of the Past", *The Việt Nam Forum*: 8.

[9] Vũ Hồng. "Sự ra đời của Đảng và bước ngoặt lịch sử của chủ nghĩa anh hùng" (Birth of the Party and the important stages in heroism), *Học tập*, Hanoi, no. 4, 1967: 75–81.

[10] "When men and women die for the country, the mountains and rivers transform the goodness of their existence into spirit. And the sun and the moon will shine in all their brightness." This is a couplet from one of the "parallel sentences" dedicated to Trương Công Định (1820–1864), a South Vietnamese patriot who rose up against the French. Cited in Phạm Cao Dương, *The Việt Nam Forum*: 13.

space of the nation is a key element of Vietnamese culture. The heroism of their ancestors allowed them to successfully resist being completely sinicised, so the modern citizen had to prove himself worthy of such a heritage. The myth of the heroic origins of the Vietnamese nation appears obsessively in the political rhetoric of the communist regime. In the days following the victory of Điện Biên Phủ, the DRV reinterpreted the stories of its historic figures in order to infuse this national spirit into the bodies of its new men.

In pre-communist Vietnam, the national hero alone represented the land of the ancestors in the villagers' daily lives, so the new government had to establish a genealogical dynastic continuity in order to gain legitimacy. They did this by invoking the nation's glorious ancestors, but they had to know what they were doing.[11] The people and the State looked to the heroic, mythic, and historic ancestor for the form and development of a historic continuity to ground their identity.

Vietnamese leaders had relied on this principle for centuries to produce a official historiography celebrating a lineage rich with heroic figures. Many historical works recount the glorious days of the royal dynasties, but there are also books praising the heroic lives of its "loyal subjects, devoted to and benefactors to the fatherland". The most famous of these was written by Lý Tế Xuyên in 1329, called *The Powerful Spirits of the Realm of Viet* (*Việt diện u linh tập*). It was basically a series of biographies of "exemplary spirits" from antiquity to the beginning of the fourteenth century,[12] who had helped to spread the Vietnamese spirit and traditions. The State encouraged its citizens to venerate the model, and each new emperor adapted the nation's historic ancestors to his liking. In the fifteenth century, the eight biographical volumes of *Extraordinary Stories from Linh Nam* (*Lĩnh Nam chích quái*) listed "the people who

---

[11] Philippe Langlet. *L'ancienne historiographie d'Etat au Vietnam* (The ancient official historiography of Vietnam), vol. I, "Raisons d'être, conditions d'élaboration et caractères au siècle des Nguyên". Paris: PEFEO, 1990, p. 16.

[12] The collected legends of kings, loyal subjects, and tutelary spirits of the country, the *Việt diện u linh tập* (Collection of the invisible powers of the Viet nation) was written in 1329 and re-issued in 1919 with three additional stories by Nguyễn Văn Chất about the Trưng sisters, Thành Đông, Phạm Ngũ Lão, Từ Đạo Hạnh, Nguyễn Minh Không, and Trần Hưng Đạo. See Trân Nghia and F. Gros, eds. *Catalogue of the books of Han Nom*, vol. III, Institut Ha Nom et EFEO Hanoi. Hanoi: nxb Khoa học Xã hội, 1993, pp. 586–8.

helped found and defend the nation, and protected the people".[13] In 1623, Phạm Phi Kiến published *Presentation of the Loyalty and the Just Cause of the Southern Nations* (*Nam thiên trung nghĩa bảo lục*), dedicated to the great men of the fatherland under the Đinh, Lí, Trần, and Lê dynasties.[14] In 1771, the scholar Hồng Cẩm Hoàng published a vast collection of poems entitled *Anthology of Illustrious Personalities* (*Danh Tích Thi Tập*), dedicated mainly to the "combatants for the just cause" and "extraordinary men" from the "land of the ancestors".

National heroes were not just an example or a model for the State, but a "constantly active source of its life, its power, its success, of the continuation of the dynasty for the good of the people".[15] The function of the hero in Vietnamese civilisation should thus be analysed within the context of his link to those in power. In his study on the historiography of the Nguyễn dynasty (1802–1945), the historian Philippe Langlet describes the use of the cult of heroic ancestors in the affirmation of dynastic majesty.[16] The hero in Vietnam was first and foremost an "outstanding citizen" to whom the dynasty in power rendered homage. The biographies of the "Illustrious Loyal Officers" enumerate the "exemplary men", listing the merits that earned them the title. Dynastic leaders had to maintain loyalty and encourage the ardour of those serving them so as to strengthen the stability of their institutions, hence the creation of an official cult to that effect under the Ministry of Rites. In 1790, Nguyên Phước Ánh (Gia Long) drew up a list of "outstanding citizens", living or dead, for real or honorific promotions. In 1791, he built a temple of Illustrious Loyalties not far from Saigon to honour more than 600 heroes who had gone with him to Bangkok (1784–87), where they joined forces to take control of Gia Định (1788). In Vietnamese tradition, virtuous spirits had to be appeased, as did their descendants:

[13] The first four volumes were written by Vũ Quỳnh between 1478 and 1492. The scholars Trần Thế Pháp and Kiều Phú then took over the project. See Trân Nghia and F. Gros, *Catalogue of the books of Han Nom*, vol. II, pp. 206–7.

[14] Notably Nguyễn Điền, Nguyễn Bặc, Lê Phụng Hiểu, Trần Nguyên Hãn, Trần Quốc Tuấn, Trương Phu Duyệt, Lê Quýnh, Nguyễn Việt Triều, Trần Danh Án, etc. See Trận Nghia and F. Gros, *Catalogue of the books of Han Nom*, vol. II, pp. 353–4.

[15] Nguyên Thê Anh, "La conception de la monarchie divine dans le Viêt Nam traditionnel" (The conception of divine monarchy in traditional Vietnam), in *BEFEO*, vol. LXXXIV, Paris, 1997, p. 157.

[16] Langlet. *L'ancienne historiographie d'Etat au Vietnam*.

> Dynastic rule was that of a family patriarch, but also of important government leaders; they had to be honoured and the souls of the departed appeased by a State cult. This cult, presided over by the emperor, was also a show of respect for the fundamental principles against tyranny.[17]

A cult of outstanding citizens was organised by categories of merit, after an examination of each candidate's history. In 1810, a temple was built near Huế to venerate the accomplishments of the outstanding citizens of the Restoration. The ruling dynasty showed great prudence with respect to these "heroic spirits". By showing respect and veneration, it hoped to influence the present and guarantee the goodwill of the elements. Each new sovereign invoked the protection of illustrious spirits from the nation's past. Devotion to the heroic dead was carried out via the spread and continuation of official rites. After the death of Gia Long (1819), Minh Mạng (1791–1840) in turn reinterpreted the deeds of past heroic figures in order to draw up a list of the greatest heroes and associate them with the cult of his father. Under the Nguyễn emperors, three types of exemplary men were honoured: Illustrious Loyalties (*hiển trung*), Outstanding Citizens of the Restoration (*trung hưng*), and the Loyal and Faithful (*trung tiết*). They were showered with imperial favour and were meant to express the solidarity of the dynasty in power.

Hero worship was thus a key political act. Popular custom held that acts of piety performed for these heroic figures could bring about benevolent intercession. The wrath of unsatisfied souls was feared and the sovereign's virtue depended upon "his current behaviour, but also upon his filial, or rather familial piety, which situated him within a historical continuity. Glorifying the benevolence of his ancestors not only proved his legitimacy, but was part of the cult of universal harmony, a condition of good government".[18] The legitimate hero was one whose actions benefited those in power. When we examine the origin of the "new man" in the DRV, we must remember this ancient link between the outstanding citizen and the state. Vietnamese culture would never recognise an illegitimate heroic figure nor one dedicated to an unjust cause.[19] Ontologically, the hero served a just cause and was defined by his filial link to the secular power. While the veneration of the hero as outstanding citizen reinforced the legitimacy

---

[17] Langlet. *L'ancienne historiographie d'Etat au Vietnam*, p. 21.

[18] Ibid., p. 69.

[19] Văn Tạo. *Chủ nghĩa anh hùng cách mạng Việt Nam* (Vietnamese revolutionary heroism). Hanoi: nxb Khoa học Xã hội, 1972, pp. 7–34.

of the political authority, the relationship with heroic ancestors played a key role in the construction of national identity.

In the eleventh century, Confucian reforms within the government imposed a new regulation of society. According to ancient tradition, the Vietnamese village had an identity and a political unity unto itself. One proverb states that "[T]he law of the prince must give way to the customs of the village (*Phép vua thua lệ làng*)". At the heart of communal culture, the tutelary spirit was the most important factor in identity formation.[20] The anthropologist Lê Minh Ngọc states that this spirit "represented the shared destiny of a society living in the same territory".[21] The spirit thus defined the territorial unity of the village community. A cult was dedicated to the spirit to protect the work and daily life of the village. In Vietnam, the ruling dynasty conceived of the nation through the community of its official ancestors. The political autonomy of the commune did not diminish its existence as a part of the nation. Thus, since the Lí Dynasty (1010–1225), imperial powers have tried to increase their hold on the tutelary spirits of the commune. The cult of local spirits had to be approved by certificates or royal edicts issued by the Ministry of Rites. Under the later Lê dynasty (1428–1788), each village had to declare every aspect of its local spirit cult (history, legend, rites, dates of celebration, festivals, etc.). The central government managed to penetrate into the communal level through this control over village rites. Secular authorities could then denounce any "inconvenient cults" that did not conform to state ideology.[22]

---

[20] The tutelary spirit was the protector of the village inhabitants. The term *thành hoàng* is a Chinese word composed of two elements: *thành* (fortifications, ramparts) and *hoàng* (a dry moat dug around the ramparts). It originally referred to the space inside the fortifications and the surrounding moats, but later referred to the god who protects the fortifications.

[21] Lê Minh Ngọc. "Tín ngưỡng Thành hoàng và ý thức tâm lý cộng đồng làng xã" (Spirit beliefs and village psychology), in *Nông thôn Việt Nam trong lịch sử*, vol. I. Hanoi: nxb Khoa học Xã hội, 1977, p. 337.

[22] Léon Vandermeesch. "Remarques sur les rapports de la religion officielle et des cultes populaires dans la tradition chinoise" (Remarks on the relationship between official religion and popular cults in Chinese tradition), in A. Forest, Y. Ishizawa, and L. Vandermeesch, eds. *Cultes populaires et sociétés asiatiques* (Popular cults and Asian societies). Paris: L'Harmattan, 1991, pp. 29–37. Georges Boudarel. "L'insertion du pouvoir central dans les cultes villageois au Viêt Nam. Esquisse des problèmes à partir des écrits de Ngô Tât Tô" (The central government's involvement in the village cults of Vietnam. Sketch of some problems based on the writings of Ngô Tât Tô), in A. Forest, Y. Ishizawa, and L. Vandermeesch, eds. *Cultes populaires et sociétés asiatiques*, pp. 87–147.

By controlling the tutelary spirits, the ruling power imposed its dominance over the nation's communes. In other words, by granting titles to local spirits, the government linked the fate of the village to that of the State.

Tutelary spirits were a mix of mythological figures, celestial spirits (*thiên thần*), historical figures, and human spirits (*nhân thần*).[23] They were venerated because they had rendered great service to their country, emperor, or village during their lifetime. The ruling dynasty encouraged the establishment of these cults in communes around the nation. We know, for example, that more than 60 per cent of the spirits worshipped in Vĩnh Phú, Hà Tây, and Hà Bắc province were patriots who had fought to defend their country. The Minister of Rites held a key position within the State apparatus as he contributed to the homogenisation of the national imaginary. The hero, who was a national figure but also a provincial, or more specifically, communal one, helped establish the myth of the "great Vietnamese family", which added a sense of familial hierarchy to the relationship between the members of the national community:

> The feudal dynasties from the Lý to the Nguyễn usually tried to make popular culture serve their political interests. They made an effort to collect the legends of heroic figures from all provinces in order to touch them up, give them their stamp of approval, and then send them out into the countryside where temples and altars would be built for their veneration. From then on, every village had to organise an annual festival in honour of these benevolent spirits. This policy established and reinforced national pride and a spirit of independence, and encouraged a veneration of the heroes who helped build the nation.[24]

The historical hero offered Vietnamese dynasties a way to politically unify their territorial space. Eventually, nearly every village had a cult for Hai Bà Trưng (?–43), Bà Triệu (226–248), Lý Thường Kiệt (1019–1105), Trần Hưng Đạo (1228–1300) (born Trần Quốc Tuấn), Nguyễn Trãi (1380–1442), Lê Lợi (1384–1433), and others, who had defended the nation's independence over the centuries. Vietnamese rulers managed to establish a homology between the present and the past. The veneration of benevolent

[23] Lê Văn Kỳ. *Mối quan hệ giữa truyền thuyết người Việt và hội lễ về anh hùng* (Relationship between Vietnamese tradition and the festivals dedicated to heroes). Hanoi: nxb Khoa học Xã hội, 1997, pp. 60–70.

[24] Ibid., p. 64.

spirits was an extension of the cult of ancestor worship,[25] and fulfilled an important political function in the construction of national identity. The ritual of venerating the nation's ancestral spirits had the possibility and privilege of bringing together the "great" and the "small" family. The cult of the hero symbolised a first attempt at unifying the country and aimed to circumvent the traditional policy of local autonomy.

The Mutation of the Hero

In the early twentieth century, the scholar-patriot Phan Bội Châu (1867–1940) proposed an abrupt reinterpretation of the heroic figure, sparking his transformation from traditional "historical hero" to the progressivist "collective hero".[26] One recurring theme in Vietnamese culture is the assimilation or rejection of exogenous ideas. The adoption of Marxist-Leninist ideology in Vietnam was due in large part to the peregrinations of Nguyễn Ái Quốc (Nguyễn the Patriot) — better known as Hồ Chí Minh (born Nguyễn Sinh Cung) — who left Vietnam for Europe in 1911.[27] The imported hero could not have been simply the fruit of the internationalist rapprochement of the 1950s.

Phan Bội Châu wrote numerous books, tracts, pamphlets, moral treatises, and interviews, which fall into three distinct phases concerning the heroic figure in Vietnam. In his earliest writings on the subject, *A Tribute to Shining Lives* (*Sùng bái giai nhân*, 1907) and *Outline History of Vietnam* (*Việt Nam quốc sử khảo*, 1908), Châu advocated the traditional approach to the historical hero espoused by scholars and official historiography. Only a scholar could rally the Vietnamese people to a just cause;

[25] Nguyễn Kiến Giang. "Thờ cúng tổ tiên trong đời sống tâm linh người Việt" (Ancestor worship in Vietnamese spiritual life), *Xưa và Nay*, Hanoi, no. 23, 1 January 1996: 16–8; and Nguyễn Văn Kiệm, "Góp thêm vào tìm hiểu thờ cúng tổ tiên của người Việt" (New ideas on ancestor worship among the Vietnamese), *Xưa và Nay*, Hanoi, no. 27, May 1996: 23–4.

[26] The figure of the hero is a constant presence in: *Lưu Cầu Huyết Lệ Tân Thư* (1903), *Việt Nam vong quốc sử* (1905), *Hải ngoại huyết thư* (1906), *Sùng bái giai nhân* (1907), *Hoàng Phạm Thái truyện* (1907), *Việt Nam quốc sử khảo* (1908), *Trần Đông Phong truyện*, *Hà thành liệt sĩ truyện*, *Trùng quang tâm sử* (1913), *Ngư Hải ông liệt sĩ truyện*, *Hà thành liêt si truyện*, *Trưng Nữ Vương* (1911), *Truyện Phạm Hồng Thái* (1925), etc.

[27] Sophie Quinn-Judge. *Hồ Chí Minh: The Missing Years, 1919–1941*. London: Hurst & Co., 2003.

only he could conjure the spirit of a movement and make it a reality. Châu referred to Nguyễn Trãi and Lê Lợi as models of the national hero who, with his acute sense of political ideals blended with strong feelings of hatred toward the aggressor, was a colourful figure and shone with exceptional character. These three elements defined the hero for centuries and made it impossible for peasants and the "lower classes" to become national heroes. Intellectual training was the only way to learn the sort of behaviour worthy of the heroism of great men.

Ideologues from the DRV criticised Châu's early writing for excluding workers and peasants. But in 1907, a short work entitled *Project for Awakening the National Spirit* (*Đề tỉnh quốc dân hồn*) revealed the evolution of his thought and the first mention of the "normalisation of the hero". He argued that if the essence of the historic struggle had always been the defence of one's country, the people should now be able to share that privilege.[28] His progressivism in those years did not go much farther than that, however. He advocated a re-evaluation of the role of the masses in the origin of patriotic uprisings, but kept within a traditional framework. His "normalisation of the hero" thus heralded the arrival of patriotic heroes from a segment of the population that had always been excluded from official historiography.

Phan Bội Châu published two works in the 1910s: *The Painful History of a Usurped Dynasty* (*Trùng quang tâm sử,* 1913) and *Portrait of a General* (*Chân tướng quân*, 1917), which revealed his new conception of the heroic figure.[29] He had been heavily influenced by the fate of Đề Thám (aka Hoàng Hoa Thám, 1883–1913), instigator of the Yên Thế peasant revolt in Bắc Giang province. From this perspective, *The Painful History*

---

[28] "He was the first to propose a new criterion for judging the historical figure. Both the nation and the people could thenceforth grant historical merit to exemplary figures", in Nguyễn Đổng Chi, "Bàn thêm về quan niệm chủ nghĩa anh hùng của Phan Bội Châu" (New elements on heroism according to Phan Bội Châu), *Nghiên cứu Lịch sử* (Historical research), Hanoi, no. 111, June 1968.

[29] For the centenary of his birth (1967), numerous studies were published in the North Vietnamese press: Trần Huy Liệu, "Phan Bội Châu tiêu biểu cho những cuộc vận động yêu nước ở Việt Nam đầu thế kỷ XX" (The biography of Phan Bội Châu and patriotic activities in Vietnam in the early 20th century), *Nghiên cứu Lịch sử*, Hanoi, no. 105, December 1967; Nguyễn Đình Chú, "Tìm hiểu quan niệm anh hùng của Phan Bội Châu" (Study on heroism according to Phan Bội Châu), *Văn Học*, Hanoi, December 1967; and Nguyễn Dông Chi, "Bàn thêm về quan niệm chủ nghĩa anh hùng của Phan Bội Châu".

of a Usurped Dynasty represents the pivotal work of his career. Châu questioned the long-standing distinction between the "anonymous hero" and the "famous hero". The main axis for defining heroism had shifted from the individual to the collective. "The country needs thousands of anonymous heroes before it can have famous heroes", Châu wrote.[30] Recognising the subtle, everyday heroism of the lower classes led him to reconsider the role of the masses in general. By granting the "anonymous hero" honours previously reserved for the extraordinary "historic hero", Châu had marked the first appearance of the "collective hero" in Vietnamese historiography, wrote the critic Nguyễn Đổng Chi in the 1960s.[31] Phan Bội Châu wrote about the acts of bravery of the "humble people", allowing Mr. Xí, Old Chìm, Mr. Võ, or Madame Triệu to share the honour with their illustrious counterparts, whose heroic deeds preserved national independence. This new perspective led Châu to reconsider the position held by the mass of "anonymous heroes", that is, by the people. In this way, venerating the various acts of these "exemplary men" from everyday life endowed the collective with a higher value than the individual action itself.

Ideologues from the DRV granted that Châu's perspective led to an exceptional rupture in national historiography, but this did not turn him into a "revolutionary writer" outright. From then on, the peasant sat prominently alongside the mandarin-patriot in the hierarchy of esteemed men, but the old model had not been completely toppled; the heroism of the peasant blended in well, in fact, with traditional heroism.[32] Phan Bội Châu was profoundly shaken by the Yên Thế peasant revolt against the French and wrote *Portrait of a General* (1917) about the event. He dedicated the book to Đề Thám, the movement's leader, and enthusiastically compared him to the "bourgeois" heroes who defeated the Chinese at Đống Đa (1788). The traditional conception of heroism no longer fit his theoretical framework, so Châu decided to redraw its contours. Trần Hưng Đạo and Đề Thám found themselves on the same footing, both having shown incomparable courage and perseverance in their fight against the hostile enemies of the state. Together, Đạo and Thám represented the best of Vietnamese

[30] Phan Bội Châu. *Trùng quang tâm sử*. 1913, p. 34.

[31] Nguyễn Đổng Chi. "Bàn thêm về quan niệm chủ nghĩa anh hùng của Phan Bội Châu", p. 20.

[32] Tôn Quang Phiệt. "Cụ Phan Bội Châu trong Lịch sử dân tộc của chúng ta" (Phan Bội Châu in our popular history), *Văn Sử Địa*, Hanoi, no. 13, January 1956: 53–65.

heroism. Action, Phan Bội Châu concluded, was the only tangible component of heroism.[33]

The conception of the heroic figure continued to evolve in Châu's works throughout the 1920s and 30s. The third stage of his evolution is illustrated in his pamphlet on the young patriot Phạm Hồng Thái (*Truyện Phạm Hồng Thái*, 1924), who was killed during an assassination attempt on Governor Merlin in Canton in 1924. I will return later to this figure from Nghệ An province, to whom the North Vietnamese regime awarded a key position within the imaginary of their movement. Through the figure of Phạm Hồng Thái, Phan Bội Châu completed the transformation suggested in his previous works. The young man's life brought together two eras of the patriotic struggle. Phạm Hồng Thái (1893–1924) was born Phạm Thành Tích, the grandson and son of the scholar-patriots Phạm Trọng Tuyển and Phạm Thành Mỹ, both of whom died under colonial repression.[34] This family tragedy only strengthened his patriotism. In 1922, Thái left his native province to join patriotic organisations based in China, accompanied by the revolutionaries Lê Hồng Phong and Lê Thiết Hùng. The young Thái, according to Châu, exemplified the shift in heroism from the hands of an enlightened elite to the omnipresent masses.[35] His acts of bravery concretised the need for the "right of the lower classes" to participate in nation-building. From then on, the fatherland extended the privilege of the legitimate struggle to the people. The honour of lineage could not compete with the grandeur of the just cause.

The ambiguity of Phan Bội Châu's approach, however, kept him from being considered a precursor of Vietnamese communism. He never ventured into paradigms,[36] refusing notably to accord primacy in heroism to "the consciousness of the working class". Though Châu conferred upon the "lower classes" the means to participate fully in a patriotic movement, he maintained that the "enlightened figure" of the intellectual was still more suited to guide "the great disorder of the popular masses".

---

[33] For more on this, see the various historic portraits proposed by Phan Bội Châu in *Việt Nam nghĩa liệt sĩ* (The martyrs of Vietnam). Hanoi: nxb Văn Học, re-issued in 1984.

[34] Phạm Thị Kim, ed. *Phạm Hồng Thái*. Hồ Chí Minh City, 1994.

[35] Phan Bội Châu. "Suu tâm, văn tế liệt sĩ Phạm Hồng Thái" (Funeral oration for the martyr Pham Hông Thai), *Văn Học*, Hanoi, December 1967: 50–2.

[36] Hương Phố. "Nhân đọc một tác phẩm, góp phần đánh giá Tư tưởng Phan Bội Châu" (Measuring a work: contributions by and appreciation of Phan Bội Châu's thought), *Nghiên cứu Lịch sử*, Hanoi, no. 94, January 1967: 23–8.

DRV ideologues criticised what they called "the limits of Phan Bội Châu thought", but put it down to the nineteenth-century spirit of his era.[37] Whether he was the first Vietnamese socialist or a scholar from the previous century, Phan Bội Châu still revolutionised the conception of the heroic figure in Vietnam. His writings were the first to impose a distinction between two types of relationships to patriotic excellence within a community. He was the first to grant the people the right to take part in the just cause of the fatherland and to don the robes of the national hero.

For Phan Bội Châu, the hero was made in the way he surmounted difficulties to defend the just cause. But the grandeur of the heroic figure took on real meaning in his relationship with death. A hero did not fear death. "Death is useful; one should not die an insipid death, but in the struggle, not in the arms of one's wife," Châu remarks. The hero therewith affirmed the depth of his commitment. Phan Bội Châu was in fact falling back on a patriotic tradition that imbued martyrs, such as Trần Bình Trọng (thirteenth century), Bùi Thị Xuân (eighteenth century), Trương Định (nineteenth century), and Thủ Khoa Huân (nineteenth century), with an aura of indisputable purity. According to Châu, a hero was solely defined by his absolute self-sacrifice, be he "famous" or "anonymous". When he wrote biographies, Châu invariably recounted the last hours of the hero with emphasis and emotion. In the 1950s, government ideologues condemned Phan Bội Châu's literary style, which was stamped with the "petit-bourgeois" lyricism of the late nineteenth century. They agreed, however, on his vision of the heroic figure. The death of a hero guaranteed the continuation of an ideal and appeased the torment of the nation's spirits. Phan Bội Châu always concluded with the declaration that the hero should have

[37] Tôn Quang Phiệt, *Phan Bội Châu và một giai đoạn Lịch sử chống Pháp của nhân dân Việt Nam* (Phan Bội Châu, a historical period in the Vietnamese people's fight against France). Hanoi: nxb Văn Hóa, 1958. Nguyễn Anh, "Bàn thêm về nguyên nhân ra đời của hai xu hướng cải lương và bạo động trong phong trào cách mạng đầu thế kỷ XX" (New thoughts on the cause of insurrectional events in the revolutionary movement of the early twentieth century), *Nghiên cứu Lịch sử*, Hanoi, no. 65, August 1964: 35–42. Trần Huy Liệu, "Nhớ lại Ông già Bến Ngự" (In memory of the elder Bến Ngự), *Nghiên cứu Lịch sử*, Hanoi, no. 47, February 1963: 40–4. Nguyễn Thị Tuyết Mai, "Phan Bội Châu trong Lịch sử cách mạng Việt Nam" (Phan Bội Châu in Vietnamese revolutionary history), *Nghiên cứu Lịch sử*, Hanoi, no. 104, November 1967: 41–4. Tôn Quang Phiệt, "Phan Bội Châu trong Lịch sử chống thực dân Pháp của dân tộc Việt Nam" (Phan Bội Châu in the history of the Vietnamese people's anticolonial struggle against the French), *Văn Sử Địa*, Hanoi, no. 13, 1956: 53–65.

a certain charisma in order to fulfil the social role demanded of him by his community. This idea evolved in his work, and in the deeds of Phạm Hồng Thái, Châu found a true grandeur. The hero's charismatic nature destined him for a mission within the community. Whether mandarin, peasant, or worker, the heroic figure had to serve as a model of the morality and action of his time.

Why did historians and men of letters of the 1950s so frantically scrutinise Phan Bội Châu's legacy? What did they hope to find in the scholar-patriot's reflections about the notion of the hero? The reinterpreting of Phan Bội Châu's works was part of the North Vietnamese regime's repositioning vis-à-vis its national imaginary. Ever since Trường Chinh's speech extolling a Maoist rupture between the old and the new in May 1952,[38] the official historiography was reoriented toward the demand for continuity in national history. Ideologues sought national origins for this imported new figure. The critic Nguyễn Đình Chú affirmed that the theoretical basis for the "new man" was already found in Châu's *Painful History of a Usurped Dynasty*. He explained how, in shifting the source of heroism to the people, Phan Bội Châu was the first to affirm the existence and the primacy of the collective hero over the individual. This was clearly an effort to reinforce the Vietnamisation of a foreign concept. The same thing happened in the early 1960s when the State and the Party encouraged local governments to build memorials to new heroic figures. The desire for genealogical continuity is an old custom in Vietnamese culture. By situating the birth of the collective hero within the work of a national patriotic thinker, the DRV reappropriated the exogeneity of an internationalist myth. Our interest is less in whether Phan Bội Châu really was the first to create the collective hero in Vietnam, than in seeing how the communist Vietnamese regime sought, in the period between the two wars (1954–1964), to nationalise an imported figure in order to strengthen its hold in the countryside.

The Importing of an Internationalist Model

In just a few years' time, the DRV reappropriated the spirit of the traditional heroic figure. The birth of the new hero took place at the conference of

---

[38] Trường Chinh, "Thế nào là anh hùng mới?" (What is the new heroism?), in Hồ Chí Minh, Trường Chinh. *Thi đua và anh hùng mới* (Emulation of the new hero). Nha Tuyên truyền và Văn nghệ, 1953.

Tuyên Quang in May 1952. The new exemplary man was at the head of a restructured hierarchy of political virtue and was accompanied in official historiography by a reflection on his place within the new society. Unlike their counterparts in China, North Vietnamese leaders saw the new hero as much more than an infinite biographical source. On the contrary, he needed an air of normalcy in order to be easily understood by the average peasant, who was often far removed from the contingencies and abstractions of political discourse. The new man could now be a cadre, a soldier, or an outstanding peasant. Emulating a hero was not seen simply as a communist invention since Confucian tradition had used heroic tales for centuries to educate the people. Communism just increased the ways in which this could be accomplished: strict ideological control of the hero's character, massive and global propaganda techniques, and an authoritarian policy of mobilising the members of the collective under the exemplary banner of new virtuous figures.[39] The new man quickly became a high-priority stake for a government trying to root its political legitimacy within a new, active force. Far from all abstraction, the new bureaucracy of heroism generated a contingent of men and women who strengthened the government's power structures (administration, mass organisations, the army, etc.). These transformations directly reveal changes within the regime.

Vietnamese revolutionaries had heard about Stakhanovism even before the war through the French communist publications that were widely distributed throughout the country with the establishment of the Popular Front in 1936. The new Soviet hero extolled the superiority of the "communist man" over his "capitalist and imperialist" antithesis. Soviet society had two types of heroic figures: the "Hero of Socialist Labour" (*Geroi Socialisticheskogo Truda*) and the "Hero of the Soviet Union" (*Geroi Sovetskogo Soyuza*). The honorific title of "labour hero" had been established by a decree (*ukase*) of the Presidium of the Supreme Soviet on 27 July 1927. In December 1938, Soviet leaders replaced this with "Hero of Socialist Labour", but the aim was still to promote "people who have accomplished exceptional innovations in industry, agriculture, transport, science and technology that improve the economy, culture or science in the country, or who increased the influence and the glory of the Soviet

[39] Mary Sheridan. "The Emulation of Heroes", *The China Quarterly*, London, no. 33, 1968: 47.

Union".[40] The title of "Hero of the Soviet Union" dated from a decree issued by the Central Committee of the USSR on 16 April 1934. It was only granted to "people who have rendered an important service to the State through great heroic deeds".[41] In the 1930s, these two honorific titles determined the outlines of a new internationalist ideal ready for export to the socialist world. Within the Soviet Union, the movement for the construction of the new man gathered momentum on 30 August 1935, when a miner from Donbass, Alexei Stakhanov, single-handedly extracted 102 tons of iron ore. Beyond the mere details of the story, the productivist movement took on the name of its hero and allowed the Stalinist regime to "reaffirm its authority over the working-class through intimidation and the creation of a loyal caste of privileged workers".[42] In the Russia of the 1930s, the movement thus served more to consolidate the government's foothold than to increase their production.

The internationalist "new man" arrived on Asian shores in late 1943. In November–December of that year, the Chinese Communist Party (CCP) organ, *Jiefang Ribao* (*Liberation Daily*), illustrated its front pages daily with colour portraits of "labour heroes" or distinguished soldiers from communist-held areas in the North. On 19 December 1943, Mao Zedong's movement organised a conference to officially elect new internationalist figures from the Chinese revolutionary movement. The CCP's propaganda organ called upon "Labour Heroes" and "Military Heroes" again during the Chinese civil war to mobilise the population in Communist-held areas.

The first Vietnamese emulation tried to espouse a more flexible approach and outlook than that of the Yunnan campaign (1942–44). The new man in true Sino-Soviet form would not become a reality in Vietnam before 1950–51. The spread of "new heroism" is linked to the "conversations between leaders of the CPSU [Communist Party of the Soviet Union]

[40] From December 1938 to 1 September 1971, the title of "Hero of Socialist Labour" was awarded to 16,245 people. See articles on "labour hero" and "hero of socialist labour" in *Great Soviet Encyclopedia*, vol. 6. New York: MacMillan, 1975, p. 594 (Moscow, 1970).

[41] From April 1934 to 1 September 1971, the title of "Hero of the Soviet Union" was awarded to 12,447 people. See articles on "Heroes of the Soviet Union" in *Great Soviet Encyclopedia*, p. 594.

[42] Donald Filtzer. *Soviet Workers and Stalinist Industrialisation: The Formation of Modern Soviet Productions Relations (1928–1941)*. New York: M.E. Sharpe Inc., 1986, p. 179.

and their counterparts in the CCP" which took place in Beijing in April 1950.[43] Focusing on organisational issues within the Party and propaganda bodies in socialist countries, emissaries from the CPSU trained new Chinese advisors bound for the provinces of North Vietnam. In Vietnam in the early 1950s, the profile of the socialist new man as developed by heads of the National Emulation Committee resembled the internationalist hero that Soviet ideologues had created in the 1930s. In the Soviet Union in the 1920s, the historian Mikhail Pokrovsky (1868–1932) proposed a reform of the historic discourse which systematically did away with great men, events, and dates. But this determinist, linear, and irreversible model, governed by strict Marxist laws, was criticised by the Bolshevik intellectuals Anatoli Lunacharski (1875–1933) and Nikolai Bukharin (1888–1938). Both men died in the purges of the 1930s, however, and Stalin rediscovered the advantages of nationalism, which reinstated the prominence of the personalised heroic figure before the renewed outbreak of war.[44] The debate also shook up leaders in Hanoi in the 1950s, though it never reached such an abstract level. While Khrushchev's de-Stalinisation speech split the communist world,[45] intellectuals and theorists from the Workers' Party (Đảng Lao Động, or VWP) in Hanoi carried out heated discussions of the individual heroic figure, the cult of personality, and the new heroism in the journal *Văn sử Địa* (*Culture, History, and Geography*).

Communism and Official Heroism in Vietnam

During his speech at the Tuyên Quang conference of 5 May 1952, Trường Chinh laid out the definition of the new hero in North Vietnam:

> The hero is oriented towards the party, dedicated to serving the people. He does not oppress the people and takes part in the liberation of the masses. Most heroes are workers and peasants. For the good of the masses, the hero is a dedicated volunteer, exemplary in production and labour. The hero follows the political line of the Vanguard Party and the government. The hero has a close relationship with the masses; he

---

[43] Conversation between leaders of the central committee of the CPSU and leaders of the CCP, in Archives of the Central Committee of the CCP. Moscow, files no. 1200 and 1201, April–December 1950.

[44] Martin Malia. *The Soviet Tragedy: A History of Socialism in Russia, 1917– 1991*. New York: Free Press, 1995.

[45] The Khrushchev "de-Stalinisation" speech was made on 24 February 1956, before the 1,436 delegates of the twentieth congress of the CPSU.

> must belong to the masses. The hero is neither proud nor conceited; he tries to learn; he practices criticism and self-criticism in order to make constant progress. The hero has a revolutionary spirit, initiatives, knowledge, and a new discipline that stems from a rich experience derived from contact with the masses. The hero has a strong sense of class. He can distinguish between good and bad, friend and enemy. He is selfless, and has a responsible attitude towards leaders and the masses. His participation in the struggle and in production is not driven by individual interest but by a collective one.[46]

DRV leaders wanted to impose a new model of society, so they had to renew the link between the government and the governed. The people had to understand that only by acting in line with the legitimate government would they approach a promised era of "economic prosperity and social equality".[47] Peasants, workers, and small shopkeepers had to be realigned in their responsibilities towards the community. The new man satisfied a juxtaposition of three criteria: political (total Party loyalty), technical (exceptional combative or productivist qualities), and social (being from and remaining in close contact with the masses). Heroism officials singled out the most virtuous of these subjects. They honoured the discipline and dedication of these exemplary men and women in an effort to keep their hold on the social space.

The criteria for civic exemplarity had to be understood by all cadres in leadership positions, starting at the communal level. The new man was the fruit of a new socio-economic environment which would be the basis for the reorganisation of society. The State promoted the man of the people and a new community solidarity, and rejected outright a model of society that had championed individualism since the beginning of French colonisation.[48] Paradoxically, the road towards the new man offered leaders the hope of a restoration, a return toward the holistic values which placed the members of the community in a relationship of dependence with the nation. Hồ Chí Minh stated that "socialist morality is not the same everywhere.

---

[46] *Đại hội toàn quốc các chiến sĩ thi đua và cán bộ gương mẫu từ 1.5.1952 đến 6.5.1952 tại Việt Bắc* (National conference for emulation combatants and outstanding cadres in the Việt Bắc from May 1–6 1952), in AVN3, BLD, file no. 432, 1952, pp. 34–5.

[47] Văn Tạo. *Chủ nghĩa anh hùng cách mạng Việt Nam* (Vietnamese revolutionary heroism). Hanoi: nxb Khoa học xã hội, 1972, p. 6.

[48] Nguyễn Văn Kỳ. *La Société vietnamienne face à la modernité. Le Tonkin de la fin du XIXe siècle à la seconde guerre mondiale* (Vietnamese society confronting modernity. Tonkin from the late nineteenth century to World War II). Paris: L'Harmattan, 1995.

Figure 2. The "New Heroes" of the conference at Tuyên Quang (1952)

In our country, it is synonymous with diligence and frugality. Everyone who practices emulation studies with the spirit of socialism, works within a socialist framework, and has a socialist morality."[49] By joining mass organisations and the Party, the Vietnamese new man was "liberated from the yoke of individual self-interest and took possession of himself".[50]

To better understand the role of the new man, we must look at Hồ Chí Minh's place in the Vietnamese community. His intellectual training in the 1920s was mainly in Marxist-Leninist thought though he later advocated a more moderate ideological approach to the movement. Upon his return to Vietnam in 1941, Hồ managed to make himself the sole model of

[49] Hồ Chí Minh. "Nói chuyện với sinh viên và cán bộ Việt Nam đang học và công tác" (October 1961) (Discussion with Vietnamese students and cadres in training), in *Toàn tập*, p. 115.

[50] Nguyễn Khánh Toàn. "Việc xây dựng con người mới và trách nhiệm của khoa học xã hội" (On the construction of the new man and the responsibility of the social sciences), *Học Tập*, Hanoi, no. 8, 1968: 51.

legitimate virtue.[51] He chose Marxism-Leninism, it was repeated throughout the countryside, because it was the best choice for the country. The veracity of such a choice left no room for debate. Only one who could distinguish good from bad could legitimately hold the reins of power, and his position as head of state conferred upon him this gift. The new society was a sort of dynastic rupture, but Hồ Chí Minh and his Party would see to the formation of the people's spirit. The new man was the product of a new society built on the principle of the right political leader. The regime made him the most ardent defender of State values, of revolution, of socialism, and of the struggle for national unification. Hồ's life symbolised the very essence of the nation's advance towards socialism. He had such "love for his fellow man", explained government propaganda, that from a young age he naturally turned towards the truly oppressed of his era — the workers and peasants. His humanity, continued Party hagiography, made injustice unacceptable. For the head of state, injustice stigmatised the "imperialists and the oppressing classes". Hồ's love of justice led him to become the defender of the "poor and oppressed".[52] Hà Huy Giáp saw Uncle Hồ's humanism as the path that would lead the government to Marxism-Leninism; it was reason and the love of one's neighbour — he continues — that eventually brought Vietnam into the fold of socialism. Liberating the country meant releasing the people from the yoke of oppression. Independence would usher in the systemic arrival of a new man, born of the humanism that the father of the country had for his legitimate children. Every member of the community was indebted to him for his kindness. In return for this love for his fellow men, Hồ deserved the utmost respect from his citizens. The balance of society depended on it. Since the father of the country had sacrificed himself, the good citizen was called upon to do the same. For the people, the new man was simply the result of the affirmation of this traditional duality.

The new man was thus based on two types of veneration, one linking him to the people and one to the ideology of his leaders. In the end, both

---

[51] Helmut Martin. "Canonical Writings and Forms of the Personality Cult at China's Periphery (Vietnam: A Hồ Chí Minh Cult Without an Orthodox Canon)", in *Cult and Canon, the Origins and Development of State Maoism*. New York: Sharpe, 1982, pp. 150–4.

[52] Hà Huy Giáp was quick to give Hồ's humanism a Biblical tone. "Jesus Christ said: a man who has committed a mistake and begs heaven's forgiveness is better than ninety believers." Hà Huy Giap, "Một vài suy nghĩ về đạo lý làm người của Hồ Chủ tịch" (Some reflections on Hồ Chí Minh thought), *Học tập*, Hanoi, no. 5, 1969: 29.

exploited the same key element: his discipline. He was a man of results. His actions alone determined the strength and also the limits of his importance within society. The transformation of men seemed to be the fruit of his good management. He was not asked to think but to work and join in. In the Stalinist and Maoist world, the production of thought was allocated to intellectuals. The Party encouraged initiatives on the part of the new man, but only in the area of production, not ideas. He had a disciplined respect for his creator, and action brought him into a Promethean face-to-face encounter with his hostile environment.

Mencius defined righteousness (*vì nghĩa*, *chính nghĩa*, or *nghĩa*) as the only conceivable path. Political action in a Confucian society was judged according to this principle, and any ruler who failed to honour it could lose the Mandate of Heaven. The question was to determine the natural limits of what was right and wrong. In the twentieth century, Hồ Chí Minh summed up what was "right" in a maxim: "*Vì Độc lập — Tự do của tổ quốc*" (Independence and freedom for the fatherland). The just cause was that of the fatherland, so the just man could only be one who fought to defend it. Patriotism was the flesh and blood of politics in a nation repeatedly coveted from abroad. The just cause was that of the nation's glorious ancestors, those who had fought to defend the country against the string of Chinese, French, and then American invaders. Governance by a foreign power made a mockery of the founders' spirits. The insurrection of August 1945 — whereby Hồ Chí Minh declared the country's independence from France after the Japanese surrender — pitted the just against those who illegitimately held power. Once the Japanese and the French were driven out, Hồ Chí Minh's rule attained a primacy that no opposition force had managed to obtain. The victory of the Việt Minh helped realise the legitimacy of the new regime. It was then up to the government to secure its power to the virtue of illustrious ancestors, and to the loyalty of the new outstanding citizens. Hồ Chí Minh, the Party, and eventually the working class symbolised this defence of the just, and the new man owed them absolute loyalty. In the government's quest for exemplary men, it always took into consideration a potential candidate's loyalty or "political positioning".[53]

[53] *Hướng dẫn về việc lựa anh hùng thi đua Ái quốc (Phong thi đua ái quốc Trung ương)* (Recommendations on selecting heroes of national emulation [Central department of national emulation]), in AVN3, Coll. BLD, file no. 510, unnumbered document, December 1956, p. 2.

In Confucian thought, the just was something unique and indivisible, and under a Marxist-Leninist government it was beyond all dispute. Only loyalty to the just cause could attain the good positioning of Man in society. To define the new man, one needed only to follow the model of virtue (*Đức*) laid down by historic figures from the nation's past; every period had figures whose lives could be personified into examples.[54] Hồ Chí Minh himself symbolised this symbiosis in Vietnam. For Phạm Văn Đồng, "President Hồ not only asked the people for more solidarity, he put this solidarity into practice. What's more, President Hồ was not only the symbol of solidarity, he alone was this solidarity."[55] Hồ Chí Minh was the personification par excellence of the new man. Revolutionary heroism represented the most modern and most developed version of the nation's heroic tradition. Hà Huy Giáp even asserted that its leader's exemplary journey illustrated the progressive gestation of the new man in North Vietnam, who existed only with respect to his model. The new man was the anthropomorphism of a "body-nation", an idea to which I will return in the following chapters. In choosing the just cause, the exemplary man showed a natural "greatness of soul". Society simply offered him respect and veneration in return.

Morality, Heroes, and the Revolutionary Ideal

Scholars and ideologues often debated whether the hero was the product of his environment, or vice versa.[56] Much has been written about the primordial influence of the Vietnamese land on the greatness of its people. According to popular belief, climate changes, natural disasters, typhoons, and deadly floods only strengthened the vigour of the Vietnamese people and their attachment to their native land. Chinese geomancy admitted that there existed a "land that gave birth to heroes and that it had to be kept in order". Vietnam was this land, its patriots claimed incessantly. The birth

---

[54] Trần Dân Tiên (pseudonym of Hồ Chí Minh). *Những mẩu chuyện về đời hoạt động của Hồ Chủ tịch* (The important phases of President Hô's activities). Hanoi: nxb Văn học, 1960.

[55] Phạm Văn Đồng. *Hồ Chủ tịch, lãnh tụ của chúng ta* (President Hô, our leader). Hanoi: nxb Sự thật, 1963, p. 10.

[56] Trần Huy Liệu. "Anh hùng tạo thời thế hay thời thế tạo Anh hùng?" (Does the hero create the environment or does the environment create the hero?), *Nghiên cứu Lịch sử*, Hanoi, no. 96, March 1967: 1–57. Hồng Quang, "Lịch sử và chủ nghĩa anh hùng" (History and heroism), *Nghiên cứu Lịch sử*, no. 99, June 1967: 1–9.

of the Communist Party in 1930 was but another stage in the heroic destiny of their nation. It was born of the actions of the men and women touched by the grace of a heroic ancestral land:

> Born in a land of radiant beauty, but a narrow one, wedged between the mountains and the sea, our people had to live for centuries under the continual threat of foreign invaders and natural disasters. They needed an immense greatness of spirit to withstand hurricanes, floods, and droughts month after month, and not die of hunger or the cold.[57]

The new man, with his close filial link with the new political authority, showed the same "greatness of soul" as his ancestors. He was not merely the product of an imported internationalism, but primarily the product of the "culture, spirit and spiritual beauty of the Vietnamese nation". The new man, as eponym for the outstanding citizen of the past, was defined by his close association with the ruling power. For his sacrifice to the just cause and his great filial piety to the nation, society — in the form of each member of the community — had the duty to help educate these "virtuous men". The State, out of respect for an ancestral principle, had to forge the spirit of its citizens. In the beginning, each man was like a blank slate, and his socialisation was the duty of those in power. Every man could aim to become a new man. His "greatness of spirit" was already present in the blank slate of his life. Only a collaboration with "reactionary forces" (landlords, the colonial administration, etc.) could drive it away. But in that case it was already too late, the period of "harmful socialisation" had already taken place. The new man did not bear re-education since he had never supported the unjust cause.[58]

The new man's "greatness of spirit" stemmed from his irremediable bond with the land of his ancestors, with his own virtue, and from his ability to follow the teachings of a worldly power bearing the "Mandate of Heaven". A just society sought balance. To this end, political leaders

---

[57] Vũ Hồng. "Sự ra đời của Đảng và bước ngoặt lịch sử của chủ nghĩa anh hùng" (Birth of the Party and the important stages of heroism), p. 75.

[58] The myth of the "blank slate" was an essential part of Vietnamese culture. It was more important than an individual's social origins. Indeed, it was better to be from a bourgeois family but decide early to fight for the "just cause" than the opposite, to be from the working classes but let oneself be led astray by the enemy. There were quite a few government leaders (Hồ Chí Minh, Võ Nguyên Giáp, etc.) and new heroes (Tôn Thất Tùng, Phạm Ngọc Thạch, etc.) who were not from the working class. None, however, skipped the important early stages in the socialisation process.

had to show unfailing respect to their most distinguished citizens. Their pride in the heroes of yesterday and today was matched only by their need to venerate them in return. As Krushchev's de-Stalinisation policy spread throughout Asia in 1956, North Vietnamese ideologues quickly stepped forward to make the distinction between the cult of personality (*sùng bái cá nhân*) and the veneration that the State traditionally bestowed on those who served it well (*tôn kính anh hùng*).[59] Paying respects to a heroic figure, the VWP repeated, was primarily an homage to the spirit of the nation. This principle led to a symbiosis between the hero and the nation's history, which was completely different from the deification of an individual personality that was being condemned by the new leaders in Moscow.

The government's homage to its heroes initially had an internationalist bent, but gradually shifted towards a cultural hierarchy in the 1960s. Confucious, who saw reality as something in perpetual transformation, declared, "I hate stubbornness", since the judgment and the conduct of the "virtuous man" should not become ossified.[60] Thus, the definition of the new man has more to do with morality than ideology, more with wisdom than philosophy. He was indeed considered a man of national virtue. Collective morality was at the very heart of orthodox Confucianism. The wise man was a good man, a man of the middle ground, and a moral one. He was, as Confucious propounded in his *Analects*, in harmony with nature (the earth, sky, etc.). Unfailingly, his way of being enabled him to adapt to changing reality. In 1946–48, when the DRV broached the question of the new life (*đời sống mới*), their policies required such adaptiveness. What looked like an internationalist-style rupture was more a question of immanence, as the government simply reacted to changing circumstances to suit their cultural needs. It was an ambitious goal, to "launch a transformation of popular consciousness".[61] This re-calibration of society along class lines implied de facto a re-centering of the middle ground.

Despite their occasional rejection of Confucian principles, ideologues never strayed from the idea of the just, the true, the middle ground, the wise, reasonable, or possible. Instead, they simply slightly altered the definitions. Within such a system, morality only served to legislate the relationship to the just (*lí*); the legitimacy and perenniality of society were at stake.

---

[59] Trần Huy Liệu. "Bàn thêm về vấn đề chống sùng bái cá nhân" (New reflections on the the cult of personality), *Văn Sử Địa*, Hanoi, no. 19, July 1956.

[60] François Jullien. *Un sage est sans idée ou l'autre de la philosophie* (A sage is without ideas, or the other in philosphy). Paris: Seuil, 1998, p. 22.

[61] Shaun Malarney, *Culture, Ritual and Revolution in Vietnam.*

In his essay on the responsibility of the social sciences in the creation of the new man, Nguyễn Khánh Toàn wrote that the new man could only be defined by his relationship to the collective. His ideology tied him to the present, and his ethics determined the stability of his role within the community. The new man strove to be the personification of the just. Hồ Chí Minh often said that "morality is the primary — if not the essential — quality of revolutionary fighters".[62] The morality of the new man lay in his self-sacrifice for the good of the nation. In one of Hồ's key texts from 1958, he writes (under the pseudonym Trần Lực), "real self-interest is collective interest", so "Trần Phú, Ngô Gia Tự, Lê Hồng Phong, Nguyễn Văn Cừ, Hoàng Văn Thụ and Nguyễn Thị Minh Khai were the real precursors of the new revolutionary morality".[63] One could, in fact, wonder what was really "new" about this perspective, and whether that term was warranted. For Hồ Chí Minh, revolutionary morality had to satisfy four essential elements. One had to: "make a life-long commitment to fight for the Party and the revolution; strive to work for the Party, obey its discipline, and correctly implement its policies; put the interests of the Party and the people first, before self-interest; devote oneself to studying Marxism-Leninism, and always apply oneself to practicing criticism and self-criticism to improve one's mind."[64]

Revolutionary morality dictated the limits of the possible within the community. "The Path is not far from man," we read in the *Analects*. As a tool for group cohesion, the revolutionary ethic in Vietnam sprang from within and did not tolerate excessive theorising. Hồ Chí Minh stressed that civic morality was meaningless unless put into practice:

> The morality of a citizen leads him to respect certain principles: obey government laws; be disciplined in one's work; conform to collective directives; pay your taxes in full to serve the collective interest; take part enthusiastically in collective works; protect the public good; protect the nation.[65]

---

[62] Trần văn Giàu. *Giá trị tinh thần truyền thống của dân tộ* (The value of the traditional spirit of the people). Nxb Khoa học xã hội, 1980, p. 306.

[63] Trần Lực (aka *Hồ Chí Minh*). "Đạo đức cách mạng" (Revolutionary morality), *Học tập*, Hanoi, no. 35, December 1958: 11.

[64] Trần Lực (aka *Hồ Chí Minh*). "Đạo đức cách mạng":12.

[65] Hồ Chí Minh. "Đạo đức công nhân" (Workers' morality), in *Xây dựng con người mới* (Constructing the new man). Hanoi: nxb Chính Trị Quốc Gia, 1995, p. 103.

Defending the integrity and stability of the "great Vietnamese family" thus became the driving force of the new man. "In armed battle as in production", the Party tried to animate the spirit of victory within the Vietnamese people.[66] It made heroism the basis of revolutionary morality.

Cultural scholar Vũ Khiêu writes that the Party, by aligning itself with the new man, restored the immanence of a revolutionary morality inherent within its "four-thousand-year history". The new man was a model of revolutionary moralism. However, the government expected neither speeches nor eloquent writings from him. All he had to do was conscientiously practise the four founding virtues in his work and in his daily life: Thrift, Diligence, Integrity, and Honesty (*Cần, kiệm, liêm, chính*). Vũ Khiêu maintains that Hồ Chí Minh gave a totally new meaning to these key values of Confucian morality.[67] He even added a fifth element to these four "golden rules": "Everything for the collective and nothing for self-interest." Still, it would be wrong to call this a revision. Hồ Chí Minh himself bore the stigmata of the new moral ideal. As proof of his dedication to the nation, Party chiefs pointed to his selfless decision to not have a family:[68] "Hồ never once thought about himself. His family was a family in the larger sense, that of a global working class, of the Vietnamese people." The myth of this self-sacrifice by the "father of the people" for the collective was firmly anchored, and was in itself an essential part of the revolutionary ethic they

---

66 Vũ Khiêu. "Đảng ta và chủ nghĩa anh hùng" (Our Party and heroism), in *Anh hùng và Nghệ si*. Saigon: nxb Văn học, nxb Giải Phóng, 1975, p. 176.

67 Vũ Khiêu. "Tấm gương sáng ngời ở Hồ Chủ tịch" (Wholeheartedly with our model President Hồ), in *Anh hùng và Nghệ si*, p. 247.

68 In 1993 Sophie Quinn-Judge published an article about the romantic life of the young Nguyễn Ái Quốc in the 1920s–30s proving that he had a relationship with the militant Nguyễn Thị Minh Khai. Vietnamese authorities were adamant that the article not circulate in the country. See Sophie Quinn-Judge, "Hô Chi Minh: New Perspectives from the Comintern Files", *The Viêt Nam Forum,* Yale University, no. 14, 1993: 61–81. The writer Dương Thu Hương wrote her novel *Au zenith* (At the zenith), published in 2009, about this taboo subject: "In 1953, the president [the president is not named but it becomes obvious soon enough that the author is referring to Hồ Chí Minh] falls madly in love, at sixty-something years old, with a very young woman. He has a family with her and takes them to Hanoi after retaking the capital. But he is not an ordinary man, he is the father of the country. When he wants to make his union official, the ministers, whom he helped put in power, make him understand that this private affair would pull him down from his political pedestal. The president gives in, believing that he is making a legitimate choice for the State. From that day forward, his life would never be the same." Paris: Sabine Wespieser, 2009.

wanted to pass on to the people. The well-being of the group depended on the affirmation of this patriotic duty. The actions and the daily life of the new man materialised the essence of the five virtues.[69]

On the other hand, the weaknesses of the new man were also brought into play as the model spread through society. Pointing out the "wrong-doing" and "social evils" of the present time led back to the affirmation of the new man's ethical role in society. The accusations ran from waste to theft, bureaucratism, sectarianism, narrow-mindedness, corruption, formalist indiscipline, pride, egotism, laziness, provincialism, individualism, or excessive self-interest. The spread of the criteria for the new man allowed Party cadres to catalogue the weaknesses to be eradicated. The enumeration of his sins presented a negative image of his virtues to a population now on the path to a "new life". The creation of the new man concretised the State's new civic morality.

The heroes of Tuyên Quang did not need facts to prove their existence; the Party had conjured biographies for them while avoiding detours into their private lives. The new man was a man of action. The State asked him to be loyal and efficient, and in return he received a shining tribute. His sudden appearance in collective memory (administrative archives, books, films, etc.) provided the historian with a new object of study.[70] The new man became the incarnation of a society in transition. In the following chapters, I look at the movements of these peasants, artisans, and labourers whose everyday actions make up the "works and days" of the common people and whom we now look at with new eyes. It is a history of the trivial, like a history of daily life, of things that we do every day without really thinking about them. The new man is part of this amplified quotidian, a man of the people who has been struck by a surprising and unexpected historiographical collusion.

---

[69] *Hồ Chủ tịch dân chủ, kỷ luật và đạo đức cách mạng* (The democratic President Hô). Hanoi: nxb Sự thật, 1967, p. 35.

[70] On this subject, see the excellent study by Michel Foucault, "La Vie des hommes infâmes" (The lives of infamous men), *Cahiers du chemin,* Paris, no. 29, 1 January 1977: 12–29. Reprinted in Foucault, *Dits et écrits 1954–1988,* vol. III: 1976–1979. Paris: Gallimard, 1994, pp. 237–53.

CHAPTER 2

Patriotic Emulation (1948–1952)

> What is the goal of patriotic emulation? It is to fight famine and poverty, to fight ignorance, and to fight the foreign invaders. The way to do this is to rely upon the people's forces and the people's spirit, in order to bring happiness for the people.... The first results of patriotic emulation will be the following: the entire people will have enough food and clothing, [they] will have learnt to read and write, the entire army will have enough food and armaments to wipe out the invaders, and the whole nation will be completely unified and independent.
>
> Hồ Chí Minh[1]

> Lord, it is through greater obedience to your will that I feel the most free.
>
> Saint Augustine

With the outbreak of war with France in 1946, the Việt Minh resistance was isolated on the international scene. At the close of World War II, the Soviet Union had openly ignored the Indochinese question to avoid jeopardising their policies in Europe.[2] In addition, the traditional disinterest of Soviet leaders for this Asian peninsula had turned to discord when Hồ Chí Minh decided to dissolve the Indochinese Communist Party in November 1945. After that, the DRV remained politically open to dialogue with any country willing to support its demands for independence. Moscow held this against Hồ Chi Minh for a long time. Vietnam remained only of secondary importance to both the

---

[1] "Appeal for Patriotic Emulation" (Lời kêu gọi thi đua ái quốc), in Hồ Chí Minh. *Selected Writings*. Hanoi: Foreign Languages Publishing House, 1977, pp. 84–5.

[2] Stein Tønnesson. *Vietnam 1946: How the War Began*. University of California Press, 2009.

Cominform and its little-known Asian wing. In 1947, a report on Indochina by the Soviet Ministry of Foreign Affairs praised Hồ Chí Minh as a "high-quality journalist with good theoretical training".[3] The Kremlin continued — though not publicly — to see Hồ as a potential "Asian Tito".

Meanwhile, the French were pushing for a solution under Bảo Đại, which further confused the situation. Paris excluded any possibility of negotiation with the DRV as per the Halong Bay Agreement of 5 June 1948. The Việt Minh fought to increase its presence within the country and transform the chaos of its rise in 1945 into political stability. In late 1947, Trường Chinh's *The Resistance Will Win* proposed the first theoretical outline of the movement, declaring that the Việt Minh defended a just cause — it was not a question of politics but ethics. Hồ Chí Minh wanted to usher in a "new life" whereby a society based on a horizontal relationship between the members of a group would replace the old and perverted vertical relationship linking an individual to his sovereign. But in 1948, the DRV was not Vietnam; its territorial roots did not encompass all of the nation's cultural, ethnic, or political diversity. The peasantry was not as won over as the official historiography has claimed since 1954.

Thus the first order of business for the Việt Minh was mass mobilisation. The DRV counted on emulation campaigns to mobilise the people as these had already proven to be a great success throughout the communist world. During the war with France (1947–1954), Vietnam organised not one but two distinct emulation campaigns. The first, launched in June 1948, promoted patriotism under the term "patriotic emulation" (*phong trào thi đua ái quốc*). The second was embarked upon in the early 1950s and was entirely concerned with "socialist emulation" (*phong trào thi đua xã hội chủ nghĩa*). Until 1950 the aim had been to reformulate the individual in his relationship with the group, but now socialist emulation demanded the opposite: a transformation of society through the example of a new figure — the internationalist new man. In the winter of 1951–52, the second emulation campaign brought forth the emulation fighter (*Chiến sĩ thi đua*) and the new hero (*Anh hùng mới*). The Việt Minh government hoped the movement would strengthen its political influence on the nation and increase its "ideological legality" as it resumed its dialogue with the Soviets.[4]

[3] "Information report on the situation in Indochina for Comrade Jdanov", in Archives of the Cominform, Coll. no. 575, file no. 21, document no. 25/F 25116, 13 September 1947, p. 18.

[4] "Documents from the Information Services of Vietnam (Prague)", in Archives of the Cominform, Coll. no. 575, file no. 118, document no. 195, 6 February 1949.

Emulation and Collective Morality

In 1948, patriotic emulation tried to reposition the Vietnamese citizen at the centre of his community. The revolution — or more precisely, the revolutionary struggle — was first and foremost a moral issue. Hồ Chí Minh wrote, "Like a river that is fed by its spring, and dries up without it, a tree needs to have roots, and dies without them. A revolutionary needs to have morality; without it, regardless of his abilities, he cannot lead the people."[5] This transformation of morals did not, however, aim for a rupture between the old and the new. Hồ Chí Minh had mastered the art of gradual change and tactical moderation to a much greater extent than had Mao. The new Vietnamese Republic, based in the Việt Bắc province until the end of the war with the French, initially hoped to gain the upper hand over the pro-French nationalist government of General Nguyễn V.ăn Xuân (1948–49), its primary political rival. The revolutionaries were not trying to orient the country towards a foreign model of a progressivist society; rather, they wanted to create a homegrown alternative[6] and to renew their political purity, rejecting the compromises of the outdated, traditionalist ideology of the provisional central government. President Hồ hoped to win over the peasantry, who tended more towards conservatism than Bolshevik conversion.[7] By the end of the 1940s, efforts towards the "new life" were much more concerned with opposing "collaboration with France" than with aping an internationalist movement. The DRV sought a new legitimacy of power centred on collective morality, and concepts of family and filial duty underpinned these patriotic emulation campaigns.

The new man was first of all an enemy of the Nguyễn regime. The Việt Minh did not approach their patriotic war in terms of class; it was a *just war* that they fought against "invaders and oppressors, safeguarding the freedom and independence of the entire nation".[8] The myth of national purity was not set against feudalism in the Marxist-Leninist sense. The DRV was engaged in a progressivist struggle since it was founded on defending the vital interests of the common people; the government thus

---

[5] "Sửa đổi lề lối làm việc" (Correct the way we work), October 1947, in Hồ Chi Minh, *Về xây dựng con người mới* (On constructing the new man). Hanoi: nxb Chính trị Quốc gia, 1995, p. 86.

[6] Tân Sinh. *Đời Sống Mới* (The new life). UBVDDSM, 1948.

[7] "Sur la modification des mœurs" (On the changing of customs), in CAOM, Coll. du HCI, file no. 6–36, document no. 1376, 8 August 1948.

[8] Hồ Chí Minh. *Thi đua yêu nước* (Patriotic emulation), p. 8.

wanted to improve living conditions and increase democratic rights. Declaring its intention to defend the people helped to anchor the DRV's legitimacy in the countryside and facilitate a general mobilisation of the nation's working population. DRV leaders claimed a direct lineage with the heroes and heroines of the nation's glorious past. The discourse was about unity, but a union that the revolutionary movement wanted to take credit for. Patriotic emulation would first serve to "train new cadres and improve old ones in a new spirit of collective solidarity".[9] The government evoked the need to promote collective heroes capable of guiding the people towards the path of "people's liberation", a heroic collective mass which would give rise to a few exemplary individuals.[10]

As the war progressed, the Việt Minh had to step up its mobilisation. Though they had not invented the concept of the new man, the Vietnamese resistance hoped that emulation would strengthen the bonds of solidarity in a nation that had been divided by the colonial administration. In January 1948, DVR leaders reacted to several military setbacks by announcing the beginning of a second phase, one of "equilibrium". Patriotic emulation campaigns were launched as part of this change in strategy. The DRV increased the numbers of its regular troops, provincial forces, and local militia groups: from 50,000 at the beginning of the war to 250,000 soldiers and militia forces in 1948. Even though the French still occupied most of the area around the Red River Delta, the Việt Minh launched a "phase of pacification of the free zones" to strengthen its political activities in the villages. Võ Nguyên Giáp, Minister of National Defence, affirmed that guerrilla warfare no longer suited the political objectives of the new phase of action.[11] They had to take command on the battlefield and increase their mobilisation. Already in December 1945, the DRV had instituted administrative reforms to increase its hold on the local elite.[12]

---

[9] *Trường Chinh's Speech at the Congress for Party Cadres (14–18 January 1949)*, in CAOM, Coll. du CD, file no. 105, document no. 1417, 2 February 1950, p. 12.

[10] Lê Ngọc. "Nước ngoài thi đua, từ Xit Ta Kha Nop đến Ngô Man Hữu" (Emulation abroad, from Stakhanov to Ngô Man Huu), in *Sự thật*, no. 95, 19 June 1948, p. 10.

[11] Võ Nguyên Giáp. *People's War, People's Army*. Hanoi: Foreign Languages Press, 1962, p. 92.

[12] On the reform of the revolutionary administration, see George Ginsburgs, "Local Government and Administration in North Vietnam, 1945–1954", *The China Quarterly*, London, no. 10, April–June 1962: 174–204; and B. Fall, "Local Administration under the Viêt Minh", *Pacific Affairs*, Vancouver, no. 1, 1954.

Việt Minh leaders had a second objective in 1948: the rapid unification of a population that was "dismembered, forced together, and heterogeneous". The unanimous support of the people for the Việt Minh is a myth of communist historiography. In July 1945, Trường Chinh had already criticised the people of Tonkin for their poor engagement in the struggle to liberate their country. In his study on the August Revolution, the historian David Marr points out that barely 10 per cent of the population from the liberated mountainous regions in the North were actually enlisted in the National Liberation Army.[13] The August insurrection was not the sole effort of the Việt Minh, since there were many other local groups that called themselves Việt Minh without having the slightest idea about the Party line. Two years later, in late 1947, the Việt Minh was confronted with not only the advances of the French army but also an erosion of their political legitimacy in the countryside due to the waves of repression and the decline of communal autonomy. Since the 1930s, the Party fought to safeguard its influence in rural areas by lowering taxes, abolishing monopolies, and distributing rice paddies. When the war resumed in December 1946, the DRV again offered to reduce interest rates and farm rents in order to secure peasant support.

On the eve of the first emulation campaign, the DRV's activities to mobilise the population turned out to be rather disappointing on the ground. Trường Chinh admitted that their measures had done little to win the good graces of poor peasants. For the most part, new Việt Minh recruits came from the urban and industrialised areas of the country while the rural population was reluctant to join mass organisations in the villages. Peasants' Associations loyal to the Việt Minh barely garnered 820,000 members throughout the country.[14] For Defence Minister Giáp, the key priority was not so much to combat French occupying forces but to rebuild "the spirit of the Vietnamese man", so he could distinguish for himself the just cause — that of the Việt Minh. Propaganda organs repeated that the resistance would lead to the "metamorphosis of the Vietnamese people".[15] DRV

---

[13] David Marr. *Vietnam 1945: The Quest for Power*. Berkeley: University of California Press, 1995, p. 239.

[14] Văn Tạo. "Vài nét về quá trình xây dựng và Phát triển của Nhà nước cách mạng Việt Nam 20 năm qua" (A few notes on the evolution of the construction and development of the Vietnamese revolutionary party in the last 20 years), *Nghiên cứu Lịch sử*, Hanoi, no. 77, August 1965: 23.

[15] Võ Nguyên Giáp. "Đẩy mạnh kháng chiến cứu quốc" (Reinforcing the resistance for national liberation), *Sinh Hoạt Nội Bộ*, December 1947.

leaders would have to establish a new mass mobilisation movement that would finally reach their objective — transforming Man to better secure his allegiance to their cause. The patriotic emulation campaign of 1948 was their attempt to resolve the political and moral dysfunction in society. Emulation was supposed to be a springboard towards a "new life" whereby the Việt Minh would offer the peasant class a "legitimate reason" for mobilising and uniting under the flag of patriotism. The formation of minds was to be the final step in the DRV's attempt to allay the chronic weakness in their quest for support in the countryside.

The First Patriotic Emulation Campaign

The first campaign for patriotic emulation was laid out in the spring of 1948. The movement, it was announced, would acquire the human and material means to victory and would strengthen the credibility of the Việt Minh resistance in the eyes of the communist world.[16] On 19 June 1948 — the thousandth day of fighting against France — patriotic emulation was officially launched throughout the country:

> What is the patriotic emulation competition? Competing with patriotic feeling in everything one does in order to obtain good results. Mobilising the masses to achieve victory. Exterminating the three enemies: invaders, hunger, and ignorance. What are its main goals? Politically, we must establish the basic organisations of the Party, the people, and political authority in the occupied zones. We must develop and consolidate the popular organisations of the Liên Việt [the reformed and renamed Việt Minh] and set up autonomous cells. Economically, we must make weapons, increase the production of rice and rice paddies to put aside reserves, reorganise the cooperatives and create new ones, reduce farm taxes by twenty-five percent, and sabotage the enemy's economy. Culturally, we must eradicate illiteracy and advocate the new life. Lastly, militarily we must develop the people's war, create the foundations for a guerrilla war, buy resistance bonds and contribute to the Resistance Fund. The patriotic emulation competitions must have the characteristics of a popular movement.[17]

[16] Chiến Hữu. "Thi đua ái quốc" (Patriotic emulation), *Sinh Hoạt Nội Bộ*, no. 8, May 1948: 16–7.

[17] *Chương trình cơ sở* (Basic programme), in CAOM, Coll. CP, single document, 1950, 70 pp.

A national emulation committee or bureau was created to oversee the programme. It was made up of government representatives, delegates of the National Assembly, and members of the leadership committees of all mass organisations. Each level (national, zone, province, district, and commune) was supposed to have a branch office staffed by three or four people to organise local campaigns. The government wanted them to pay particular attention to the make-up of the committees, suggesting they assign people who were not Party members.[18] Villagers deemed progressivist were the natural choice to lead these new bodies. They were told to avoid village elders or scholars and to choose instead people who were active and successful in their field, since it would take a well-selected committee to win over the rural population, which traditionally shied away from change.

On the communal level, the emulation bureau made a list of its model citizens, then shared their stories with people in the area. These men and women were part of a vanguard that had to go out and educate the villagers. In reality, however, not many of these branch offices saw the light of day. At the end of the first season of emulation, only the military zones or a few provinces had emulation facilities. At the village level, the president of the commune or the Party secretary was in charge. In response to this shortfall, the government shifted the main burden of its emulation policy to provincial authorities. Delegates from provincial committees received training in the military zones and served as a relay between the central government and the local collectives within their area. The province delegated two types of officials: emulation cadres who devised programmes adapted to the particular conditions of their area, and itinerant cadres who would help implement the movement throughout the territory. In 1949 there were only a few itinerant cadres, so the provinces sent them first to the more populated villages in the valleys or low mountains. Lacking time, they would just hold short informational meetings to explain how people could benefit from participating in the emulation campaigns. Cadres from the provincial apparatus ran up against the conservatism of the villagers, who were not very open to new ideas.[19] Absenteeism was high.

---

[18] *Trường Chinh's Speech at the Congress for Party Cadres (14–18 January 1949)*, p. 10.

[19] "Le Parti doit agir contre l'esprit 'régional', borné de paysans" (The Party must combat the "regional", narrow mindset of the peasants), in CAOM, Coll. du HCI, file no. 253/34, document no. CP 867/0, 8 August 1947. In a later document, the specific characteristics of peasants are listed as: "self-interested and egotistical, conservative, servile, pacifistic", in CAOM, Coll. HCI, file no. 245–718, no. 9868 (summer 1950), 3 November 1950.

To combat this lack of interest, cadres wrote down the names of those who did not show up and later paid them a visit to explain the error of their ways. The organisation of this first emulation campaign in the provinces of North Vietnam was carried out by these small groups of itinerant cadres (sent by the province or, when not available, by the district).

Communal authorities launched collective operations (cleaning and draining canals, clearing land, etc.) to show the benefits of group work and its advantages in terms of productivity and effort. Village chronicles by the new government describe the "collective and jovial [atmosphere] that suddenly arose among the villagers" whenever they came to help each other. The National Emulation Committee printed out patriotic songs that cadres handed out to the local people to sing as they worked:

> Uncle Ho called for emulation, let's see who succeeds and who fails. Go to the Front to fight the foreigners, and to the fields for the harvest. If you are poor you'll stay poor, since you cannot fight alone against the morning heat and the afternoon rain. If you want enough rice and money to feed every soldier, you must boldly take a stand. Young children must stand by their aging mothers, older ones by their younger siblings. And you, you must try to see farther, fight on so many fronts, cut down so many heads; to every husband and every wife, tell me who will receive recompense — the ones who take the lead in emulation.[20]

Educational groups used Hồ's declaration of 19 June to launch emulation as a pedagogic tool. Youth organisations sent groups of two or three children to villages to recite poems and sing songs about emulation. They had to overcome the prejudices and mistrust of the peasants. In each hamlet, government representatives created emulation units made up of 20 to 50 families.[21] Provincial cadres studied the data to establish "programmes adapted to local conditions". The division of land was carefully examined; the various professions and modes of production were indexed as well as the standard references (gender, age, family situation, attitude towards the resistance, etc.) and the physical ability of the inhabitants. The province

---

[20] Song written in 1948 by Thôn Nữ for the first emulation campaign, in *Vận động phong trào thi đua ái quốc* (Activities of the patriotic emulation movement). Central Bureau of Patriotic Emulation Activities, Information Departement of South Vietnam, 1949, p. 13.

[21] Chính Nghĩa. "Phát triển thi đua ở xã" (Developing emulation at the village level), *Sinh Hoạt Nội Bộ*, no. 16, April 1949: 6.

asked its cadres to talk with village elders to avoid the risk of confrontation (mainly hostilities among families), which would impede the campaign's progress. Finally, villagers were gathered together to present their assessment of the operation. The government advised its cadres to "speak quite firmly, if necessary, to show the villagers what they had to do" but "with a spirit of simplicity and flexibility".[22] Emulation leaders first brought up the "congenital" bond between the villager and his nation before explaining the organisation of a local competition for patriotic emulation.

The notion of a competition was familiar to the people but in its traditional form. Before, gruelling competitions were held to elect officials of the imperial state; now the key to success rested on one's patriotism and allegiance to the Việt Minh struggle. It was no longer a question of competition but of solidarity between the members of a community; one did not have to study Chinese classical literature but government directives. The winner was the one who most enthusiastically responded to the government's productivist, military, or political needs. At the end of each emulation season or campaign (lasting three to six months), the government selected the "most progressive elements". In the villages, cadres awarded all participants an emulation certificate with a simple inscription: "I take part in emulation" (*tôi thi đua*). They had to display it at home so that cadres could freely control their participation in the movement. Within the ranks of the army (both regular and regional forces) or the people's militia, the certificate was in the form of a pennant or flag issued by the Minister of Defence.[23] Within each sector of activity, steering committees organised closing meetings to elect the best representatives of the season. The National Emulation Committee explained to the people what they personally stood to gain from taking part in the movement.[24]

---

[22] *Vận động phong trào thi đua ái quốc*, p. 24.

[23] *Về việc khen thưởng cho các dân du kích 1948* (On the distribution of recompense to our resistance fighters in 1948), in AVN3, Coll. Assemblée Nationale, file no. 59, document no. 53/LQCT, 19 July 1948.

[24] "All services rendered must be rewarded and encouraged in order to create good soldiers. Offenders must be punished so that they comform to the rules of discipline, which is the driving force of an army." Directive by the Foreign Affairs Commission in Nam bô, in CAOM, Coll. du HCI, file no. 314/863, document no. 5165/S, 5 September 1949. See also Khổng Minh, *Cách huấn luyện cán bộ Quân sự* (Training of military cadres), 1948 (translated from the Chinese by Hồ Chí Minh); and *Cuốn sách của chính trị viên* (Manual for the political cadres), Hội tan văn hóa, 1948.

In the Soviet Union, socialist emulation took pains to "offer all Stakhanovites special privileges in kind or in services that were previously unavailable to their income level".[25] In the same vein, the Vietnamese government promised to reward "virtuous people" for their engagement in the struggle of "legitimate forces". In Asian societies, a medal was like a gift. A gift demanded reciprocity, not a quantitative one, but one based on honour. The recipient becomes a debtor and must return the gift in order to ease the temporary imbalance in social order. The gift brought about a distinction that was unacceptable to the perenniality of the collective. A family rewarded by the State gained legitimacy over those around them, thus creating a source of disorder. The cultural continuity of the principle of "gift/counter-gift" gave the State a vector for further emulation to strengthen its mobilisation of the masses. A reward pay scale was drawn up by the Standing Committee of the National Assembly in May 1948.[26] An Institute of Decorations was created to award new patriotic titles to the "exemplary men of the DRV": the Hồ Chí Minh Prize, the Medal of Military Merit and Medal of the Combatant, the Gold Star, the Hồ Chí Minh Medal, the Medal of Independence, and the Medal of Resistance. These individual and collective awards came with a small sum of money. The government saw this reward policy as a way to strengthen its influence on the minds of the people.

Emulation in Nghệ Tĩnh Province

Long considered by the government as a pillar in its efforts to establish authority, Nghệ Tĩnh province (which encompasses the territory of Nghệ An and Hà Tĩnh) had been a defensive shield against the south for centuries.[27] The Party's Central Committee chose Thanh Hoá and Nghệ Tĩnh

---

[25] Donald Filtzer. *Soviet Workers and Stalinist Industrialisation: The Formation of Modern Soviet Production Relations, 1928–1941*. New York: M.E. Sharpe, Inc., 1986, p. 186.

[26] Directive 139/CT, May 1, 1948, in Coll. de l'Assemblée, file no. 59, document no. 53/LQCT, 19 July 1948.

[27] The poet and strategist Nguyễn Trãi (1380–1442) saw Nghệ Tinh as the "third shield" in the South, and the historian Phan Huy Chú (1782–1840) wrote that "Nghê Tinh was a strategic region, a defensive shield throughout the dynasties", in Phan Huy Chú, *Lịch triều hiến chương loại chí* (Institutions of different dynasties), vol. 1. Nxb Bộ Văn hóa Giáo dục và Thanh niên (published between 1809 and 1819, re-issued in 1974).

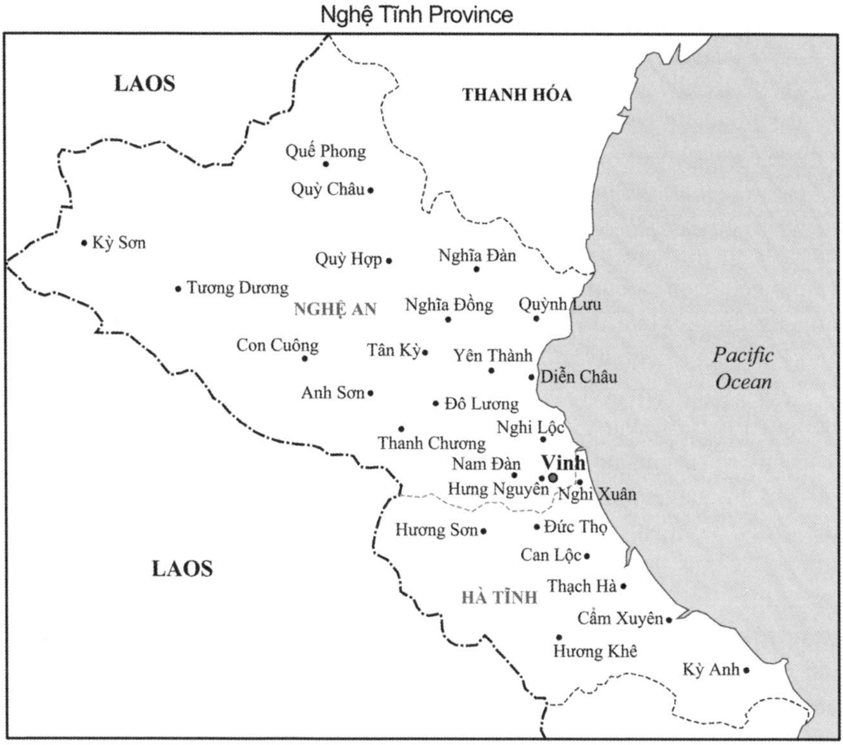

Figure 3. Map of Nghệ Tinh province

in early 1947 as rear bases for the battles to come in the centre of the country. Their watchword was "Protect the South, advance towards the South, push the enemy towards the South", and Thanh Hoá and Nghệ Tĩnh were to be bulwarks against the advances of the French army. In mid-1947 the region of Bình Trị Thiên fell into the hands of Franco-Vietnamese forces, so the strategic importance of Nghệ Tĩnh increased and the mobilisation of its people became a priority.

The first campaign of patriotic emulation was meant to follow the popular mobilisation movements put into place when the war with France began. As of the summer of 1947, the Women's Association from Nghệ An had been put in charge of creating units of mothers of combatants from each commune. Other groups were in charge of collecting food, clothes, and money. Patriotic emulation was a variant of these campaigns of patriotic solidarity. A conference was organised in Nam Đàn (seat of Nam Đàn district) in June 1948 to outline the nature and objectives of the movement.

Under the supervision of the local branch of the Party, the Provincial Committee of Resistance and Administration brought together representatives from the people's assemblies, the Liên Việt, mass organisations, and from each administrative level in the area to explain the procedure. The emulation campaign was spread over eleven months and comprised two distinct phases, from 1 August–23 December and from 1 March–19 June 1949. The Ministry of Labour advised the communes and districts to create special bureaus to manage the programme, but this was largely ignored. Instead, communal cadres entrusted the dissemination of the movement to mass organisations, while the management would be shared between themselves and Party representatives.

In 1948, however, not all communes had Party cells (it should also be noted that the Party had been officially dissolved in November 1945 as a means of disguising its leadership over the provisional government established in September).[28] The movement had the quickest success within the army. Political commissioners held informational meetings with their troops (within the military zone of the district) and then offered courses in politics, military strategy, and guerrilla tactics. The government wanted to increase the number of revolutionary organisations, communal forces of the People's Army of Vietnam (PAVN), the People's Militia, and guerrilla units. In June, the province launched a movement called "One month in the people's militia forces". All men from 18–45 years of age and women from 18–35 were encouraged to join local resistance groups. Official statistics show excellent results: in just a few weeks, membership in the provincial people's militia went from 166,460 to 387,530. Security forces were established on the communal and town levels. Village security groups, made up of five families, were formed and put in charge of neighbourhood safety. In February 1949, the district of Nam Đàn created the first group of "senior" soldiers in North Vietnam, attracting 43,380 people before the year was out. By the end of the year, the Supreme Council for National Defence entrusted the financing of the people's militia forces to the provinces. The Party organised a collection in the villages of the area to raise

[28] *Rapport sur la situation du PCI en 1948 et sur la planification du travail intérieur en 1949 du comité exécutif de la section du PCI* (Report on the situation of the ICP in 1948 and on domestic planning in 1949 by the executive committee of the section of the ICP), in CAOM, Coll. CD, file no. 105. document no. l0234, 24 October 1949.

the necessary funds. In January 1949, the village of Ốc Khê in Can Lộc district (Hà Tĩnh) was chosen to test out the new campaign.[29]

> After increasing membership in the patriotic forces, the emulation movement added a second objective: improving agricultural, artisanal and industrial production. People were encouraged to clear new land and plant on tracts that lay fallow. Official sources confirm that Nghệ An increased its cultivable land area by almost two thousand hectares (nearly five thousand acres) in November 1948. The government encouraged peasants to improve their productivity with the help of fertilizers, both natural (vegetable and animal manure, compost) and industrial (phosphates). Cadres explained that it was more productive to get together in small groups, to share the workload, encourage each other, and provide criticism. They explained how to set up support cells. In June 1949, the district of Nghi Lộc (Nghệ An) had 462 collective production groups, with the participation of some twenty thousand peasants.

On the provincial and district level, agricultural committees were created to train new "cadres of agricultural production". These technicians would be the link between the communal committees and mass organisations, and would help choose the outstanding workers of the village. It was thus that in 1948, the agricultural committee from Nghệ An province awarded the first award to the Catholic peasant Hoàng Hanh (Xuân Lậc, Nam Đàn), four years before he was given the first title of "Hero of Agricultural Labour" during the conference at Tuyên Quang in May 1952. In the area of artisanal and industrial production, however, the patriotic emulation movement turned out to be less effective. In the late 1940s, Nghệ Tĩnh's industrial infrastructure was still very poorly developed. Only the provincial seat, Vinh, and the surrounding areas, had a few factory workshops — but in 1948 the small town of Vinh was still solidly held by the French. In the outlying areas, however, there were a few workshops in the hands of the Việt Minh, such as the grenade plant in the district of Nam Đàn.

[29] From February to December 1949, Nghệ Tinh province managed to collect the following for the resistance: 1,800 *mẫu* (600 hectares) of land, 195 homes, 2,679,213 *dông*, 886 tons of paddy, 8 tons of salt, 2,967 water buffaloes, 7,000 swing-plows, 5,361 pigs, 50 gold ingots, 6 silver taels, 6 gold rings, 1,397 bracelets, 3,948 earrings, 17,308 vases, etc., in *Lịch sử Đảng bộ Đảng cộng sản Việt Nam tỉnh Nghệ Tĩnh* (History of the Vietnamese Communist Party section of Nghê Tinh province), p. 267.

Official statistics showed that these small Việt Minh-controlled plants saw a real increase in production as a result of the emulation movement.

Patriotic emulation also helped in the fight against illiteracy. The DRV had already established mass education in 1945, but in 1947 only 15 per cent of the population of Hà Tĩnh could read and write. The government made it a point of honour to fight against what it considered a "deficiency of the colonial administration". In Confucian societies, it was the ruling power's duty to teach its citizens and its legitimacy depended on its ability to educate the people. The DRV's mission was thus a traditional one. In 1949, the provincial administration rewarded Hoàng Thị Liên, a former illiterate, for her work as a teacher in the village of Nghi Hượng (Nghi Lộc district). Resistance committees tried to reach out to teachers who had been trained and employed by the French, encouraging them to "return to the village" to host mass education groups. In exchange, the government awarded certificates of patriotism to those who wanted to erase their "collaborationist indiscretions". In Quỳnh Lưu, an Association for Educational Development was created to persuade the nation's scholars to teach in these "official training programmes". The administration solicited donations from the people to cover costs. Within the people's militias, those who could read were placed in cultural groups and sent to teach in their hamlets or families. In 1949, the government proudly proclaimed a "total victory against the scourge of illiteracy, one month before the close of the first phase of patriotic emulation".

Lastly, patriotic emulation aimed at creating a "new life". Local cadres praised government efforts in public hygiene. The Việt Minh press claimed that within a few months, latrines, collective showers, enclosures for livestock, and hundreds of hospital beds had been set up around the communes of Nghệ Tĩnh. In reality, however, the number of places that actually had these facilities in the late 1940s were still rare or even nonexistent. The government also encouraged participation in sports and fought to eradicate opium use, prostitution, feudal beliefs, etc. In the spirit of "Cultivate the mind, build the nation", local cadres urged young women to cut their hair short and stop wearing traditional necklaces and bracelets in order to "espouse the spirit of patriotic emulation". In the village of Văn Hải (Quỳnh Lưu district), the Party cadre Hoàng Ngọc Oanh suggested that people get together to destroy the communal halls and pagodas in the area and use the building materials (bricks, stones, wooden beams) to build "progressive buildings". However, aside from the actions of a few cadres in a couple of villages, most Vietnamese villages did not undergo any profound changes in the late 1940s.

In Nghệ Tĩnh as in the rest of the country, the emulation campaign served primarily to further establish the mechanisms for ideological training in the countryside. In May 1949, the district of Nghi Lộc had five new organisations: a group of local officials, a network of cultural groups, an association for Marxist studies, a teachers' federation, and a student group. New Party cells were created by the hundreds throughout the area. The sudden increase in membership of "progressive organisations" was amazing. According to official statistics, Việt Minh membership went from 21,160 to 31,050, the Liên Việt from 10,307 to 32,957, the youth association from 6,070 to 10,450, the association of women grew from 300 to 5,212, and the Association of Mothers of Combatants from 1,700 to 3,540. Cadres of the DRV saw patriotic emulation in 1948–49 as a tool for winning over the villages. But one year after the start of the first campaign, several government reports pointed out weaknesses in the operation. DRV leaders noted with some disappointment that "many provinces were still barely affected by the movement",[30] but admitted that "patriotic emulation was a new movement that had disoriented the people and cadres to some degree".[31]

Once a province had established a broad ideological infrastructure, the State sometimes criticised its cadres for seeing emulation only as a way of increasing Party membership or improving the training of local leaders while offering nothing to the people. By following only the directive "Emulation to help build the Party", these zealous cadres were accused of showing a "segregationist attitude that threatened national unity", while the government wanted to rely more on people who were outside of the Party.[32] Hồ Chí Minh brought up this issue during a public speech on 1 August 1949 and said it was because "Party cadres did not understand the meaning of the patriotic emulation campaign".[33] Local cadres were criticised for not explaining the notion of emulation well enough to the

---

[30] *Về Quốc quân khu VII* (On the people's army in zone VII), no. 9, 17 November 1949: 2.

[31] Thoại Sơn. "Đẩy mạnh phong trào thi đua ái quốc" (Strengthening the patriotic emulation movement), *Sự thật*, no. 106–107, 2 January 1949: 4.

[32] L.T. "Thi đua ái quốc, một ý kiến về thi đua" (Patriotic emulation, an opinion on emulation), in *Sinh Hoạt Nội Bộ*, no. 11, November 1948: 5.

[33] Hồ Chí Minh. "Lời kêu gọi thi đua ái quốc" (Call for patriotic emulation), in *Thi đua yêu nước* (Patriotic emulation). Hanoi: nxb Sự thật, 1984, p. 13.

villagers, for forgetting to nominate leaders in the communes, for not encouraging the sharing of experiences, for not sending enough activity reports from their level, or for neglecting the standard forms of propaganda (arts, popular theatre, etc.) to spread "the spirit of the campaign to the popular masses". The campaign's poor implementation at the communal level sometimes made it seem like just a new patriotic tax imposed by the central government. Hồ Chí Minh reminded the people that "patriotic emulation was in their own best interest, in the interest of their families, the village, and the nation, regardless of one's ethnicity".[34] Most importantly, patriotic emulation was not a passing phase but defined "the new life of the Vietnamese people".[35]

The Sino-Soviet Reform of Emulation

Since its creation in 1941, the Việt Minh's political strategy was that of a united front. Trường Chinh stressed the need to "rely on the solidarity of an entire nation" in the country's resistance against France. It would take the land itself, insisted Hồ Chí Minh, to win over the favour of the rural population. Resistance against the foreign oppressor should be accompanied by agrarian reform. In 1948–49, however, word from Hồ's entourage was that agrarian reform was not ready yet for implementation. Trường Chinh reiterated that progressive land reform had always been envisaged so as not to alienate a segment of the population.[36] Prudence on the part of the government resulted in the less-than-rigorous implementation of the programme in the countryside. The DRV was not officially looking for a model, but it was also not in a position to defend one. The journal *Sự thật* (*Truth*) discussed this issue in its edition of 6 January 1950.[37] Government

[34] Hồ Chí Minh. "Lời kêu gọi thi đua ái quốc", p. 14.

[35] Chính Đạo. "Tổ chức và lãnh đạo thi đua" (Organizing and running emulation), *Sự thật*, no. I/5, 7 October 1949: 10.

[36] In 1949, Trường Chinh explained the three stages of agrarian reform: 1) Reduce farm taxes, distribute the land from colonialists and traitors to peasants, and force the rich to donate parcels of land; 2) Abolish the dominance of large farms through expropriation with indemnity; and 3) Abolish all exploitative systems and prepare for the socialisation of land. See *On Vietnam*, in Archives of the Central Committee [CC] of the CPSU, file no. 425, document no. 89 357, 1 April 1950.

[37] "Đẩy mạnh phong trào thi đua ái quốc" (Strengthening the patriotic emulation movement), *Sự thật*, no. 126, 6 January 1950: 10.

leaders sought a third way between Stalinist emulation and capitalist-style competition, while hardliners defended the higher principle of solidarity within the community. But this concept of solidarity — which I call "filial" or "Confucian" for convenience — was different in many ways from the internationalist understanding of the term. After quite prudently affirming that the class struggle was also a reality in Vietnam, the government advocated a national specificity in their conception of emulation policy. The goal of Vietnamese-style emulation was to unite the people to better fight "foreign oppression" — basically they wanted a patriotic emulation that was adapted to the socio-cultural conditions of the country.

This stance was not universally supported within the Party. In the autumn of 1948, the communist Trần Ngọc Danh criticised the Party's approach in the Cominform journal, *For Lasting Peace, for People's Democracy*, a diatribe against the excesses of Hồ Chí Minh's system that circulated for a long time among high Soviet authorities.[38] Trần Ngọc Danh accused North Vietnamese leaders of repudiating proletarian internationalism, of being obsessed with nationalism, and for lacking solidarity with the causes of a progressive world. Shortly before the official diplomatic recognition of the DRV by Beijing and Moscow in January 1950, the victory of the Chinese Communist Party in the fall of 1949 marked an important turning point. The defence of national specificity was not a new concept for leaders of the Việt Minh, but this was the time of the schism in Yugoslavia and the communist world was divided. Any nationalist deviation from the Marxist-Leninist line was harshly condemned by Stalin. In December 1949, Mao Zedong cleverly dedicated his victory against the nationalist forces of Chiang Kai-shek to the Russian leader. His government made sure to increase its acts of deference toward the lord of the Kremlin as Stalin dreaded the emergence of a challenger to his supremacy in the communist world.

In January 1950, Hồ Chí Minh and Trần Đăng Ninh set out for Moscow where a new partnership was hammered out between the Soviets, Vietnamese, and Chinese. The Kremlin demanded that the Vietnamese take the path of "internationalist progressivism".[39] An agreement was secretly

---

[38] *Report on the DRV by Comrade Trần Ngọc Danh*, in Archives of the CC of the CPSU, file no. 425, document no. 89357, 4 January 1950, 20 pp.

[39] Chapter 2, "Le héros, une affaire de diplomatie" (The hero, a question of diplomacy), in Benoît de Tréglodé. *Héros et Révolution au Viêt Nam*. Paris: L'Harmattan, 2001, pp. 81–128 (this chapter has been removed from the current translation).

signed between the Soviets and the Chinese — with Vietnamese representatives conspicuously absent — entrusting the supervision of Vietnam's revolutionary development to China. The stakes were high for the DRV as they needed to regain the confidence of the socialist world as well as secure military help from Beijing and, to a lesser degree, from other Eastern European countries. It seems clear that the agreement was more of a diktat than a free political choice, but the resumption of hostilities did not allow them much choice. The Soviet government demanded a profound recasting of the system of ideological training in North Vietnam in order to propel the country quickly into agrarian reform. Patriotic emulation was entering a totally new phase, and the arrival of Chinese advisors in the northern provinces announced a complete transformation of patriotic emulation nationwide.

In the spring of 1950, Hồ Chí Minh knew these reforms were crucial if he wanted to retain the military, economic, and diplomatic support of the communist world. In 1947, General Nguyễn Sơn, known for his Maoist leanings,[40] was the first to propose the organisation of "rectification sessions".[41] Việt Minh leadership, however, deemed the method unsuited to the "Vietnamese spirit": "Hồ Chí Minh did not want to change Man from one day to the next, but to teach him gradually to help him evolve. He did not like to rush into things. The idea that consciousness could leap forward did not even cross his mind."[42] The Việt Minh criticised China's approach for its anti-intellectualism and ideological orthodoxy. In the spring of 1950, however, Beijing went even further and oriented itself towards "an operation to remodel the character, temperament, ideas, or basically the entire psychology of Man. The goal was not intellectual but emotional: it was a matter of creating a new mentality, a new behaviour."[43]

On 6 May 1950, Hồ Chí Minh finally decided to bring up the issue during a "training and study meeting" in which he openly criticised the

[40] At the time, General Nguyễn Sơn (1908–1956) was the president of Zone IV. He was a colourful figure who had spent ten years fighting the Japanese in China. Hồ Chí Minh always mistrusted him because of his strong "Maoist" stance. Close rival and enemy of Võ Nguyên Giáp, he was sent to Korea as the representative of Vietnamese support. He returned in 1953 to the Party's Central Committee, but died prematurely of liver disease.

[41] Hoàng Van Chi. *From Colonialism to Communism: A Case History of North Vietnam*. New York: Praeger, 1964, p. 126.

[42] Georges Boudarel. "L'idéocratie au Vietnam avec le Maoïsme" (Ideocracy in Vietnam with Maoism), in *La Bureaucratie au Vietnam*. Paris: L'Harmattan, 1983, pp. 66–71.

[43] Ibid., pp. 60–1.

Maoist model of re-education, advocating a closely supervised reform of the Vietnamese man:

> The process of re-education must be positive and meticulous. One must know exactly who needs to be re-educated, who should be in charge, of what this should consist, how to do it and on what basis. One must be sure to follow closely the training process and the driving force of this teaching. One must correct overzealousness immediately and without hesitation. One must know how to use one's principles well rather than use them too much; it is useless to open re-education classes anarchically, if a class has too many participants then the levels are not equal, the program will not be suitable … and this will undoubtedly have an effect on the whole re-education process.[44]

Bùi Tín, a former colonel in the PAVN who ran afoul of the government and went into exile in Paris in 1990, writes in his memoirs that Hồ Chí Minh clearly feared a Chinese takeover of the ideological terrain at the time.[45] When Hồ spoke of self-criticism he was referring more to a therapy that could bring out the best in community members. The Vietnamese method left room for difference and flexibility and its aim was to garner the people's support for the just cause.

In the spring of 1950, however, the Maoist model of re-education dominated, despite Hồ's reservations. From changing its citizens to creating the new man, the recasting of Vietnam's emulation policy aimed to produce a whole cache of new men, which was necessary for the launching of large-scale agrarian reform. The Soviet Union was especially keen for Vietnam to speed up changes in this regard. After the agreement reached in Moscow in February 1950, the CPSU sent a group of cadres specialising in ideological matters to Beijing to organise a training seminar for Chinese advisors bound for Vietnam.[46] From 17–28 April 1950, several conferences were held on organisational matters. The Soviets stressed the key role played by socialist emulation in the formation of the masses. 27 April was entirely dedicated to "the work, Party organisation, and socialist emulation

---

[44] *Hồ Chi Minh — Biên niên tiểu sử* (Hồ Chi Minh, biographical records), vol. IV. Hanoi: nxb Chính Trị Quốc Gia, 1994, pp. 424–5.

[45] Bùi Tín. *Following Hô Chi Minh: The Memoirs of a North Vietnamese Colonel*. Honolulu: University of Hawaii Press, 1995, p. 28.

[46] The conversations between the CPSU and the CCP from 17–28 April 1950 were transcribed into two files in the archives of the CC of the CPSU (no. 1200 and no. 1201), amounting to more than 720 pages (in Russian and Chinese).

experience of the Serp & Molot [Russian: sickle and hammer] factory in Moscow". Soviet instructors explained in detail how to organise a socialist emulation campaign. They sang the praises of the emulation fighter and explained to Chinese cadres the advantages of the Soviet experience and the way to adapt its model in China and Vietnam:

> As for developments in the culture and the consciousness of our workers, we have already accomplished a lot, seen a great show of will, and had many victories. The extraordinary qualities of the Soviet man are clearly expressed via the socialist emulation movement. For the Party, emulation means: telling workers about a certain work experience, generalising it, making it clear to everyone, and sharing it as much as possible with others. In practice, this happens in the following way: a worker has a high rate of production, so his success puts into question his neighbour's methods; the neighbour then understands the error of his ways and doesn't want to be considered a bad worker, so he learns from his neighbour's experience, corrects his faults, and becomes an exemplary man himself. The workers sign an agreement on emulation and take it upon themselves to improve performance. Our job is to support such initiative and support emulation champions for taking such interest in their work. In factories, top workers are awarded certificates of honour and their names and photos are inscribed in a book and in an honour roll. Their stories are shared in magazines, newspapers, on the radio and in meetings. We have organised Stakhanovite conferences in order to change work habits via shared successful experiences. Thanks to emulation, we feel a great force pushing our society forward every day. Emulation has become a social movement, one that is alive, indispensable, and an integral part of individual consciousness. The Communist Party supports new emulations and supervises the movement.[47]

Mikhail Chiaureli's epic 1949 film about a labour hero (Ivanov), *The Fall of Berlin*, was cited as an example.[48] It showed how traditional heroism

---

[47] *Conversation with the CCP delegation on the organisation of socialist emulation campaigns in the Serp & Molot [Sickle and hammer] factory*, in Archives of the CC of the CPSU, file no. 1201, unnumbered document, April–December 1950.

[48] *The Fall of Berlin* (Padenie Berlina). Directed by Mikhail Chiaureli, 1949, screenplay by Pyotr Pavlenko, starring Mihail Gelovani (Stalin), Oleg Frölich (Roosevelt), Viktor Stanitsyn (Churchill), Boris Andreyev (Ivanov), Marina Kovalyova (Natacha), 165 minutes.

Figure 4. Mikhail Chiaureli's film, *The Fall of Berlin*

based on success in battle, found its modern-day counterpart in productivist performance. In North Vietnam, the Ministries of Labour and Culture were given the order to use the film to spread the new socialist emulation through the countryside. The "Ivanov syndrome" was supposed to penetrate into youth organisations, professional groups, and other mass movements. In the autumn of 1950, the Vietnamese delegate to the PRC, Hoàng Văn Hoan (1905–1991), proudly announced to the Soviet ambassador that Vietnamese audiences were flocking by the thousands to see *The Fall of Berlin* in the border provinces of Hà Giang, Cao Bằng, and Lạng Sơn.[49] The propaganda machine extolled the virtues of "the glorious Red Army and its eternal victory over Nazi Germany", and Ivanov's struggle was now that of the exemplary Vietnamese worker, and what's more, that of the patriot seeking freedom.[50] Starting in 1950, DRV leaders sent bi-annual reports to the Soviet Union detailing their progress in organisational matters, of which a large part was devoted to the creation of the new man[51] whose transformation was brought about by emulation. Phạm Văn Đồng soon announced to the Soviets that they had elected the first seven heroes in the history of the DRV, "a huge success in the resistance and the national construction of the Vietnamese people".[52] Thanks to the help of their Chinese advisors, he explained, the figure of Ivanov served as a model for Ngô Gia Khảm, Ivanov's Vietnamese alter ego who was awarded the title of "labour hero" in the mountains of Tuyên Quang in May 1952.

In March 1950, China sent a first preparatory mission to Vietnam under the supervision of Luo Guibo (1908–1995), Central Committee representative, head of the committee overseeing the Chinese advisors in Vietnam and special advisor to Hồ Chí Minh from January 1950 to August 1954. The question of patriotic emulation was at the very heart of ideological reform, which called for the DRV to "align itself absolutely with its Chinese allies". Beijing insisted that the North Vietnamese regime rethink its entire ideological programme for mass ideological training.

---

[49] *Conversation between Comrades Phin (Hoàng Văn Hoan) and Rochin (9 November 1950)*, in Archives of the CC of the CPSU, file no. 425, document no. 01486, 20 December 1950 (archival recording date 4 January 1951).

[50] A bi-annual report given by Hồ Chi Minh for the New Year 1952 is exemplary in this regard. See Hồ Chí Minh, "Letter from Vietnam" (24 pages), in Archives of the CC of the CPSU, file no. 951, unnumbered document, 19 March 1952, pp. 1–3.

[51] "Vietnamese Society and Revolution", in Archives of the CC of the CPSU, file no. 740, single document, March 1951.

[52] *Report by Phạm Văn Đồng in 1952*, in Archives of the CC of the CPSU, file no. 951, document no. 65 271, 4 September 1952 (archival recording date).

Hồ Chí Minh admitted several years later that "what had happened in China really did help the emulation movement work better in Vietnam."[53] In 1950, Chinese advisors increased the number of training sessions with Vietnamese mass organisations, holding conferences for the Student Union, the Youth Movement, the Peasants' Association, the National Union, etc. In August, the Việt Minh Youth Movement was unified;[54] and in late September, the Peasants' Association divided the peasants into two distinct groups: landlords and rich peasants joined the Liên Việt, while poor and middle peasants were accepted into the Peasants' Association for National Salvation once they turned 18.[55] From then on, the government demanded increased vigilance from Party leaders in their choice of members. Potential members had to undergo probation while the merits of their candidacy were being examined. The waiting period before integration varied according to the candidate's social standing. A worker had to wait two months, a peasant four, a scholar or businessman six, and former members of other organisations had to wait at least a year.[56]

For the celebration of Workers' Day, 1 May 1950, the DRV created a new medal for its exemplary blue- and white-collar labourers.[57] This had three ranks, with the highest distinction awarded by the President of the Republic while the others were issued by the office of the Prime Minister. The government set up local bureaus under the Institute of Medals to manage candidate files and gather information.[58] On the local level, this new institution was made up of the president of the province, the head of the provincial Labour Department, delegates from the professional branch (head of Economic Department and the Bureau of Rural Affairs, for example), and finally the representative of mass organisations (the peasant

---

[53] *Báo cáo thi đua trước Đại hội chiến sĩ thi đua và cán bộ gương mẫu toàn quốc từ 1.5 đến 6.5.1952* (Report on emulation for the national conference of emulation combatants and exemplary cadres), in AVN3, BLD, file no. 422, May 1952.

[54] *Résolutions de la session du Parti (20.8.1950)* (Resolutions of the Party session [20 August 1950]), in CAOM, CD, file no. 105, document no. 9243, 7 October 1950.

[55] *Synthèse hebdomadaire de la radio et de la presse en Indochine (2–9.10.1950)* (Weekly round-up of the radio and print media in Indochina [2–9 October 1950]), in CAOM, HCI, file no. 8/48-60, document no. 3229/SC, 13 October 1950.

[56] *Rapport exécutif de la section centrale du PCI (12.1950)* (Executive report on the central section of the ICP [December 1950]), in CAOM, CD, file no. 105, December 1950.

[57] *Hồ Chí Minh — Biên niên tiểu sử* (Hồ Chi Minh, biographical accounts), vol. IV, p. 423.

[58] *Tài liệu về việc thưởng Huân chương Lao động* (Documents on the awarding of work medals), in AVN3, BLD, file no. 402, document no. 16 110, 16 November 1950.

union or association). The Institute of Medals oversaw these activities on the national level (the institute was replaced by a medals commission in 1961).[59] The State propaganda machine continually repeated to the Vietnamese people that "the exploits of the workers deserve this new reward hierarchy to speed up the mobilisation of the masses".[60] Virtuocratic regimes use honorific distinctions as key elements in their education and propaganda efforts.

While the medals given out during the first years of the war were distributed by the central government or the office of the president, the recasting of the system in 1950 aimed at a more popular broadening of the system. The theme was changed to: "More individual awards than before; more people who deserve it." The DRV wanted to reach out to more people and a more diverse crowd — in other words, to democratise its patriotic awards. Two new awards were created: the Certificate of Satisfaction and the Certificate of Merit. At the village level, local cadres selected individuals, production units, and exemplary cells, then distributed Certificates of Satisfaction to the deserving candidates. The Certificate of Merit was awarded by the province, the regiment, the military zone, or directly by the administrative branch in charge of the deserving subject. Local cadres (from the commune or district) were told to organise solemn award services "as often as possible", in conjunction with provincial administration committees. The award (be it a medal, certificate, or some form of decoration) linked its recipient to a world of "respectability and patriotic exemplarity". Titles and decorations created, in return, a feeling of duty in those honoured. The newfound pride earned by the peasant or labourer had no quantifiable value. The State used "the honour won by the common people" as a springboard for the conquest of minds.

From then on, emulation policy fell to the Ministries of National Defence, Labour, and Agriculture. Following the model of its brother nations,

---

[59] In 1961 the awards commission had 11 members. Lê Thanh Nghị (Vice-Prime Minister) was president and Nguyễn Khang (Government Minister) was vice-president, with the following nine other members: Nguyễn Văn Tạo (Minister of Labour), Vũ Dương (second-in-charge of organisation for the Central Committee), Xuân Thủy (Secretary-General of the Fatherland Front), Lê Tất Đắc (Minister of the Interior), Trương Quang Giao (Vice-Director of the Committee for Unification), Bùi Quý (member of the standing Committee for Unions), Hoàng Thị Lý (Vice-Director of the Women's Association), Dương Công Hoạt (Vice-President of the Committee for Nationalities), and Vũ Quang (Secretary of the Youth Steering Committee), in AVN3, BNV, file no.1722, 1961.

[60] *Tài liệu về việc thưởng Huân chương Lao động*, document no. 16 116, 18 November 1950.

the DRV created its first title of emulation fighter in 1950, reserved for workers, peasants, and outstanding combatants. The Ministry of Agriculture, symbolically, bestowed the first title of Agricultural Fighter on 4 November. The journal *Nhân dân* (*The People*) explained to its readers:

> … in order to achieve positive results in the selection of emulation fighters, we must encourage and honour the exemplary men and women within the agricultural emulation movement. This selection must be completely democratic. Representatives of each family at the village level must select the best among them, a similar choice will then be done at the communal level, then the district, province, and finally zone. When the selection process is finished in all military zones of the country, all exemplary individuals will be summoned to a national conference to select emulation fighters on the national level. The selection must be a popular one, the people must be active participants.[61]

By the end of 1950, the DRV had a new administrative hierarchy of patriotic merit. At its base, in the villages, communes or production units, the government nominated "exceptional workers" (*lao động xuất sắc*) at the end of each emulation season. The units got together every three months to choose their best workers. Local cadres in charge of emulation then took up these lists and went through another selection to determine the outstanding workers of the year. Until 1953–54, a distinction was made between those nominated for short-term efforts and those who were selected for longer periods, but eventually the certificate of exemplary worker was only given to the former, while the latter received the title of "emulation fighter" (*Chiến sĩ thi đua*). Finally, in the spring of 1952, the DRV crowned this new hierarchy of merit with the selection of the first contingent of "new heroes" (*Anh hùng mới*), thus achieving in scarcely two years the recasting of the hierarchy of patriotic merit.

In order to produce a new society made up of outstanding citizens and new men, the government and its foreign advisors had to increase the rate of recruitment. The old emulation system had two large-scale campaigns per year (from February–May and June–December), but now they had to do more, and in less time. From then on the government organised three separate campaigns per year. A first session opened on 3 February

[61] "Kinh nghiệm bầu Chiến sỹ nông nghiệp ở Liên khu Việt Bắc" (Experience in the election of agricultural emulation fighters in the Việt Bắc zone), *Nhân dân*, no. 5, 22 April 1951: 1.

(the anniversary of the foundation of the ICP) and closed on 19 May (Hồ Chí Minh's birthday). The second began as the first one ended and continued until 2 September (Independence Day); and the third session lasted from 19 December (celebrating the creation of the PAVN in 1944) to 3 February, dedicating itself to a review of the year's activity.

The arrival of the new man in Vietnam was accompanied by the creation of a bureaucracy of heroism to manage the patriotic competitions. In 1948, a national committee began coordinating the emulation activities of each ministry. Then in the summer of 1950, Chinese advisors were sent to re-evaluate the efficiency of the system, from the central level to the de-localised bureaus in the provinces and military zones of North Vietnam. The DRV needed a solid response to the failure of the first emulation campaign. On the advice of Chinese experts, Vietnamese cadres reorganised the emulation campaigns according to the type of activity (agriculture, light industry, heavy industry, arms, education, etc.). Each ministry created an emulation planning cell, with Chinese advisors active in the decision-making process. The programme elaborated by the ministerial branch was then communicated to the administrative committees of the military zones, which supervised the implementation of these directives on the provincial level. Emulation bureaus in the zones and provinces were led by a representative of the administrative committee and comprised six members: the director of the Department of Labour, the secretary of the Communist Workers' Union, the director of the Propaganda Department, the director of Public Works, the president of the Peasants' Association, and a representative from the Department of Social Assistance.

As a relay between communes and the central government, the provincial emulation commissions transmitted ministerial instructions to their areas via mass organisations and collected the end-of-year reports by the various branches of activity for submission to their respective ministries.[62] This was supposed to revive the dialogue with the countryside, but reform did not come easily. In late 1951, the provinces still had problems estimating the results of their emulation activities. Nguyễn Ba Kính, President of the Administrative Resistance Committee of Sơn La province, explained that in his area, "the population is quite backward and is battling hunger,

[62] *Thông tri của UBND Khu Hồng Quảng thành lập Hội đồng Thi đua các cấp* (Decisions of the people's committee of the zone of Hồng Quảng on the creation of a multi-level emulation commission), in AVN3, BLD file no. 491, document no. 1139, 26 September 1955.

[so] the emulation movement did not take hold among the people."[63] In April 1951, the journal *Nhân dân* criticised the town of Bắc Giang for not working actively enough with the Peasants' Association to set up emulation campaigns.[64] Since no committee had actually been created on the provincial level, the government suggested that the Peasants' Association take over emulation activities in the area. The situation was even more uncertain for industries or businesses. The lack of steering committees for emulation led the government to strengthen cooperation between the Party and the Communist Workers' Union in order to improve awareness among workers. State enterprises (weapons, consumer goods, mining, etc.) had to serve as examples for the private sector. The government stressed that the emulation campaign would only succeed with a strict collaboration between mass organisations and the administrative apparatus in the nation's districts and communes.[65]

The selection of an emulation fighter was a novelty in Vietnamese villages. The State wanted to base the programme on productivist merit and class origin, which then freed it from the traditional age requirements. The DRV sent itinerant cadres into villages, accompanied by a "Chinese comrade" when possible, to explain the validity and necessity of reform to the people. Traditionally, peasants respected and feared cadres from other places. A high-placed cadre had more success implementing change than his counterpart in the commune, who was often just a neighbour, a cousin, or even a family enemy. The selection of new exemplary men offered the central government a way to reaffirm its control over the commune and "perfect the education of cadres, train new servants of the State, and correct the ideological deviations of some local officials".[66] The government took advantage of this to increase its patriotic tax and recruit new members to the VWP. Government leaders understood that villagers would not accept the appointment of this alter ego without explanation or through intimidation:

---

[63] AVN3, regional coll. (Sơn La), file no. 15, document no. 70/NC, 12 January 1952.

[64] "Kinh nghiệm bầu Chiến sỹ nông nghiệp ở Liên khu Việt Bắc". *Op. cit.*, 22 April 1951.

[65] *Tài liệu hướng dẫn thi đua của Tổng Liên đoàn LDVN năm 1951* (Orientation documents for emulation from the Vietnamese general confederation of labour), in AVN3, BLD, file no. 408, single document, 1951.

[66] *Tổ chức Đại hội chiến sĩ thi đua và cán bộ gương mẫu* (Organisation of the conference for emulation fighters and exemplary cadres), in AVN3, 30 October 1951.

> To avoid misunderstanding in the process of selecting an emulation fighter, which has happened in some provinces, we must clearly understand the meaning of these selections. Choosing an agricultural emulation fighter consists of singing his praises and sharing his experiences in agricultural production… To achieve this end, each administrative level must send cadres to the level below. They must go into the communes, to each village, and correctly explain the reasons for these selections and the criteria required to obtain the title.[67]

Once the candidates were nominated by village production groups and mass organisations, a file on each "exemplary worker" was to be sent to the next level up. Once the province received the files, they could start preparing conferences by branch (peasants, workers, the military) to choose which "outstanding citizens" would represent the jurisdiction at the national congress.

On 16 January 1952, the People's Committee of Vĩnh Phú province gathered its 24 agricultural emulation fighters.[68] After an inaugural speech by the president of the province, and in the presence of a representative from the ministry, the peasants seated on the podium read out a résumé of their productivist and political performance. Three of them were then chosen to represent their province at the next national conference for peasant emulation fighters: Tạ Văn Cừu (Phương Khoan commune, Lập Thạch district), Khổng Văn Cúc (Cao Phong, Lập Thạch), and Nguyễn Thị Hiên, a young woman from the village of Văn Quán (Lập Thạch). The title of provincial emulation fighter was awarded to all 24 participants and the day ended with a buffet. At this stage, the number of candidates receiving awards varied from one province to another. Lạng Sơn, for example, sent 7 outstanding combatants to the national conference, among the 32 nominated.

The penultimate step in forging the new hero in Vietnam was to hold national conferences with all provincial winners, grouped by branch of activity. For the national conference of outstanding peasants in the spring of 1952, 42 emulation fighters were invited: 8 from guerrilla zones and 34 from liberated zones. The national committee chose 11 exemplary combatants from ethnic minorities (6 Thổ, 2 Nùng, 2 Mường, and 1 Yáo), some women, and some youth representatives. The day began with labour

---

[67] *Tổ chức Đại hội chiến sĩ thi đua và cán bộ gương mẫu*, p. 1.

[68] "Để chuẩn bị Đại hội chiến sĩ thi đua toàn quốc" (Preparing the national emulation conference), *Nhân Dân*, 17 January 1952.

meetings led by Party cadres, during which the exemplary peasants studied theory on new heroism and the Party's role in society. In the evening, everyone got together to watch plays, films, or concerts, to "facilitate the education of these men and woman and make it enjoyable".[69] The peasants were thus able to share their professional experiences. The meeting ended with an awards ceremony to issue certificates, special prizes, and the title of "national agricultural emulation fighter" for all participants. In 1952, 5 peasants received a title of the First Rank, 5 got the Second Order, 27 the Third, and 5 were ranked as "encouraging."[70] During the first season, the emulation movement in industry chose 1,221 exemplary workers, 41 of whom were invited to the national conference in April.[71] Finally, within the army, 50 combatants from 5 sectors were invited: 16 per cent were cadres working in defence, 12 per cent were guerrilla fighters, 22 per cent were from communal forces of the PAVN, 44 per cent from the PAVN itself, and 6 per cent were technical specialists.[72]

All of these outstanding peasants, workers, and soldiers were carefully selected for their productivist or military performance, but also for their social or ethnic backgrounds. Among the 50 emulation fighters chosen from the army, 42 of them (82 per cent) had been classified "proletarian-peasant" and "poor peasant."[73] Since 1945, government leaders had fought to offer the classes once oppressed by the previous regime a special place within the new system. An "exemplary society", by giving rise to the emergence of a virtuous elite, led to the reform of the social link among members of the community. The "new honourees of the DRV" were primarily recruited according to the social criteria established during the classification campaigns organised by Chinese advisors.

---

[69] *Directive no. 58 LD/P5*, in AVN3, file no. 415, document no. 3.7489, 26 December 1951.

[70] *Báo cáo Tổng kết Hội nghị chiến sĩ thi đua nông nghiệp toàn quốc lần thứ nhất tháng 4.1952* (Final report from the fourth national conference on agricultural emulation fighters), in AVN3, BLD, document no. 182 B1/NDTQ, April 1952.

[71] Hoàng Quốc Việt. "Lao Động Việt Nam phải làm gì?" (What does the Vietnamese worker have to do?), in *Nhân Dân*, April 1952, p. 1.

[72] Võ Nguyên Giáp. "Nhân Hội nghị Chiến sĩ thi đua toàn quân: Quân đội thi đua lập công" (On the occasion of the national emulation conference: emulation exploits in the army), *Nhân Dân*, no. 54, 17 April 1952: 1, 4.

[73] There were seven "middle peasants", one rich peasant, and one from the "petite bourgeoise". See Thép Mới, "Quân đội ta là Quân đội anh hùng" (Our army is a heroic army), *Nhân Dân*, no. 59, 29 April 1952: 1.

In the spring of 1952, the war hindered the efforts of agrarian reform teams to reclassify and select a new patriotic elite. The spread of emulation was deemed satisfactory in the military Interzones IV and V, and in the Việt Bắc, while nothing was done in Interzone III or anywhere in the South. Regardless of these disparities, the national congress for the first heroes of the DRV was still held on 1 May 1952 and 230 emulation fighters from the national level (peasants, workers, and soldiers) were invited to Tuyên Quang province. In his opening speech, Hồ Chí Minh re-situated the Vietnamese experience in a context of internationalist cooperation, declaring to his foreign guests that the success of the reorganisation of Vietnamese emulation since 1950 was due entirely to the experience of the Soviets and Chinese.[74] North Vietnamese leaders chose seven of those selected on the national level to receive the title of "new hero" of the DRV (one of them posthumously). Among the 50 emulation fighters from the PAVN, 4 received the certificate of "military hero": La Văn Cầu, Nguyễn Quốc Trị, Nguyễn Thị Chiên, and the martyr Cù Chính Lan. Of the 42 distinguished workers on the national level, 2 were awarded the title of "labour hero": the engineer Trần Đại Nghĩa, who invented the Vietnamese bazooka, and the arms specialist Ngô Gia Khảm. Lastly, the peasant movement was represented by 42 national figures, of whom only one won the title "agricultural hero": Hoàng Hanh, an elderly Catholic farmer from Nghệ An province.

In the traditional agricultural societies of Southeast Asia, the recognition of an individual's heroic qualities "inspired loyalty that could help form groups and gain political influence. Their extraordinary individual abilities reveal leadership qualities and confer upon their ruler an aura of miraculous virtue, and thereby his affinity with supernatural powers."[75] The Tuyên Quang conference of 1952 marked the high point of the reorganisation of the bureaucracy of heroism, carried out with the help of Vietnam's brother nations, especially China.[76] This was all part of an evolution —

[74] Hồ Chí Minh. "Lời phát biểu trong buổi lễ khai mạc Đại hội chiến sĩ thi đua và cán bộ gương mẫu toàn quốc" (Speech for the inauguration of the national conference of emulation fighters and exemplary cadres), in *Thi đua ái quốc*. Hanoi: nxb Sự thật, 1984, pp. 30–1.

[75] Nguyễn Thế Anh. "La conception de la monarchie divine dans le Viêt Nam traditionnel", p. 147.

[76] *Đại hội toàn quốc chiến sĩ thi đua và cán bộ gương mẫu (1–6.5.1952 tại Việt Bắc)* (National conference on emulation fighters and exemplary cadres held from 1–6 May 1952, in the Việt Bắc province), in AVN3, BLD, file no. 432.

Figure 5. Ngô Gia Khảm

whether desired or suggested by the government — to remodel the social relationship between members of the community. The government still lamented the poor implementation of some of its directives, which had led to the unequal development of the programme around the country. Yet, despite the internal weaknesses of the movement, the DRV had at least shown to the communist world its respect for the decisions of January 1950. Hồ Chí Minh liked to tell Soviet authorities: "The Chinese people are very close to us, we are exalted by their example."[77] The new heroic figure answered Stalin's demand that they quickly develop new "exemplary men" in order to launch agrarian reform. But — and this is especially true of the heroes at Tuyên Quang — the "newly elect of the DRV" were there mainly to rework the hierarchy of patriotic merit in order to solidify the new government's hold on power. Though the turning point of 1952 did not lead to any real reflection on the role of the new heroic figure, it answered the demands of the era, quickly transforming the emulation fighter and the new hero into the exemplary citizen of past times.

[77] *Letter from Vietnam*, in Archives of the CC of the CPSU, file no. 951, document no. 4531k259, 19 March 1952.

CHAPTER 3

The Emulation Fighter (1950–1964)

> An emulation fighter's mission is to always try, always progress. They should be modest and close to the people, and set an example for them. They should study political texts and have a spirit of emulation that is both patriotic and internationalist. They should avoid pride, self-importance, and isolation from the masses. They should always bear in mind that their performance is a collective one, a collective heroism, not an individual act. It reveals the collective honour of the people and not the particular honour of one individual.
>
> Hồ Chí Minh[1]

The emulation fighter in Vietnam never represented a sociologically distinct group but was consubstantial with the group. To Vietnamese leaders, he offered an idealised image of the community. He was a kind of Trojan horse in the village square, bearing with him an image of the new national virtues. The emulation fighter was disciplined and helped reaffirm the cohesion of the social fabric that had been damaged by the West since the end of the nineteenth century. Before becoming workers for internationalism, these exemplary men were to be the craftsmen for the reconstruction of national identity. After the election of the first emulation fighters in January 1951, their numbers continued to grow. There were barely 1,000 in early 1951, but some 3,000 in 1953, 30,000 in 1956, 65,000 in 1961, and more than 100,000 in 1965.[2] This increase went

[1] Hồ Chí Minh, *Báo cáo về sự mở rộng và nâng cao phong trào thi đua sản xuất và tiết kiệm ở nông thôn* (Report on the development and reinforcement of the productivist emulation movement in the countryside), in AVN3, BLD, file no. 52, document no. 12/bld, March 1956.

[2] *Báo cáo công tác thi đua 1952 của các UBKC khu, tỉnh* (Report on emulation activities in 1952, all zones, all provinces), in AVN3, BLD, file 1952. *Về Hội nghị anh hùng và chiến sĩ thi đua toàn quốc lần thứ ba* (On the third national conference on heroes and emulation fighters), in AVN3, QH, file no. 367, 1962. *Báo cáo tổng kết công tác thi đua 1965* (Summary of emulation activities for 1965), in AVN3, BLD, file no. 576, 1965.

hand in hand with national reconstruction. The swelling numbers revealed the government's desire to rebuild a virtuous administrative elite at each level of its apparatus.

In 1950, the Soviets demanded that Vietnam implement large-scale agrarian reform, which formed the real impetus for the DRV's new bureaucracy of heroism. Emulation fighters were created to help build the new structures of production and ideological training (production groups, cells of mutual aid, mass organisations, Party apparatus, etc.), and the first emulation campaigns in the villages were usually organised by agrarian reform cadres.[3] From 1954–56, the partial dismantling of the old communal elite necessitated a reshuffling of local leaders. Agrarian reform cadres had divided the peasantry into five distinct social groups (landless peasants, poor peasants, middle peasants, rich peasants, and landlords), creating a void of leadership at the village level that only the new exemplary men and women could fill. In December 1953, Hồ Chí Minh called "the entire nation, soldiers and emulation fighters to enthusiastically carry out the two main missions of 1953: strengthen the resistance and implement agrarian reform".[4] In response, men and women from unsullied backgrounds were elected "vanguard workers" and "emulation fighters" to answer the call. The second phase of the making of the new man dates from 1955–56. Following the Geneva Agreement of 21 July 1954 (marking the end of France's presence in the North), more than 7,300 North Vietnamese officials took refuge in the South, paralysing 70 of the 131 government agencies formerly held by the French in the DRV.[5] In the northern provinces (from Quảng Trị along the thirteenth parallel to Hà Giang), they desperately needed new cadres to reclaim the occupied zones and rebuild the government apparatus.

---

[3] On 4 December 1953, the National Assembly of the DRV enacted decree 197/SL, instituting agrarian reform. A pilot programme was put in place in Thái Nguyên province between December 1953 and March 1954. To date, the best study on agrarian reform in Vietnam is that of Edwin Moïse, *Land Reform in China and North Vietnam: Consolidating the Revolution at the Village Level*. Chapel Hill: University of North Carolina Press, 1983.

[4] Hồ Chí Minh. "Lời kêu gọi nhân dịp kỷ niệm 7 năm toàn quốc kháng chiến" (Call for the seventh year of national resistance), *Nhân Dân*, no. 156, 26–31 December 1953: 1.

[5] Võ Nguyên Giáp. *On the Implementation of the Geneva Agreements*. Hanoi: Foreign Languages Publishing House, 1955, pp. 13–4.

Portrait of a Combatant

Class was a key element in a candidate's selection, so village cadres chose people from the lower ranks of society who were classified as "landless, poor, or middle peasants".[6] The average peasant, however, usually associated personal magnetism with the ability to attain material success. Many local authorities thus chose middle peasants rather than the landless or the poor since they had a greater chance of inspiring others to follow them. The candidate's respectability played an important role. The emulation fighter should be admired by his peers and reflect the dynamism and youthfulness of the regime. In areas where ideology had not yet taken hold, the government chose middle-aged men and women (30–45 years old). In Nguyên Bình district (Cao Bằng), more than half of the emulation fighters were older than 30. Elsewhere, however, the "young" (20–30 years old) were still the privileged target for selection committees. In Thuận Thành (Hà Bắc) and Quỳnh Lưu (Nghệ An), for example, 75 per cent of emulation fighters were from that age group. Official documents confirm that the average age of recruitment was between 20 and 30 years old. Since anyone up to the age of 30 could join the Patriotic Youth, youth was clearly an important criterion for anyone aspiring to the title of emulation fighter.

As a representative of the lower classes, the emulation fighter had to illustrate the benefits of popular education and continued training. Government propaganda often emphasised his lack of education in order to highlight its own role as tutor to the nation. The emulation fighter was a man of the people, and the government relied on those who had been excluded from the educational system of the old regime. Most had spent only a few years at school when they were young, and many of them learned to read and write while in the people's army. They usually had no more than

[6] This was true for 95 per cent of the emulation fighters whom I interviewed in the three areas of research (Nguyên Bình, Thuận Thành, and Quỳnh Lưu). Among them, 45 per cent had been classified "middle peasants", 42 per cent were "poor peasants", and 8 per cent were "landless peasants" (the remaining 5 per cent were rich peasants). This data is corroborated by the statistical lists in the Vietnamese national archives. See *Báo cáo danh sách Chiến sĩ thi đua đơn vị Lao động 1958* (List of emulation fighters/ production units for 1958), AVN3, BLD, file no. 299, 1958. *Danh sách và số huy hiệu Chiến sĩ thi đua và khen thưởng năm 1956 của các cơ quan Trung ương* (List and insignias of emulation fighters and medals given in 1956 from all bureaus of the central government), in AVN3, BLD, file no. 282, etc.

a primary education when the government selected them as models for their peers.[7]

The National Emulation Committee recommended that candidates be chosen from outside the ranks of the VWP.[8] In the early 1950s, the percentage of Party members who became emulation fighters was still low. Less than 15 per cent of the people I interviewed in the districts of Nguyên Bình, Thuận Thành, and Quỳnh Lưu had been members of the Party before receiving their title. The government expected these outstanding workers to have acted valiantly for national resistance, but they did not gain automatic entry into the Party — even if the process was undeniably accelerated. Three-quarters of them, however, joined the VWP within three years of being selected. Nevertheless, many candidates failed to meet the expectations set for them during an initial probationary period. The title itself did not necessarily favour admission to the Party but padded a candidate's résumé.

Following an appointment, the government offered additional training to the honourees to improve their "political, technical and cultural levels to secure their place at the heart of their community". In 1952–53, the National Emulation Committee suggested its local branches follow a four-point programme: require emulation fighters to take political training courses; help them study political documents; offer additional training courses on general culture (usually just a matter of basic literacy classes);[9] and lastly, coach them on public speaking so that they could address the local government and mass organisations.[10] In the year following an appointment, the emulation fighter had to sign up for political and cultural training.[11] Reports from the Ministry of Culture frequently lamented the

[7] In 1955, the educational system was comprised of primary schools (with 257,518 students) and secondary schools (with 5,860 students). See Thaveeporn Vasavakul, *Schools and Politics in South and North Vietnam: A Comparative Study of State Apparatus, State Policy, and State Power (1945–1965)*. Ph.D. diss., Cornell University, 1994.

[8] Chiến Hữu. "Thi đua ái quốc" (Patriotic emulation), *Sinh Hoạt Nội Bộ*, no. 8, May 1948: 16–7.

[9] Between 1954 and 1956, 9,500 cadres enrolled in additional classes. At the beginning of 1960, of the 3,477 "top-level cadres with responsibilities" within the DRV, 343 were uneducated, 1,373 had reached the fourth grade, and 1,761 had completed secondary or university education.

[10] *Thông tư về việc bồi dưỡng chiến sĩ* (Note on encouraging emulation fighters), 6 September 1953.

[11] *Báo cáo tổng kết công tác đào tạo và bổ túc công nhân trong ba năm (1958–60) của các Bộ các ngành và các địa phương* (Review of educational activities and training for workers from 1958–1960 by sector and province), in AVN3, BLD, file no. 998, 1960.

"extremely weak theoretical competence" of the candidates.[12] In 1956, the Ministry of Education estimated that more than 3.4 million people in North Vietnam were illiterate. In most communes, groups of cultural cadres offered weekly courses on general culture and political training (each one lasting two-and-a-half hours) to their outstanding workers and peasants. For most of them it was their first exposure to organised education.

The Emulation Fighter and the Commune

In the North Vietnamese countryside, the agricultural emulation fighter represented the "new order". In November 1950, the National Emulation Committee established a number of criteria for those seeking nomination. The candidate had to: be active in more than one field of production (farming and animal husbandry, etc.); help increase yield and production; apply technical innovations; show great initiative and have a sense of responsibility that would allow him to coordinate community projects guaranteeing increased production and real savings.[13] The new government wanted the agricultural emulation fighter to be a pillar in the reorganisation of the Vietnamese village.

In the beginning, provincial People's Committees chose a certain number of "test communes" or a particular experimental zone in its jurisdiction. The Bureau of Emulation and the Peasants' Association then took over the operation. Groups of emulation cadres were sent to meet with villagers; until 1955, itinerant cadres were regularly accompanied by Chinese advisors.[14] Upon arrival, they had to explain to the people how they could take part in the movement, for example, by joining mass organisations such as the Patriotic Youth, Peasants' Associations, Association

[12] *Chỉ thị về đẩy mạnh học tập trong các đơn vị lưu động* (Directive on reinforcing training within itinerant units), in AVN3, BVH, file no. 696, document no. 377/VH/VP, 1962.

[13] *Nghị định số 6-QT-CN-ND ngày 4.11.1950 đạt danh hiệu chiến sĩ Lao động trong nông nghiệp thưởng tặng những nông dân có thành tích đặt biệt về tăng giá sản xuất* (Decree no. 6-QT-CN-ND of 4 November 1950, regulating the awards of peasant fighters/workers, recompense for outstanding peasants who had the highest increase in production), *Công báo*, no. 12, 1950, p. 281.

[14] *Báo cáo tổng kết kinh nghiệm bồi dưỡng chiến sĩ tại Liên Sơn, huyện Gia Viễn, tỉnh Ninh Bình* (Review of attempts to encourage combatants in Liên Sơn, Gia Viễn district, Ninh Bình province), in AVN3, BLD, file no. 277, document no. 5559, 1 August 1955.

of the Mothers of Combatants, senior citizens' groups, etc., which could nominate them on their behalf. In Diễn Sơn district (Nghệ An), the first emulation campaign in 1948 led to the creation of new structures for ideological training within the commune: 50 cells of the Peasants' Association, each with 12–15 families, and 108 production groups, each with 5–8 families, were created in the 6 hamlets within the commune.[15] In 1950–51, emulation teams sent by the provincial People's Committee relied on these groups to spread the principles of emulation and its proper use in order to select outstanding workers. They explained to the people what they had to do to obtain the new patriotic title, and itinerant cadres recounted the exploits of outstanding combatants from other provinces. Many people, however, still did not understand the movement. Some villages, for example, posted slogans that said "Emulation for a beautiful wife". The novelty of the operation required some explanation.

Once a first selection was made within production units and the hamlet, the commune held a conference with all exemplary workers from their jurisdiction. Official documents specified that this step should be done by popular vote, but people were usually happy to accept whatever the authorities (emulation cadres, the local Party cell, etc.) proposed, since they were "in the know". Nguyễn Thị Nhờ, a peasant from the village of Ngũ Thái (Thuận Thành) tells of how this first selection phase was not very well understood in his commune: "The first time, not many candidates were chosen from the hamlets. The people didn't understand why. Some people started to cry when they found out they had not been chosen."[16]

On 21 January 1954, 12 outstanding peasants, 3 teachers, and 4 civic workers were brought together by the commune of Diễn Sơn (Nghệ An). Throughout the morning, the president of the commune and the Party secretary explained what the Party meant by "new heroism" and outlined the course of the emulation movement. They stressed the brilliant prospects that awaited future emulation fighters. In the afternoon, the peasants

---

[15] In 1954, the commune of Diễn Sơn had 1,889 inhabitants (894 men and 995 women) in 19 hamlets of varying size (from 25 people in Ngoc Minh to 184 elsewhere). The agrarian reform team noted 2 "landlord" families, 47 "rich peasants", 541 "middle peasants", 1,171 "poor peasants", 1 "worker family", and 1 "shopkeeper" family. See *Số lượng tình hình xã Diễn Sơn* (Inventory Diễn Sơn commune), in AVN3, BLD, file no. 270, 1954, p. 2.

[16] Interview, Ngũ Thái commune (Thuận Thành, Hà Bắc). I conducted numerous interviews throughout the country over the past 15 years, and have not used names here out of respect for my interviewees' privacy.

were invited to talk "in a relaxed atmosphere" about their performance in their production groups. It was quite a challenge for these men and women who were not used to speaking in public. At the end of the meeting, local cadres reviewed the performance of each candidate and wrote a short individual biography before sending the files to the provincial emulation committee (via the administrative committee of the district), which had the final word. Writing the official biography of an outstanding worker was an important step, and the meeting often gave rise to animated discussions. Candidates who were literate sometimes brought along a draft, which was then collectively discussed and then rewritten by the local emulation authority or, in his absence (which was most often the case), by the communal Party secretary.[17] In principle, each commune had to nominate one or two candidates for the title of emulation fighter. The commune awarded a certificate of "exemplary worker" to those who failed to make the cut.[18] Before the conference began, campaign organisers made the newly benighted patriots promise they would spread the movement within their families, neighbourhoods, hamlets, and production groups. The operation at the village level was then complete. They then had to wait three or four weeks for provincial authorities to announce which peasants would receive the title of emulation fighter. In practice, however, provincial opposition to communal recommendations was extremely rare.

Several weeks after this stage in the campaign, a conference was organised in the provincial seat.[19] The meeting always began with a general review of the emulation movement in the jurisdiction. Speakers encouraged the audience to "persevere in their efforts to eradicate weaknesses in the movement". After the introduction, provincial cadres gave the floor to that day's heroes, dressed up for the occasion. The stories succeeded each other in a steady rhythm as the candidates took to the stage to read the résumé of their performance. The crowd of officials erupted in applause. When one sector, production unit, or commune had too many nominees, one of them was designated to speak for the group. After the presentations, a provincial cadre handed out the certificates of emulation

---

[17] Interview, Nghĩa Đạo commune (Thuận Thành, Hà Bắc).

[18] *Báo cáo tình hình chung chung về phong trào thi đua ái quốc xã Diễn Thắng* (Report on the patriotic emulation movement in Diễn Thắng commune), in AVN3, BLD, file no. 270, 1955.

[19] During the first few years, provinces organised conferences for all the different branches of activity at one time. Starting from 1956–57, however, the increased number of nominees led provincial authorities to hold separate meetings for each profession.

fighter. They came with a small badge and a payment in kind, a financial bonus equal to a third or half of the average monthly salary, and a small gift (clothing, fabric, a toy, alcohol, a flashlight, photos of political leaders, patriotic literature, etc.). A photographer was on hand to capture the emotion of the glorious day. And finally, the new "distinguished children of the province" were invited to a banquet organised in their honour.

The newly decorated peasant or cadre's return to his village was the next important step. The emulation fighter would carefully unfurl his new certificate next to the Party secretary (or a village cadre, if there was no secretary), and the communal government invited him to a banquet with representatives of the collective. When possible, a feast with plenty of food and rice wine was held for the new honouree. Trần Văn Chiến recalls the huge get-together organised by the Communal Hall in his honour when he returned to his village of Nguyệt Đức (Thuận Thành) in January 1954: "At some point somebody asked me to take the place of honour, and then cadres read the details of my performance and everybody cheered for me."[20] After another ceremony held by the People's Committee, the new emulation fighter was congratulated by the members of his work unit, who paid their respects in the name of the collective. Then the new local hero had to speak before his friends, neighbours, and family. His prestige was important to the village. Mass organisations discussed his life story, he was asked to lead informal talks, and his photo was posted in government offices, cooperatives, or the cultural centre. The emulation fighter was no longer an anonymous subject but had become the object of conversation; word of mouth and official meetings elevated him to a special status within the village. They had to use this tactic sparingly, however, since the value of this new patriotic honour also depended on its rarity. It was an honour for the entire collective if a child of the village received recognition by the province. In the early 1950s there were still very few agricultural emulation fighters in North Vietnam, but a decade later the situation was quite different.

A New Local Elite?

The new heroes may have gained prestige, but did they attain any real power within their communes? In many areas in the 1950s–60s they did not actually have much real influence. Outside of the industrialised areas,

---

[20] Interview, Nguyệt Đức commune (Thuận Thành, Hà Bắc).

which produced so many "new men" that their prestige was somewhat diluted (such as in Tĩnh Túc in Cao Bằng province, where the Kim Loan company alone elected at least 50 distinguished workers per session), less developed regions were slow to accept these new mid-level honorary positions. In the Red Yáo village of Vũ Nông (Nguyên Bình, Cao Bằng), for example, Triệu Thùng Chòi was the only emulation fighter to receive the award between 1951 to 1965. He believes that the "new hero" saw no increase in prestige or status because the local people failed to grasp the implications or felt somehow excluded:

> The villagers were not very interested, and didn't understand the real meaning of the title anyway. Some of them did come up to meet me and ask me questions about it, but in the end it didn't change anything for them, they didn't really know what it was all about. From what they understood, being chosen as an emulation fighter meant you had to leave your home and family. This made them afraid, and to be honest, nobody really wanted it.[21]

The emulation fighter's entrance into the village value system was concretely experienced as a rise in professional and social status. His connections with political leaders strengthened his image and legitimacy with the villagers. The DRV paid special attention to the hierarchy of honours.[22] The emergence of a new mid-level honorary position destabilised the traditional social balance within the community to some degree, but this was not due solely to the title of emulation fighter. Every award also implied a collective shift. Sometimes the government preferred to select its outstanding citizens from among powerful and respected families. Indeed, the National Emulation Committee had suggested that the award be given to influential people within the commune. In the village of Thuận Thành (Hà Bắc), for example, the peasant Nguyễn Văn Hợp told me that his status in the community did not change at all following his decoration as it merely confirmed his superior social status.

Consequently, can we really speak of the emergence of a new local elite in North Vietnam? The DRV had made a point of focusing its efforts on people who had previously been excluded from power. The emulation

---

[21] Interview, Vũ Nòng commune (Nguyên Bình, Cao Bằng).

[22] Nguyễn Từ Chi. *Góp phần nghiên cứu văn hoá và tộc người* (Contribution to the study of culture and man). Hanoi: nxb Văn hoá thông tin-Tạp chí Văn hóa Nghệ thuật, 1996, pp. 235–8.

fighter and his family now received both the interest and esteem of their friends and neighbours. One popular saying goes: "A bowl of rice with the entire village is better than a feast at home." Everyone benefited from the prestige of this official honour, and traditionally they had always respected the notion of the reward. An entire lineage would be proud to have one of its members honoured by the government. They could be proud to have been chosen over their neighbours and to have attracted the attention of those in power, which legitimised their actions. The family's reputation in the community was enhanced by visits from local cadres, annual gifts, or the new honouree's participation in local meetings and events. Sometimes neighbours would drop by to seek information, or just out of respect for the honour made to the village, which further solidified the new hero's symbolic position within the community. A moral and pedagogic responsibility fell on the newly elect. People now came to them for advice on making their lives a little bit easier. The new outstanding citizen was often summoned by production groups to raise the spirit of collective solidarity, and the most articulate ones had to spread the spirit of emulation. With this political responsibility, the "common man" found himself thrust into the centre of a new symbolic space.[23] In Linh Xá (Thuận Thành, Hà Bắc), the prestige conferred upon young Nguyễn Như Nguyện forced him to play a central role during ritual ceremonies: "Since I was an emulation fighter, they asked me to speak at funerals and marriages in the village, even though I was still quite young."[24] Moral and patriotic pride, as well as the promise of elevated status, seduced many villagers who were eager for respectability. The neighbours, friends, and relatives of a new awardee could also try their hand at winning with the help of the latter's reference or introduction. The structures of mass mobilisation were very good at manipulating the psycho-cultural mechanisms of the people. The State sparked an organisational disorder within the commune, creating the need for social reciprocity that facilitated its conquest for hearts and minds.

In Vietnam, appealing to individual interest is not a sign of ideological weakness but shows the ingenuity of DRV strategy. On patriotic holidays, government authorities on each level, along with Party leaders

---

[23] In 1952, only 40 per cent of emulation fighters were carrying out such activities, however, as regrettably noted in an official document from the Military Interzone III. See *Báo cáo công tác thi đua 1952 của các UBKCHC các khu, tỉnh* (Report on emulation activities in 1952 from all resistance authorities at the zone and provincial level), in AVN3, BLD, file no. 426, 1953.

[24] Interview, Linh Xá commune (Thuận Thành, Hà Bắc).

and mass organisations, renewed this social pact by distributing gifts to outstanding citizens. They stressed the importance of practical application. The State asked that particular attention be paid to "progressivist workers",[25] and made the patriotic gift a nationwide practice. People's Committees had their cadres hand out gifts to the "vanguard families" in their district during patriotic holidays. For Tết (Vietnamese New Year), 1 May, and Independence Day (2 September), soldiers' families, veterans, workers and outstanding peasants were given a small cash bonus drawn from collections taken up during the year. This of course was "terrible for those families who got nothing, who thought it was deeply unfair. Material things got the people excited, and sometimes, we must admit, that was the motivation behind the mass engagement hiding behind all the grandiose words."[26] Families who were blessed by these rewards cast dishonour on those who were not.

In 1961, the Party's political journal *Học tập* (*Studies*) stressed the "need for material disinterest" in matters of popular motivation.[27] By rewarding an outstanding citizen for his good and loyal service, the State was not only bestowing its favours on an isolated individual but on the members of a family, a lineage, or a generation. Financial incentive and the patriotic gifts were a way for government representatives to rebalance the contractual relationship with their communities. Anyone who received a gift had to respond with a counter-gift, though not more than what they had received. A balance within the social exchange was achieved by the distribution of "parallel sentences" (a classical Vietnamese literary style involving two matching verses), certificates, diplomas, and orders of merit. Gift-giving was a rite, and had been an essential strategy for kings and emperors for centuries. The distribution of food, goods, or titles conferred upon the "representative of heaven" the loyalty of his subjects. At the end of a war, kings would offer their officers silk or cotton robes. The more a

---

[25] *Báo cáo về công tác bồi dưỡng Chiến sĩ thi đua năm 1953 của các Khu Lao động III, IV., Việt Bắc và một số địa phương* (Report on encouragement efforts for emulation fighters in 1953 in zones III and IV, in the Việt Bắc, and some provinces), in AVN3, BLD, no. 443, document no. 1951 UT/QT, 6 September 1953.

[26] Interview, Hanoi.

[27] Quyết Tiến. "Cần quan tâm đến lợi ích vật chất của xã viên, Kết hợp đúng dân lợi ích cá nhân với lợi ích tập thể, đẩy mạnh hơn nữa phong trào thi đua đại phong" (On the need to consider the financial interest of communal cadres, and the positive addition of individual and collective interest in order to better strengthen popular emulation), *Học Tập*, Hanoi, no. 8, 1961: 40.

ruler gave, the more he asserted his authority. DVR policy was thus totally in line with this time-honoured tradition. A gift from the central government required a commitment by the recipient, especially if the latter was from low social origins. This principle ensured the cohesion of the group. The government's gift paid off by securing the unfailing loyalty of the contractant. The peasant thus offered himself up in a patriotic communion.

The various certificates of good conduct also brought access (in theory, temporary) to social assistance normally reserved for the most deserving families.[28] Some outstanding citizens were also offered trips in return for their service. In 1962, for example, Đàm Thị Thuỷ, a worker from the tin mine at Tĩnh Túc, was invited to Hanoi to visit the Văn Hô Exposition Centre. Given his background, this was a great honour for the young man. Lastly, the regime granted certain exemptions to some emulation fighters. In 1958, an official document stated that "heads of families who received a decoration or honorary title or resistance medal" could be exempted — in theory, non-transmittable — from certain days of mandatory civic labour.[29] On this level, the title of emulation fighter conferred concrete favours upon the recipient. He gained real access to the decision-makers within local government, and some did not hesitate to take advantage of it. All of these material incentives raise a difficult issue: the commodification of the new heroism. Revolutionary morality should theoretically oppose the monetisation of patriotic exemplarity. The DRV skirted this issue by broadening the idea of gift/counter-gift — the emulation fighter's material gain was simply a legitimate homage from the collective to its best subjects. In no case should it seem like a tool of "petit-bourgeois, capitalist" greed.

Nevertheless, the title of emulation fighter had the material result of raising the recipient's salary or monthly wages:

> In the 1950s–60s, to be named an emulation fighter was already a big reward for a peasant. Beyond the personal prestige they always acquired, it also meant real financial gain, a step up in their wages, and especially

---

[28] A directive from the national emulation committee from 13 September 1958 states that only those emulation fighters invited to a national emulation conference were eligible for a stay at a rest home. See *Thông tư về tổ chức cho Anh hùng Lao động và chiến sĩ thi đua đi nghỉ dưỡng sức năm 1958* (Announcement on the organisation of rest home use by labour heroes and emulation fighters), in AVN3, BLD, file no. 553, document no. 25-TDLD, 13 September 1958.

[29] *Tập liệu phổ biến học tập điều lệ dân công của khu, tỉnh năm 1958* (Information documents on the regulation of collective works organised in zones and provinces in 1958), in AVN3, file no. 414, document no. 343/BLD, 19 March 1958.

a promotion in their professional pay scale and sometimes access to foreign goods at the government-owned shops.[30]

The title of exemplarity was thus not only symbolic, but carried with it a variety of material gains. As a tool for mobilisation, it handily tapped into the common quest for financial advancement to ensure the people's allegiance. Undoubtedly, the itinerant cadres and their Chinese advisors had to cope with the pressures of family solidarity. A Vietnamese proverb states that "when someone receives the title of mandarin, his whole family line benefits." The anthropologist Christine White wrote about the importance of family lineage in Vietnam in her article about the ideological changes brought about by agrarian reform.[31] Our interviews were also very revealing on this score:

> Each village has two or three powerful families. They are often members of the Party, so frequently everything was discussed within the family. Little has changed, in fact. Each lineage has its supporters, and the choices made by those in power followed this traditional logic. The elected official chose men from his lineage. The Party tried to combat this by sending in men from outside, but often this didn't go well. This also happened in the local emulation committees. Everything was decided by vote, so the most senior communist of the village decided to appoint members of his own lineage to the local Party cell.[32]

Agrarian reform teams tried to fight against the weight of family ties while they visited a village, but old habits usually took over after they left.

In the towns of Thuận Thành (Hà Bắc) and Quỳnh Lưu (Nghệ An), more than two-thirds of those who received titles came from the most powerful lineages of their village. Their emulation fighters had family members in key positions within the local government (president of the commune, communal party secretary, security attaché, and head of the cooperative).[33] I have already mentioned the importance of the intermediary,

---

[30] Interview, Hanoi.

[31] Christine White. "Mass Mobilisation and Ideological Transformation in the Vietnamese Land Reform Campaign", *Journal of Contemporary Asia*, London-Stockholm, vol. 13, no. 1, 1983: 74–90.

[32] Interview, Hanoi.

[33] For example, Vũ Văn Liêm, an emulation fighter in education, was from the main lineage (Vũ) of the village of Quỳnh Xuân (accounting for more than 50 per cent of the population). At the time of his appointment (1956–58), he belonged to the same lineage as the president and secretary of the communal Party. See Interview, Quỳnh Xuân commune (Quỳnh Lưu, Nghệ An).

"the presenter", in the nomination process. The writer Nguyễn Khắc Trường brings up this issue in her novel *Ghosts and Men* (*Mảnh đất lắm người nhiều ma* [1991]): "And if I wasn't a Party member, how could I have kept my job as president of the cooperative six or seven years running? And how do you think the young people of our lineage got admitted to the Party? If it wasn't for me, they would still be waiting!"[34] The strength of family ties may have been shaken up by agrarian reform, but they were eventually able to adapt to the new socio-political context. Class competed poorly against family, and had to adapt. There might have been a reconstruction of social relationships centred around loyalty and the political merits of exemplary men from the community, but it could never totally do away with the traditional role of lineage within a village.

The recomposition of the village elite in North Vietnam is thus a particularly complex issue. Did the exemplary worker or the emulation fighter really help usher in a new local elite? Or was it more a question of heightened resistance by the traditional village hierarchy to the arrival of "reformist types" with conspicuous ties to the central government? Indeed, available statistics show clearly that these certificates were awarded to only a small number of people spread unevenly throughout the country.[35] In 1958–59, the production units and communes of Lào Cai province elected 1,441 "vanguard workers", but the title of emulation fighter was only given to 154 of them, or less than 10 per cent (the percentage is even lower if you consider the total population of 130,000 in 1960).[36] Likewise, figures from 1957 on the distribution of emulation fighters per village in Vĩnh Linh province show that it was still a relatively rare honour:

[34] Nguyễn Khắc Trường. *Mảnh đất lắm người nhiều ma* (Men and as many ghosts and sorcerers). Hanoi: nxb hội nhà văn, 1991, p. 28. Translated into the French as *Des fantômes et des hommes* by Picquier (Arles) in 1996.

[35] *Báo cáo thành tích phong trào thi đua yêu nước 1959 và nhiệm vụ thi đua yêu nước năm 1960 tỉnh Lào Cai* (Report on the patriotic emulation movement of 1959 and tasks for emulation in 1960 in Lào Cai province), in AVN3, BLD, file no. 583, document no. 3866, 29 April 1960.

[36] Moreover, this was despite a good number of businesses in the province under ministerial guidance (an apatite mine, power station). See *Thống kê số lượng công nhân sô luong công nhân các Ngành Năm 1959 của Sở Lao động* (Statistics on workers by sector for 1959, Department of Labour), in AVN3, BLD, file no. 449, 1959.

Commune	*Adult Inhabitants*	*Emulation fighters*
Vĩnh Kim	395	1
Vĩnh Tu	1693	4
Vĩnh Lam	538	1
Vĩnh	88	3
Vĩnh Hoà	636	2
Vĩnh Giang	905	4
Vĩnh Long	819	3
Vĩnh Thương	117	2
Vĩnh Thạch	595	6
Vĩnh Hiên	1,090	2
Vĩnh Quang	547	3
Vĩnh Trung	545	4
Vĩnh Sơn	784	1
Vĩnh Hà	100	1
Vĩnh Chấp	576	4
Vĩnh Thủy	586	3
Vĩnh Trường	117	3
Vĩnh Nam	791	2

Number of emulation fighters/number of eligible inhabitants (Vĩnh Linh province) in 1957.[37]

We must consider what actually became of them and how they were integrated professionally into the organisation of the commune. What jobs did they hold? Did they really serve as a counter-weight to the tenacity of the traditional Vietnamese elite? In the 1950s, the Vietnamese commune was comprised of an administrative apparatus on the communal and village level, an ideological apparatus centred around the local Party cell, an economic sector made up of cooperatives and production groups, mass organisations, and social services for medical care and education.[38] In Nghệ An province in 1962, records show that exemplary workers and emulation

[37] Table taken from *Danh sách thành tích đơn vị và cá nhân được BLD đề nghị khen thưởng Huân chương Lao Động 1957* (List of outstanding units and individuals nominated by the Ministry of Labour for a work medal in 1957), in AVN3, BLD, file no. 291, document no. 57/VL, 1958.

[38] On the organisation of the North Vietnamese commune in the 1950s, see the excellent study by Diệp Đình Hoa, *Tìm hiểu làng Việt II* (The Nguyên village: Research on the Vietnamese village II). Hanoi: nxb Khoa Học Xã Hội, 1994, pp. 267–309.

fighters barely held 20 per cent of the seats in the People's Assembly.[39] At the highest level of the communal hierarchy (party secretary, president of the commune, and head of the cooperative), the percentage is even lower. In the districts of Nguyên Bình, Thuận Thành, and Quỳnh Lưu, just over 5 per cent of the emulation fighters became president of their commune in the year following their election; 8 per cent became communal party secretary, and 11 per cent took over as head of the cooperative.

Be as it may, reports collected by provincial emulation bureaus in the 1950s show that the title of emulation fighter still led to a quicker ascent up the communal ladder. Indeed, emulation fighters were not only assigned honorary positions but often held more technical positions: head of the production group, security chief, head of the department of economic affairs, chief of cultural affairs and of literacy, leading cadre from the hamlet, accountant for the cooperative, etc. In communes with a weak ideological base, however, emulation fighters were more likely to receive a key position in village government. In Vũ Nông (Nguyên Bình, Cao Bằng), the Red Yao cadre Triệu Thùng Chòi easily became president of the commune, chief of security, and head of the small trade cooperative. In the absence of a traditional local elite, the emulation fighter could become a key player in the modernisation of the village administration.

Occasionally there were problems with bad behaviour following the election of a "new man", though such cases were rarely mentioned in official documents. The Interior Ministry asked provincial authorities in charge of emulation to carry out an annual follow-up of "breaches of collective discipline" among the newly elect. "Normally people have great respect for emulation fighters, so it is unacceptable that some of them, after achieving great things and obtaining their title, let themselves go and behave poorly with the people."[40] In Nghệ An province in 1961, of the 3,376 emulation fighters and vanguard workers, 148 were sanctioned for collective indiscipline. Four types of offences were mentioned: poor implementation of the central government's policies, ill discipline, theft, and distance from the

[39] *Thống kê Kết quả bầu cử hội đồng nhân dân tỉnh Nghệ An Khoa IV năm 1962* (Statistical result from the people's assembly elections of Nghê An, fourth session, 1962), in AVN3, BNV, file no. 1778, document no. 23/NA, 1962.

[40] *Báo cáo tổng kết kinh nghiệm bồi dưỡng chiến sĩ tại Liên Sơn, huyện Gia Viễn, tỉnh Ninh Bình* (Review of encouragement efforts for emulation fighters, Liên Sơn commune, Gia Viễn district, Ninh Bình province), in AVN3, BLD, file no. 277, document no. 148 TD/LD, 27 July 1955.

masses.[41] Punishment was light, however. Only 7 of the 148 sanctioned were called before the People's Tribunal, and of these, only 3 were handed harsh sentences.[42] Two-thirds of the offenses required only that a warning letter be sent to the Party member. Expulsion or outright dismissal was to be applied in less than a third of offences, the government preferring to demote the offender by one rung in order to reduce his salary.[43]

Ultimately, the government rarely punished their "new men", even though several inspection reports indicated that a number of them did not take their role seriously. They were frequently criticised for not attending official meetings or sharing their experiences adequately with villagers. When one exemplary worker tried to apply himself, he was criticised for "lack of clarity, incoherency, and shyness, which made the audience laugh and damaged his credibility."[44] Some of this was due to a lack of education and a poor understanding of class by the newly elect. While some were reluctant to take on their responsibilities, others seemed to throw themselves into it with a bit too much zeal. In Nghi Lộc (Nghệ An), the district head of emulation criticised some exemplary workers of spending too much time at public meetings since it took them away from their regular jobs.[45] Moreover, since participation in events was also remunerated (for participation and transport), he also condemned the potential professionalisation of heroism in the countryside.[46]

---

[41] *Báo cáo thống kê tình hình cán bộ được khen thưởng và kỷ luật năm 1961 của các tỉnh* (Statistical report on cadres who were decorated or sanctioned in 1961, all provinces), in AVN3, BNV, file no. 1726, UBND [people's committee] Vinh, 4 May 1962.

[42] Two of them were "outstanding workers" accused of theft in the workplace, and the third was punished for "distance from the masses". Other cases involved a second-rank cadre who was given a suspended sentence for insubordination, and three others whose fate had not yet been decided but were under investigation. *Báo cáo thống kê tình hình cán bộ được khen thưởng và kỷ luật năm 1961 của các tỉnh.*

[43] Within the province, a leading cadre was demoted a rank for theft in 1961. Seven workers were accused of the same crime, and three others for "distance from the masses". See *Báo cáo thống kê tình hình cán bộ được khen thưởng và kỷ luật năm 1961 của các tỉnh.*

[44] *Ban tổng kết kinh nghiệm bồi dưỡng chiến sĩ nông nghiệp xã Nghi Thu, huyện Nghi Lộc* (Review of encouragement efforts for agricultural emulation fighers in Nghi Thu commune, district of Nghi Lộc), in AVN3, BLD, file no. 277, document no. 4822, 9 August 1955.

[45] *Ban tổng kết kinh nghiệm bồi dưỡng chiến sĩ nông nghiệp xã Nghi Thu, huyện Nghi Lộc.*

[46] *Đề án của Ban Thi đua trung ương về tổng kết công tác thi đua và lựa chọn anh hùng chiến sĩ thi năm 1956–57* (Project of the National Emulation Bureau on the closure of emulation activities and the selection of heroes and emulation fighters for 1956–57), in AVN3, BLD, file no. 532, 1956.

Minorities, Revolutionary Heroism, and Exclusion

In the 1950s–60s, mobilisation activities were not organised evenly throughout North Vietnam. This was due in part to the poor reception given to the government's campaigns by ethnic minorities in isolated areas and in provinces with a strong Catholic base. One must remain a bit sceptical, then, regarding the claims of the "enthusiastic participation of the Vietnamese people in the DRV struggle" that the government continues to spout to this day. During the Franco-Việt Minh war, colonial French forces and the communist Vietnamese continually competed for the support of ethnic minorities and the Catholic community.[47] The appearance of the new man in North Vietnam basically relied on a community of ethnic Kinh (almost 90 per cent of Vietnamese were Kinh) who were already won over by the ideas of the VWP. The historian Andrew Hardy showed the importance of economic migration in the DRV's conquest of the nation.[48] In the "Red Hills" of North Vietnam, for example, the new man was not easily accepted by the local population.

Vietnam has 54 different ethnic minorities, who make up 11 per cent of the total population and whose allegiance has always been a key political stake. In 1947, a Việt Minh document reports the problems encountered in mobilising them:

> As far as the minority peoples are concerned, on the one hand it makes sense to buy out the chiefs and mandarins with bonuses. We must have their leaders well in hand. On the other hand, we have to be forceful with the reactionaries. We learned at Lạng Sơn that the more concessions we make to the Nùng, the more they will want. A great many of them followed the bandits. Once we used a firm hand to control them in some areas, they quieted down, and what's more, some of them even came to give themselves up.[49]

---

[47] Hélie de Saint Marc wrote an interesting account of his stay with the Thô in Cao Bằng province in *Mémoires. Les Champs de braises* (Memoirs: fields of embers). Paris: Perrin, 1995. One of the key works in this field is the account by Bế Viết Đẳng, *50 năm các dân tộc thiểu số Việt Nam (1945–1995)* (Fifty years of ethnic minorities in Vietnam). Hanoi: nxb Khoa Học Xã Hộ, 1995.

[48] Andrew Hardy. *Red Hills. Migrants and the State in the Highlands of Vietnam*. Singapore: NIAS Press-ISEAS, 2005.

[49] *Tract Viêt Minh*, in CAOM, CP, file no. 15 suppl., document no. 2264/C, 28 March 1947.

For many of these mountain people, the idea of family, race, or clan was much more familiar than the abstract concept of a nation. Of course, the various ethnic groups spread throughout the mountainous areas did not all follow the same trajectory, so one should examine their relationships with the Kinh separately, and over time.[50] The Tày, for example (the largest ethnic minority), are very assimilated into Vietnamese culture — their mores, customs, language, and surroundings were often similar to those of the Kinh.[51] Conversely, the rites, language, way of life, and cosmology of the mountainous Red Yao minority was quite distinct from the world of the Kinh. The government translated several books into Tày and Nung in the 1950s, but did nothing in Yao. Very few minority peasants knew how to speak Vietnamese. Of the 1,500 inhabitants of the commune of Vũ Nông (Nguyên Bình), only 20 could speak it in 1960; and this was more than in the other villages of the district, such as Yên Lạc, La Thành, Mai Long, Phan Thanh, and Thành Công, each of which were several hours from the district seat by foot. Until the mid-1970s, most of these mountain villages were not targeted by a single act of propaganda. It was obviously not here, then, that the government would find the first exemplary workers and emulation fighters of Cao Bằng province.

Nestled in the valley, the small town of Tĩnh Túc (Nguyên Bình) was the industrial powerhouse of Cao Bằng, thanks to an open-air tin mine that had been in operation since the 1920s. The DRV decided to make it the showcase of the province's economic development. With the signing of the new economic partnership between the USSR and the DRV (1955), Soviet engineers and their families began to move into the area. At the time, Tĩnh Túc was composed of 200 Red Yao, White Yao, and Hmong families. When the French were in control of the mine, they did not want to hire locals, claiming that they were incompetent and unable to communicate with the French engineers or their Vietnamese assistants. When operations began again in 1955, the Vietnamese followed the same tack. Before the arrival of the Soviets, authorities moved the inhabitants of this narrow little valley to nearby villages.[52] The government claimed that this

---

[50] Chu Văn Tấn. *Reminiscences on the Army for National Salvation, Memoir of General Chu Van Tan*. Data paper no. 97. Ithaca & New York: Cornell University, 1974, p. 30.

[51] Nguyễn Văn Thắng. *Ambiguity of Identity. The Mieu in North Việt Nam*. Chiang Mai: Silkworm Books, 2007.

[52] *Histoire de la compagnie Kim Loan (données statistiques)* (History of Kim Loan company [statistical data]), roneotyped document, 19 August 1996.

was because of overpopulation, but it was obviously more concerned about meeting the demands of the Kim Loan mining company. General and agricultural taxes were raised dramatically in an effort to force the minorities out of the valley. Extreme measures were taken, and in just a few months the transfer of the local population was complete. The Yáo, Hmông, and Ngai families relocated to host-villages in the surrounding mountains, and the terrain was set for a new economic resettlement. By the late 1950s, Tĩnh Túc had only 7 families who were neither Kinh nor Tày (3 of them were Hmông) in a population of 6,000. In 1960, the town was finally officially classified as a New Economic Zone; the mine was then recruiting workers and cadres from the entire area (5 years later, 80 per cent of the new economic immigrants were still all from Cao Bằng). The DRV obviously sought their "new men" in the town of Tĩnh Túc, and more specifically within the Kim Loan company, not the ethnic minority community.

It took a similar approach in Quỳnh Lưu district (Nghệ An province). In the 1950s, the western, mountainous part of the district had 150 ethnic Thái families (2 per cent of the total population estimated at 80,000), spread throughout the villages of Quỳnh Thắng, Quỳnh Châu, and Quỳnh Tam.[53] These 3 communes were 2 hours from the district seat by horseback (11 km/7 miles). Originally from Hòa Bình and Thanh Hóa province, the Thái had arrived in the early nineteenth century; in 1955 they made up 70 per cent of the minority population of Nghệ An, and so were the second largest ethnic group after the Kinh.[54] In the 1950s, Thái families did not take part in the political activities organised by district cadres, in stark contrast to those who lived along the coast or in the central plains. In 1953, a law on ethnic policy advocated "choosing minorities who worked well, then educating and training them to become key cadres of their area",[55] but it was not well implemented on the ground. The three villages of Quỳnh Thắng, Quỳnh Châu, and Quỳnh Tam remained untouched by the government's mobilisation efforts. Thái households continued to cultivate their

---

[53] The ethnic Thái from the mountainous regions of Nghệ An were broken up into three main groups: the Táy Mương (or Tay Chiềng, Hàng Tổng); the Táy Thanh (or Man Thanh), and the Táy Mười. The Táy Mương were the biggest and most long-standing group in the province. See *40 Năm chặng Đường* (A forty-year journey). Vinh: nxb Nghệ Tĩnh, 1985, pp. 157–8.

[54] *Quỳnh Lưu-huyện địa đầu xứ Nghệ* (Quỳnh Lưu: the land, the history). Ban chấp hành Huyện Đảng bộ và UBND Huyện Quỳnh Lưu, Vinh, 1990, p. 12.

[55] *Tài liệu học tập cho chiến sĩ và dân công năm 1954* (Study documents for civic combatants and workers, 1954), in AVN3, BLD, file no. 315, document no. 3/DT, 1954.

own land as always. No-one made a list of landlords. The district decided that it was useless to send an agrarian reform team except to the village of Quỳnh Thắng, where a group of cadres had gone in 1954 before giving up all social reorganisation efforts. It was not until 1959 that Quỳnh Thắng, Quỳnh Châu, and Quỳnh Tam organised their first emulation campaigns, and their brand new agricultural cooperative produced the first exemplary workers. Once again, as in the case of Nguyên Bình, the emulation at Quỳnh Lưu did not focus on the good works of the minority peoples but on the "revolutionary activism" of resettled Kinh immigrants. In the late 1950s, 6,000 Kinh were sent from South Vietnam to ethnic Thái villages, and even more arrived in 1963–64. Once in the majority, these minority people were gradually marginalised in their traditional homeland; many of them moved into even more remote areas.[56] With the massive influx of Kinh, mobilisation efforts could now begin. Cooperatives were established in nine hamlets in the commune of Quỳnh Thắng, but "in spite of this, the movement was still extremely weak in the predominantly Thái neighbourhoods".[57]

The minority peoples thus remained relatively untouched by the emulation campaigns; the same was true of the Catholics in North Vietnam. During the Franco-Viet Minh War, Catholics were an important stake for both camps, not only for military purposes but especially regarding ideology and identity.[58] The DRV kept the Catholic peasant Hoàng Hanh (from Nghệ An) on the list for the first new heroes at Tuyên Quang in 1952 as part of their global strategy for strengthening national unity. During the Geneva Accords (1954), Clause 14d announced the exchange of populations between the North and South over a period of 300 days. The commissioner for refugees in Saigon estimated that 794,876 Catholics fled the North between 21 July 1954 and 21 May 1955 — about two-thirds of

[56] Interview, Quỳnh Châu commune (Quỳnh Lưu, Nghệ An).

[57] Ibid. The provincial department in charge of ethnic issues said that 95 per cent of the Thái families in Nghệ An had joined cooperatives between 1958 and 1965. See *40 Năm chặng Đường*, p. 169. Another source, however, showed that the participation of minority households in the communes of the mountainous district of Quỳnh Lưu barely reached 65 per cent of the total in 1965, in *Quỳnh Lưu: huyện địa đầu xứ Nghệ* (Quỳnh Lưu: the land, the history), p. 113.

[58] Trần thị Liên. *Les Catholiques vietnamiens pendant la guerre d'indépendance (1945–1954). Entre la reconquête coloniale et la résistance communiste* (Vietnamese Catholics during the war of independence [1945–54]: between Colonial Reconquest and the Communist resistance). Unpublished thesis, I.E.P., Paris, 1996, p. 576.

the nation's total.[59] The historian Trần Thị Liên points out that those who stayed often did so less out of deliberate political choice than out of attachment to their homeland, or because they did not have the money to leave. Officially, the DRV espoused a policy of openness and solidarity with its Catholic minority. One critical event — that has since been erased from the history books — left a deep division, however, between the communists and the Catholics, and led to the latter's refusal to participate in the emulation movement.

In August 1956, several weeks after the official close of the population exchange between the North and South, requests for permission to leave continued to flood the People's Committee of Quỳnh Lưu. They were systematically denied by the district cadres, leading to friction between the two camps. In theory, any Catholic who wanted to move needed government authorisation, to avoid "acts of treason", they claimed, but a tacit solidarity between Catholic villages allowed them to bypass these measures. In 1947–48, Catholics made up more than 10 per cent of the population of Quỳnh Lưu district (6,500 people).[60] Despite calls for reconciliation and the government's promises of goodwill (their resolution of 26 March 1955 and the fundamental law granting religious freedom of 14 June 1955[61]), Catholics continued to head south in large numbers. An account from Quỳnh Thọ reports that 1,728 Catholics (more than 60 per cent of the commune) left their village during this period.[62] The Party, however, continued to extol the merits of its Catholic members: the exemplary figures of Nguyễn Thinh and Ngô Thành symbolised the solidarity that still stirred the hearts of the Catholics from Quỳnh Lưu in its struggle against the foreign invader. Following the victory of Điện Biên Phủ, the mass exodus of Catholics toward the South was a clear sign that Vietnam was not yet "one great family", as the government had claimed since the resumption of hostilities in 1946. The Catholic community was basically grouped into four villages in the district: Quỳnh Thanh, Quỳnh Yên, Quỳnh Lâm, and Quỳnh Lộc. Right in the middle of them, however, lay the commune of

---

[59] According to Trần Tâm Tính, in 1954 Catholics made up 10 per cent of the population of the DRV (1,390,000 out of 13 million), which fell to 6.5 per cent (550,000) in 1956. See Trần Tâm Tính, *Dieu et César. Les Catholiques dans l'histoire du Vietnam* (God and Caesar: Catholics in the history of Vietnam). Paris: Sudestasie, 1978, pp. 45, 102.

[60] *Quỳnh Lưu: huyện địa đầu xứ Nghệ*, p. 99.

[61] *Hồ Chí Minh – Biên niên tiểu sử*, vol. VI. Nxb Chính Trị Quốc Gia, 1995, p. 108.

[62] *Quỳnh Thọ*, đảng uỷ [published directly by the committee in question] UBND xã Quỳnh Thọ, 1990, p. 53.

Quỳnh Đôi, known for the political intransigence of its cadres and its long-standing ties with the central government. The Catholic exodus increased tensions between the communes, and in Quỳnh Đôi, this "flight to the South" was harshly condemned. A former Party secretary of the commune recalls: "In our village the only religion since the August Revolution was the Party. There were no Catholics or Buddhists. It was particularly hard for us to tolerate what was going on in the Catholic villages at the time."[63]

In early September, the situation turned into open conflict. Pro-Catholic villagers and Party supporters clashed: "The reactionary clique took advantage of our policies to pervert the backward Catholics masses, but we put up a strong resistance. The most serious incident involved the commune of Quỳnh Yên, where the Catholic villages of Hà Lang and Cẩm Trương rebelled, creating a kind of Catholic *jacquerie* [peasants' revolt in Picardy in 1358]."[64] The inhabitants of Quỳnh Đôi and Quỳnh Thanh were furious, and they sent their militia to the corridor between Quỳnh Thanh and the other Catholic villages in order to halt the outflux of villagers. Worried by this eruption of violence, the government sent a regiment of the PAVN. It took them several weeks to restore order, and a number of soldiers were killed. In early October, the army managed to bring the situation under control. The Catholics were once more redistributed through the district. In 1958, only the village of Quỳnh Thanh still had a completely Catholic population; elsewhere, the administration annexed predominantly Catholic hamlets to other non-Catholic communes in the area. The aim was to control and disperse this religious minority.

A taboo subject in contemporary history, the Catholic *jacquerie* of 1956 halted the wave of national solidarity imagined by the State. The memory of this event remained vivid within the Catholic community but was partially erased from the collective imagination. The government had been lauding the heroism of the Catholic Hoàng Hanh since 1952 to bring them back to the fold of emulation, but the events of September 1956 made any attempt at reconciliation difficult. There were no campaigns for mass mobilisation within the Catholic bastion of Quỳnh Thanh between 1956 and 1965. There was no question of nominating exemplary workers or emulation fighters. The commune did have structures for ideological mobilisation and mass organisations, but none of the villagers really participated in them. They did not get a Party cell until 1954, and this was

[63] Interview, Quỳnh Đôi commune (Quỳnh Lưu, Nghê An).

[64] *Quỳnh Lưu: huyện địa đầu xứ Nghệ*, p. 111.

placed under the supervision of the Catholic cadre Nguyễn Trương Chính; in 1965 it still had only four members. The government had tried to isolate the rebellious commune rather than integrate it — or at least associate it — with its mobilisation efforts. Contrary to the situation in Quỳnh Trang, the government did not try to include the rebel village in the new zones of economic development. They even abandoned the idea of opening a cultural centre, a people's library, or a recreation centre. Itinerant cultural groups bypassed the village. The Ministry of Education managed to send a new teacher to their primary school, but the villagers did not hide their defiance and rarely sent their children to attend: "Why go to school when we're just going to end up tending water buffalo…?"[65]

The situation was different in the village of Quỳnh Lộc. The commune was one-third Catholic in the late 1950s and had launched its first emulation campaign in 1951. The People's Committee had, however, chosen to exclude Catholics. Until 1965, none were elected as emulation fighters or even exemplary workers, even though Quỳnh Lộc had the first Catholic cooperative in the district. But fear still ran high among non-Catholics, who wondered if "these men who sprinkle water on their heads aren't actually enemy spies".[66] Since 1953, the commune of Sơn Hải had 50 Catholic families in one of its hamlets, and local authorities tried without much success to launch a "Hoàng Hanh movement". But in Sơn Hải, as elsewhere, "the villagers of Catholic faith didn't participate much in mass organisations. With the approach of war, they couldn't even become soldiers because everyone was afraid they were traitors."[67] Until 1965, some Catholic villagers managed to become members of the cooperative or of fishermen's groups from the commune, but the local government was still wary and preferred not to award them with a title of exemplarity. In theory, a predominantly Catholic hamlet could be represented in the local government by one of their own. This was the case in Song Ngọc (Quỳnh Ngọc commune), which was under the leadership of the peasant Quang Phúc from 1945 to 1965, but this was rare, especially after the arrival of agrarian reform teams. Trần Chất Hiền, a Catholic, was Vice President of the commune of Minh Châu until the team decided to relieve him of his duties in 1955. Of the 18 communes in Quỳnh Lưu, only Quỳnh Giang (which was one-quarter Catholic in 1960) saw a Catholic peasant awarded

---

[65] Interview, Quỳnh Thuận commune (Quỳnh Lưu, Nghệ An).

[66] Ibid.

[67] Interview, Sơn Hải commune (Quỳnh Lưu, Nghệ An).

the title of emulation fighter.[68] In other areas, both official statistics and collective memory confirm the presence of strong religious intolerance.

For the common people of Vietnam, the emulation fighter represented primarily the belief in a reform of the old order, regardless of the modest place that he finally assumed within society. A product of the illusion of patriotic rhetoric, he would never be totally free from the daily toil and strife of his existence. Thus, the title of emulation fighter offered its bearer less a way to compete with a local elite that was often deeply rooted within the local landscape, than access to new mid-level positions created by the DRV. Those who won patriotic awards really experienced an undeniable rise in their social status; never, however, did these awards lead to a serious questioning of traditional hierarchies. In any case, government cadres had no desire to see a new local elite acquire more power than they should. And in the end, were not those who held real power afraid of the emergence of a potential rival to their influence on the nation?

[68] The man, named Kinh, was elected agricultural emulation fighter in 1962 (date not confirmed). Interview, commune of Linh Xá (Thuận Thành, Hà Bắc).

Chapter 4

The New Hero (1952–1964)

> History without biography would be something like rest without relaxation, food with no taste, and a bit like a history of love without love.
>
> Victor Albjerg[1]

The world of the new hero is steeped in both myth and reality. The heroes at Tuyên Quang were real people, endowed with omnipotence by an authoritarian and internationalist political rhetoric. In the Vietnam of the 1950s, the new hero represents the slow and progressive disappearance of individual memory in the face of the propaganda apparatus of the State. The new Vietnamese hero differed from the emulation fighter because of his close bond with the central government. Although this close collaboration was sometimes fictitious, the heroic figure was designed to be the incarnation of a value; he was an absolute in flesh and blood presented to society as the conduit of an ideal. The new hero was a transmitter, the alchemist of a new transformation between the government and its people. He alone ushered in the acceptance of a new idea and gave life to an immaterial temporal power bearing the weight of national tradition. Since 1950, the DRV conformed to the dictates of an internationalist framework and the hero was always clad in modern-day dress, either as Catholic peasant in 1952, valiant warrior in 1955–56, or outstanding worker from 1958–1962. He fulfilled a double mission: on the international scene, he positioned the DRV on the scale of "friendships" that they had procured with their brother nations; on the domestic front, he helped the people identify with their leaders in a nation torn apart by war. By the time the war resumed with the South (1964), he had been overused, however, and

[1] Victor Albjerg. "History through Biographical Lenses", *Social Studies*, no. 38, October 1947: 243.

his efficacy dulled, to the point where popular sayings and proverbs made fun of his overexposure. The new hero inhabited the realm between myth and reality, a fragile but very real emanation of the essence of a nation born from the originary struggles of their mythic Hùng kings.

The Official Biography

Vietnam's official historiography had always made use of the official biography.[2] It was a way for the nation to give meaning to the fleeting lives of its people. The biography was grafted onto the hero's actual life and made sense out of the myriad daily activities of his existence. It diluted the details of an individual's fate within the essence of the nation. The ethnologist K.H. Schreiner explained in his study of the heroic figure in Indonesia:

> the person described is not, as it is with historical biographies, a historical figure who lived and worked in a particular era, in a particular place. At the centre of the work there is much more, an abstract form, the expression of an ideal. Any part of the character's personality that doesn't correspond to this heroic ideal is pushed aside, to the point where one loses the actual individual and his personal value. By this procedure, the hero's biography becomes a sort of heroisation process, whereby a real person's life is fused with that of a hero.[3]

Communism and decolonisation in the Third World sparked a profound transformation of identity in countries that found themselves thrust into change. In Southeast Asia, this led to a widespread re-reading of national heritage. Borders alone could not define the boundaries of a nation whose territory had been repeatedly redrawn by foreign hands. The hero's life was offered as a triumph to countries in search of a national identity. Throughout the centuries, ruling dynasties kept the flame of biographical identity alive by generating new patriotic genealogies. The communist regime in Vietnam did not question the inviolability of this principle. The hero represented the essence of the nation's cultural identity so each new generation would be nourished by the exemplary figures of their glorious

---

[2] Langlet. *L'ancienne historiographie d'Etat au Vietnam, tome I. Raisons d'être, conditions d'élaboration et caractères au siècle des Nguyên.*

[3] Klaus H. Schreiner. *Politischer Heldenkult in Indonesien. Tradition und modern Praxis.* Berlin: Dietrich Reimer Verlag, 1995, pp. 248–9.

past. In 1954–55, the DRV began to reinterpret great historical figures as well as spread the stories about new heroic lives. The new hero's story was part of a functionalist recasting of the national historiography. In Indonesia, it went against Javanese tradition to focus on the fate of one individual rather than a group, dynasty, or an entire people, but the Sino-Confucian world had always paid special attention to exceptional figures with a heroic destiny. In Vietnam, these life stories were always about a particular individual, and were officially presented by those in power. They never included any private details about a subject and his era. As far back as the fifteenth century, rulers rated the nation's heroes according to patriotic merit, awarding them posthumous titles and organising patriotic rituals in their honour. The life stories of outstanding citizens reassured the mandarin bureaucracy, which sought to establish a social contract. These stories thus had an administrative and secular function. *The Spiritual Powers of the Viet Kingdom*, written in 1329, and the five-volume *Heroes of the People's Armed Forces*, written 600 years later, provided their eras with vibrant descriptions of the heroes that protected the nation's safety.[4]

A hero's life was always recounted by those in power. In communist Vietnam, they were written under the supervision of a special committee attached to the Party's propaganda wing and followed the key principles of Hồ Chí Minh thought: "One naturally expresses what is useful to the people and to the nation. Just as one remains naturally silent on what is not useful to the people and the nation."[5] In 1952, biographical notices were entrusted to a group of progressivist intellectuals under the leadership of the writer Nguyễn Tuân (1910–1987). A member of this commission recalls:

> When we got together to discuss a hero's life, we first had to get rid of the parts that were not proper. Official biographers created idealised characters, made up on paper. But at the same time, we had to make sure we didn't lie too much. Sometimes it was indeed difficult since the intellectuals often had very little contact with these heroes.[6]

Cù Chính Thào, the younger brother of Cù Chính Lan, hero of the battle of Hòa Bình elected in 1952, affirms that the government never sent a

[4] *Việt điện u linh tập* (Collection of invisible powers from the land of Viêt [1329]). *Anh hùng lực lượng vũ trang nhân dân* (Heroes of the people's armed forces). Hanoi: nxb Quân dội nhân dân. (vol. 1: 1978; vol. 2: 1980; vol. 3: 1981; vol. 4: 1982; vol. 5: 1983).

[5] Interview, Hanoi.

[6] Interview, Hanoi.

cadre to his family to ask questions about his brother's childhood or life. Historic accuracy was obviously not essential to the hero's life story.

Nguyễn Văn Trỗi (1940–1964) is a good example of someone with a double life story. In 1965, the North Vietnamese government wanted to offer people the exemplary life of a simple young man from the central part of the country (Quảng Nam-Đà Nẵng) who went to Saigon to make his life amidst the "misery of the Southern regime". Once he saw the injustice of the system, Trỗi turned towards the Resistance. His engagement was due to his good sense, and his devotion was a model for the people of the South who were not very receptive to orders from the North. This idealised Nguyễn Văn Trỗi was pinned onto the average everyday reality of a young man "like everybody else", who even sacrificed his love for his beautiful young girlfriend Phan Thị Quyên to fight for his country's independence. In 1965, the government wanted to show the spontaneity and spirit of initiative of the South Vietnamese in their participation in the movement of national liberation. To do this, however, they had to tone down the actual influence of North Vietnam on operations so as not to offend a deeply rooted southern particularism. In 1975, when the reunification of the country was finally achieved, the government propaganda apparatus took another look at this hero from Đà Nẵng. We thus read in the army's daily, *Quân đội nhân dân*, that Nguyễn Văn Trỗi did not go of his own accord to Saigon.[7] He was apparently already an active member of the Communist Youth in Central Vietnam before his departure for the South, and had been sent by his organisation to strengthen the resistance movement there. On 17 February 1964, three months before his attack on the American Secretary of State Robert McNamara (9 May 1964), he had joined a secret commando unit of the PAVN on assignment in Saigon.

When war broke out with the South, the propaganda department of the VWP decided to promote a contingent of heroes from that area: Nguyễn Văn Tư (Bến Tre, 1966), Tạ Thị Kiều (Bến Tre, 1966), Nguyễn Văn Bé (Thủ Dầu Một, 1967), Nguyễn Việt Hồng (Rạch Giá, 1970), etc. Thus in 1965, the government tasked the North Vietnamese writer Trần Đình Vân (aided by Trỗi's widow, Phan Thị Quyên, from Hà Đông province in North Vietnam) with writing a story that would make Nguyễn Văn Trỗi the first "new hero" from the South to have national impact during

---

[7] Nguyễn Thanh. "Chiến sĩ biệt động Sài gòn" (Exceptional combatant in Saigon), *Quân đội Nhân dân,* Hanoi, 3 May 1975. These changes were made in the last edition of the repertory of heroes from the PAVN. See *Anh hùng lực lượng vũ trang nhân dân*, p. 7.

Figure 6. Nguyễn Văn Trỗi

the American War. In 1975, on the other hand, the Party was eager to show the predominance of Northern initiatives in the unification of the country. In this new version, Nguyễn Văn Trỗi was only an "agent of the North", so his work with the Resistance could not symbolise any "Cochin-chinese specificity". Trỗi's charisma and his popularity on the international scene transformed him into a key figure in the legitimacy of the government in Hanoi.

The heroic biography questioned the nature of memory, both individual and collective. A life story that was written *post mortem* anchored the fate of an anonymous figure — who seemed an unlikely candidate for such honours while he was alive — in the upheavals of a nation's history. The official biography focused on the details of daily life that had generally been overlooked by his contemporaries. With time, the memories of his close relations were reformed around the series of events reproduced in his mimeographed biography. The official life story was placed in direct competition with individual memory and transformed it from the inside. Biographical reconstruction was also applied to new heroes who were elected while still alive. The government removed the new hero from his geographical context immediately following his election, thereby hoping to sever his ties with the anonymous existence he had led until then. He was often promoted to positions outside of his native region. At regular intervals, however, they would orchestrate his return to his village, but this show of prestige barely left him time to see his own family. The propaganda apparatus wanted to limit the influence of individual memory on the construction of a new myth. A certain distance was required before the myth of the new hero could take hold in the minds of the Vietnamese peasant.

The heroic biography offered the government a great way to take control of the nation's diverse local history. Just as the heroic figures of the past fought to defend their country, the heroes of Tuyên Quang stabilised a village identity that had been shaken by the central government's intrusion behind the "bamboo hedge". The DRV was offering the commune the chance to feel that they were at the very heart of national reconstruction. In 1958, the State set up study committees on Party history at all administrative levels to develop a new historiography of the local.[8] Provincial chronicles and heroic biographies were part of a re-homogenisation of the national patrimony. Through the exemplary lives of these "celebrated children", the specific history of a village joined up with the great heroism of the entire nation.

The Myth of the Hero

The "new hero" was basically a peasant issue in Vietnam. Most heroes came from the lower classes, offering the government a powerful tool for communicating with the rural population, which accounted for 93 per cent of North Vietnam's 22 million people in 1955. Their reception varied according to the cultural milieu in which they were placed. The closer they were to the centres of power, the less effective they were. They worked best in areas with a weak cultural base, where the people were more receptive to the marvellous image of the new heroic national figure. A resident of Trạm Lộ village (Thuận Thành, Hà Bắc) remarked:

> It's impossible to become a hero! Many cadres from the province have come to talk to us about the heroes of national reconstruction. I always

[8] Lê Manh Trinh. "Nghiên cứu Lịch sử Đảng" (Study the history of the Party), *Học Tập*, Hanoi, no. 10, 1966: 48–57.

> wanted to become one of them one day, but at the same time I was discouraged by the enormity of the task. So they encouraged me to imitate the example of these men. We men of the people, we often dream of becoming heroes but we are simple people. La Văn Cầu, for example, was a Party member with close ties to the government. We, on the other hand, are simple peasants, it's just too hard.[9]

Repeated mention of the exemplary worker or farmer's exploits set the bar intimidatingly high. The State proposed a model to follow, a direction, rather than a concrete goal to attain. It expected its citizens to be totally dedicated to the collective: becoming a hero meant a reorganisation of their daily lives. By actively participating in the patriotic emulation movement, the inhabitants of Vũ Nông village (Nguyên Bình, Cao Bằng) knew they would have to leave their homes since a hero had to sacrifice his wife, family, and ancestors at the altar of the new regime. The frequent meetings and productivist requirements of the emulation campaigns were the physical embodiment of the "selflessness" demanded by the authorities. The new hero's inaccessibility was thus announced with a certain fatality, which ran counter to the usual familiarity of these new elite from humble origins.[10] For centuries, Vietnamese tradition granted secular authorities the power to "choose and endorse figures from the current dynasty". The heroes of Tuyên Quang were progressively assimilated to the figure of the outstanding citizens of the past. The well-educated initially considered him a type of high official with a long career rather than as a mythical figure.

In many areas, however, people knew nothing about government policy so continued to view the new hero as the stuff of myth. A feeling of exclusion imperceptively spread among the rural masses. The idea of coming across a real hero at a meeting organised by provincial authorities was unthinkable to the men and women whose lives revolved around working in the fields. A resident of the village of Quỳnh Bá (Quỳnh Lưu, Nghệ An) said: "A hero is somebody huge! When I went to study at the provincial People's Committee, I listened attentively to the hero Nguyễn Trung Thiếp, but I didn't dare talk to him. Everyone applauded after his speech, it was very impressive. I had a lot of respect for him and I never

---

[9] Interview, Trạm Lộ village (Thuận Thành, Hà Bắc).

[10] "Of the three essential criteria for choosing a hero, class is the most important. That is what allowed one to become a new hero." See *Hướng dẫn về việc tuyển lựa anh hùng thi đua ái quốc* (Directives on the selection of national emulation heroes), in AVN3, BLD, file no. 510, document no. 56, December 1956, p. 2.

for one moment thought I could be a hero like him."[11] In the countryside, the sacred nature of the new hero was augmented by his gift for public speaking, his ability to speak Vietnamese if he was an ethnic minority, or his close familiarity with the leading cadres. But in any case, the new hero hardly ever ventured into the countryside. The peasant could only imagine him, viewing him as someone from far away, assimilated into the milieus of power and lying "outside of normality". Cadres from the commune evoked his deeds on patriotic holidays. Within the popular imagination, the real heroic figure existed alongside one that was imagined and idealised. The less one actually saw of the hero, the more he represented an ethical absolute. By cleverly controlling his rare appearances, DRV propaganda made him into the symbol of the new patriotic and moral ideal.

The Hero's Childhood

The Party's propaganda department traced the roots of the hero's legitimacy to his childhood and early youth. Invariably full of misery and injustice, the hero's origins denied him the right to blissful innocence. An official biography always began with a litany of suffering endured by the future heroic figure. The Catholic hero Hoàng Hanh (1952) began his tale with memories of a childhood scarred by "colonial oppression". He wrote in his autobiography:

> My previous life was no different from that of an insect, of an ant. You open your eyes and see sorrow and poverty. When I was twelve I worked as a servant. I had the body of a child but was already working very hard. I had enough to eat, but I was tired of always being beaten and insulted at work. They beat me whenever they felt like it. Whenever I talked to my family about it, I cried. Then when I was seventeen, my father died.[12]

This list of injustices gave the government a way to put colonialism on trial. The hero's first accomplishment was surviving the violence of an "illegitimate oppressive system". All of the decorated national heroes from 1952–1962 were raised "under the yoke of colonial oppression". Having endured the disintegration of the family unit caused by Western influence,

[11] Interview, Quỳnh Bá village (Quỳnh Lưu, Nghệ An).

[12] *Truyện 7 anh hùng* (History of seven heroes). Hanoi: nxb Văn Nghệ, 1954, p. 113 (see the chapter on Hoàng Hanh).

the heroic child emerged with a halo of glory which remained with him throughout his career. Having managed to tolerate the intolerable with courage and dignity, he had triumphed over normality. Growing up with just one parent, or none at all, increased his aura of invincibility. A look at the first heroes elected in Tuyên Quang in May 1952 shows clearly that being an orphan increased one's chances at winning this national title: Nguyễn Thị Chiên was an orphan, Ngô Gia Khảm lost his father and father-in-law, Hoàng Hanh lost his father when he was a child, as did Trần Đại Nghĩa and La Văn Cầu, and Cù Chính Lan lost his mother when he was very young — only Nguyễn Quốc Trị escaped the family tragedy. The official biography of the hero drew a parallel between the destruction of the family unit and the taking hostage of society by French forces. The rupture of this relationship of filial protection threw the adolescent into the abyss of injustice and exploitation.

Vietnamese culture conferred upon its rightful leaders a filial responsibility towards those struck down by misfortune. According to this ancient tradition, if a government failed to shoulder this responsibility, then the people had the right to revolt against what they deemed irresponsible leadership. Government propaganda repeatedly stressed the suffering caused by the colonial administration in order to weaken the link between the people and their collaborationist leaders. In the late 1940s, the Việt Minh accused the "illegitimate" government of mistreating its citizens due to the "feudalism of the landowning classes and exploiters of the people". Under constraint, the future hero sold his "labour potential" in the hopes of surviving the disappearance of his family. A classist exploitation turned him away from the roads of knowledge and education, violating once again the traditional responsibility of the State. The labour hero Ngô Gia Khảm (1952), for example, wrote in his memoirs about the cruel treatment he received as a servant in Hải Phòng.[13] A child's life invariably deteriorated after he left home. The heros' childhood was indelibly marked by this filial bond such that the death of a parent was a trauma, yet one that the heroic child managed to rise above with fortitude.

The hero's filial piety towards his parents or ancestors was an important part of the heroic ideal. The tale of young Morosov — who joined forces against his own family out of loyalty to the Soviet Communist Party

---

[13] *Một đảng viên, Hồi ký cách mạng của Anh hùng Ngô Gia Khảm* (A member of the Party: revolutionary memoir of the hero Ngô Gia Khảm). Hanoi: nxb Kim Đồng, 1965, pp. 8–11.

— would never work in Vietnam. On the contrary, a good hero was first a good Confucian in his attachment to the family and the Party. In a biography of the ethnic Mãn hero Bàn Văn Mình (1955), the writer Hải Như devotes more time to the hero's relationship with his mother than to his connection with the central government.[14] Readers understood from the story that the energy and initiative of their hero was primarily due to his deep respect for filial piety. The hero's childhood was marked by both a traditional devotion to his ancestral spirits and a visceral hatred of the colonial government. Blasphemous foreigners were accused of undermining a relationship between members of the community that had stood for several thousand years. The heroic teen's greatness lay in his determination to preserve a moral code in the face of a decaying social order. Shaken by social upheavals, the young hero set an example for his peers; his choices and his engagements had a purely axiological meaning.

The Hero and the Party

The future hero had a double initiation into adulthood. As a child he had already learned to situate himself within the disorder of society, and was scarred in his youth by injustice. Then, carried away by his anger, the adolescent made the "wise" choice to align himself with the progressivist movement (mass organisations, military groups, self-defence units, etc.). Ngô Gia Khảm wrote in 1952:

> I got involved in the movement and gradually began to understand. One day, a guy named Nhân [one of Trường Chinh's pseudonyms] came up to me. He said that if the French imperialists stay one more day on our soil, our people won't have enough rice to eat or enough clothes to wear. Then he told me about the Soviet Union. They had a Stalinist constitution that protected the rights of all workers; there was no evil [General] Lecuyer or Americans. Workers and people worked happily and enthusiastically to ensure everyone had enough food and clothing. I listened as he spoke about the USSR, my heart full of joy.[15]

The future hero met people who helped him materialise and channel the excess anger that had been building up in him since childhood. His real intellectual apprenticeship began when he embarked upon the ideological

[14] Ten of the sixty-one images in his biography are dedicated to his mother as well. See Hải Như. *Người anh hùng Vàng Pè* (Hero Vàng Pè). Hanoi: nxb Phổ Thông, 1965.

[15] *Anh hùng lao động Ngô Gia Khảm* (Ngô Gia Khảm, labour hero), pp. 10–11.

training by the Việt Minh, which took the place of his missing family. He was welcomed and was initiated by a group that was inspired by the words and writings of the central government. Cadres talked to these promising young people and taught them to read and write. The future hero's first initiation was a moral education, inaugurating his impending entry into the universe of excellence that was the Party.

The future hero's second initiation was the moment of his induction into the Party. Becoming a Party member was the ultimate honour and the only consecration that really mattered in the future hero's life. Biographers embellished the sacred event with the tears and torments of so many sleepless nights. To earn the title of national hero, one had to undergo a political baptism into the Party. The dutiful individual finally attained the envied status of outstanding citizen within the new society. Ngô Gia Khảm wrote:

> In 1939, I had the honour of becoming a member of the Indochinese Communist Party. I still remember when Comrade Lương Khánh Thiện, one of the Party cadres at the time, said during the ceremony: now, Comrade, you are a member of the Party. A comrade must try his best to follow the Party line. You will have to fight until your dying day. A comrade must be faithful to the Party his whole life, and believe that the revolution can win. I felt like I was leaving the darkness and was bathed in light. Tears rolled down my face. I began a new life. I didn't sleep at all that night, and neither did my wife.

Becoming a Party member provided a framework for understanding the inconsistencies and shortcomings of one's time, and with it the ability to make it better. The group acknowledged the happy new arrival and his outstanding moral character. He reached the ultimate stage of knowledge during the induction ceremony. The future hero was grateful, and the Party showed that it cared about those whose lives had been shattered by the old regime. His official life story stressed the contrast between the hero's past suffering and the justice and equality of his new life. Nguyễn Thị Chiên (1952) from Thái Binh and Mạc Thị Bưởi (1955) from Hải Hưng thus found a new way to live out their lives within the community.[16] The government's solicitude flattered those of modest means and offered proof that the tide could turn in their favour. The commune became the theatre

---

[16] Trần Cân. *Mạc Thị Bưởi — truyện thơ* (Mạc Thị Bưởi — a tale in verse). Hanoi: nxb Phổ Thông, 1957. Vũ Cao, Mai Văn Hiến, *Nguyễn Thị Chiên*. Việt Bắc: Quân đội Nhân dân, 1952.

of this reorganisation, where the virtuous man played the leading role. The future heroic figure earned social recognition. He helped organise the emulation movement and became an example for his peers. The new State apparatus made professional advancement accessible to the common people, and the official biography showed clearly that active participation in the VWP brought numerous advantages. In order to position the outstanding citizen within the hierarchy of honours, the biographical committee described in detail the government's appreciation: "Núp was cherished by the villagers and his compatriots. He was elected Banner of the Emulation Movement for the Liberation Struggle of the compatriots of Tây Nguyễn. He received a medal of the highest order and Hồ Chí Minh himself presented him with some clothing and a badge."[17]

Meeting Hồ Chí Minh

The hero's meeting with Hồ Chí Minh was meant to confirm the order inherent in the new society and established a direct connection between the government and its people. He brought the common man closer to the father of the nation, who had previously been out of reach. The hero was multi-faceted: he was a worker and a peasant, a Catholic and an ethnic minority, a man, woman and child. The government could thus offer a suitable heroic figure for every stratum of society. The production of these great men allowed the regime to ground its real power in a hierarchical relationship with the "hero of heroes", the Head of State. The story of the hero's meeting with Hồ was not repeated as often as the tales of his exploits, but it offered yet another glimpse of this new figure. In order to situate the new hero in a hierarchy of power, the government had to undercut his myth somehow, since he should in no way present direct competition to the State. The meeting between the two representatives of Sino-Confucian authority — political power (leaders) and traditional power (spirits and heroes) — was described in such a way as to erase any appearance of collusion. Their respective areas of jurisdiction had been precisely delineated. Though venerated at the local level, the hero owed his existence to the central government. He was completely subservient to it. Official biographies culminated with the details of this meeting.

---

[17] *Anh hùng lao động tại Đại hội liên hoan anh hùng chiến sĩ thi đua công nông binh toàn quốc lần thứ hai* (Labour heroes from the second national conference of worker, peasant, and military heroes and emulation combatants), 1958, pp. 1–2.

Figure 7. Meeting with Hồ Chí Minh

Sino-Confucian culture rests on its sense of hierarchy. Even though the DRV claimed to be a government by the people and for the people, Hồ Chí Minh still retained his right to intercede. For the average peasant, meeting Uncle Hồ was a sacred act, a privilege reserved for extraordinary people. The new hero became part of an elite for whom the unthinkable had become reality. Patriotic propaganda related at length the meeting between the president and his exemplary servants to situate the new hero within the hierarchy of honours. The hero took on the role of child before the father of the country. His tears were proof that his commitment was sincere, and his humility reinforced the sanctity of the nation's leaders. The entire apparatus rested on Hồ Chí Minh's personification of the new

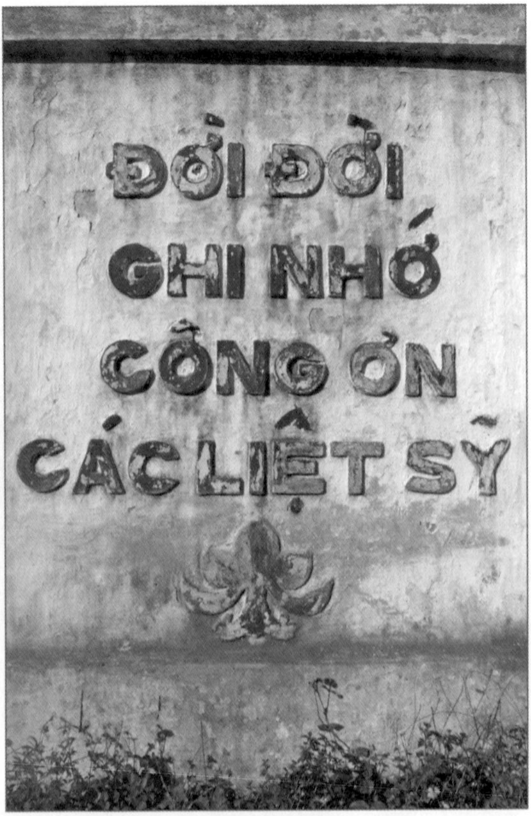

Figure 8. Hero's cemetery

regime. The tears of the young Southern combatant, Tạ Thị Kiều (1966), reaffirmed his dominance as the sole representative "of a heroic people with a heroic history" — "This afternoon I met Uncle Hồ, I was extremely happy, I looked at him and couldn't help breaking into warm tears."[18]

The Recycling of the Hero

Once awarded the national title and placed in a hierarchy according to his rank, the hero faded from the public eye. The State then elected new ones to keep up the momentum. The meeting with Uncle Hồ was the last chapter in the hero's biography and signalled his death or dissolution into

[18] Tạ Thị Kiều and Nguyệt Tú. *Lớn lên với Thôn xóm* (Growing up in the village). Hanoi: nxb Phụ Nữ, 1966, p. 42.

Figure 9. Nguyễn Viết Xuân

Figure 10. Tomb of Kim Đồng

Figure 11. Tomb of Phan Đình Giót

the illusion of an ideal. Officially, after the meeting the hero was sent back to his home province to begin spreading the movement. Once he returned to his family, his symbolic role was finished. The central government's solicitude also limited his field of action. From now on he was expected to be modest and dedicated in his new daily life. His official biography stopped at the moment of his return home. If a new hero strayed from the ideal established by the Party, his errant behaviour must not contradict the exemplary course of his official existence. The State had already turned its attention to other "wonderful stories" and the new hero was destined to be forgotten. His return home — whether idealised or real — announced the final stage of his illustrious life.

Silence was not the only way to close the book on the new hero's official existence, however. Among the 148 heroes elected from 1952–1964, 13 per cent were awarded posthumously. The dead had an advantage over the living: they offered the State a finished picture of the revolutionary ideal, one that could never be tarnished. Unlike in mainland China, only soldiers who had fallen in battle received a heroic death in Vietnam. Until 1964, workers or peasants who died in work-related accidents were not commemorated, as Maoist China did with the young work hero Lei Feng.[19] The death of a hero represented his profession of faith in the system via one final act, validating the sacrifice and the legitimacy of his martyrdom.

Just before the outbreak of war with the South, the new hero had fulfilled his mission and the DRV could now take up arms. One suspects, however, that the official depictions do not fully reflect the reality of the heroic figure. Beyond the allegory of official discourse, what was the real face of the new hero in Vietnam from 1950–1960? What role did he actually play in the building of the nation? These questions led me to probe the image and myth of the new hero to examine the areas that remain in shadow.

The Making of the New Hero in Vietnam

In 1952, the Democratic Republic of Vietnam created the titles of "Hero of the People's Armed Forces" and "Labour Heroes". Between the first national conference for emulation fighters and cadres held in Tuyên Quang

---

[19] F. Naour. "La vis et les chaussettes ou la vie minuscule de Saint Lei Feng" (The screw and socks, or the miniscule life of Saint Lei Feng), *Perspectives Chinoises*, Hong Kong, no. 20, 10–12, 1993: 62–9.

Figure 12. Hồ Chí Minh with the "New Heroes" at Tuyên Quang (1952)

from 1–6 May of that year, and the third national meeting in Hanoi in April 1962, the government elected 147 new heroes.[20] Organised around Labour Day in the liberated zone, the Tuyên Quang conference marked the end of the Chinese-led patriotic emulation campaign begun in the summer of 1950. The State brought together the elite emulation fighters from the provincial level: 154 emulation fighters, including 41 peasants, 41 workers,

[20] Transcripts of the three national conferences (1952, 1958, 1962) are available at Centre No. 3 of the National Archives of the Socialist Republic of Vietnam. See *Đại hội toàn quốc chiến sĩ thi đua và cán bộ gương mẫu (1–5.5.1952)* (National conference on emulation fighters and exemplary cadres), in AVN3, Coll. BLD, file no. 432, May 1952 (529 pp.); *Đại hội liên hoan anh hùng chiến sĩ thi đua công nông binh toàn quốc lần thứ hai tại Hà Nôi 7–8.7.1958* (National conference on heroes and worker, peasant, and military emulation fighters in Hanoi), in AVN3, Coll. BLD, file no. 574, July 1958; *Phiên họp thứ 42 của BTVQH khoa III ngày 2.5.1962 về xét duyệt Đề nghị của Hội đồng Chính phủ tặng thưởng danh hiệu Anh hùng Lao động* (On the governmental commission for the attribution of titles of labour heroes), in AVN3, Coll. QH, file no. 367, 1962.

Figure 13. Conference of 1956

52 soldiers, 5 teachers, 7 civic workers, 6 exemplary cadres, and 2 exemplary students. Awarded were 7 new hero titles — 4 to soldiers and 3 to workers.[21] The government was careful to reward all segments of the population, including ethnic minorities and Catholics, who had suffered from deep divisions during the war. During the inaugural session a special tribute was paid to Cù Chính Lan, the only posthumous recipient.

During the second awards period (on 31 August 1955 and 7 May 1956), the National Assembly simply validated the government's decision to nominate 69 soldiers (26 in 1955 and 43 in 1956) as symbols of the victory over the French. Nineteen of them were promoted to the highest rank as martyrs for the national cause. Within the hierarchy of the PAVN, the nominations of 1955–56 were based on rankings provided by each unit during annual evaluation campaigns. Once the list was drawn up at the central level, political commissioners invited the nominees to Hanoi to receive their prizes. Of course, there were exceptions. Chu Văn Mùi (1955)

[21] *Truyện 7 anh hùng. Truyện anh hùng chiến sĩ thi đua* (The history of seven heroes: tales of emulation fighter heroes). Hanoi: nxb Việt Nam, 1954 (reissue of the seven installments published in 1952).

was not rewarded as part of the emulation movement, but belonged to a guild that the DRV wanted to honour at the end of the war. Conversely, the gunner Phùng Văn Khẩu was already a famous figure when the government named him "Military Hero" in 1955. In 1952, everyone had been chosen based on the social stratum or class they belong to; in 1955–56, however, the State paid tribute to the courage and dedication of the army after the victory at Điện Biên Phủ (7 May 1954). These 69 nominations were part of the DRV's policy to celebrate the heroism of the army.[22]

With the return of peace, the DRV reoriented its emulation campaign around three distinct goals: carrying out the final phase of land reform, reorienting the economy toward socialist principles, and developing the mass culture movement. On 7 July 1958, Hồ Chí Minh opened the fourth national meeting in a spirit of internationalism. The two-day conference in Hanoi hosted the 456 people nominated during the various phases of the emulation campaign throughout the country. The government also invited 40 heroes elected in previous conferences (Ngô Gia Khảm, Trần Đại Nghĩa, Hoàng Hanh, La Văn Cầu, Núp, etc.) as well as foreign guests from brother nations, 50 government and Party officials, and 50 people from various government branches (zone, province, and city). The government's main focus was now on the working class and on refugees from the South, known as "regroupees". While ethnic and religious factors influenced the election of the first seven national heroes at Tuyên Quang, the main concern in 1958 was reconstruction and national reunification. Consequently, 76 per cent of those elected were workers (only 3 from an ethnic minority: 1 Thái and 2 Mường). In 1958, the government had other priorities. First they had to demonstrate that refugees from South Vietnam were actively working to rebuild the country. Many of them attended the conference, and six of them received the title of "labour hero". Finally, the government had to root the conference in internationalist soil, so they officially recognised their debt to the People's Republic of China by decorating the worker Hồ Xây Dậu, a miner from Cẩm Phả of Chinese origin (his family was originally from Canton).

Finally, in 1962, the DRV held one last national conference in Hanoi, their fifth, before war broke out with the South. Held in the days following

---

[22] *Tóm tắt lý lịch, thành tích cá nhân và đề nghị khen thưởng Anh hùng, Chiến sĩ thi đua các ngành năm 1956* (Personal files of candidates who obtained the title of hero and emulation fighter, all branches for 1956), in Archives of the National Union, Hanoi, Coll. Ban thi đua sản xuất, file no. 197, 1956.

Figure 14. Hồ Chí Minh, Conference of 1962

Labour Day (4–6 May) under the chairmanship of Deputy Prime Minister Lê Thanh Nghị, the meeting put an end to three seasons of socialist emulation (1959, 1960, and 1961).[23] It was part of the government's new policy of economic recovery, including the widespread creation of cooperatives (agricultural, industrial, and commercial), establishment of a five-year plan (1960–64) similar to those of other socialist countries, development of a strong cultural policy focusing on remote areas, and the opening of economic resettlement zones.[24] The 1962 conference announced a reorganisation of socialist emulation policy. Although the selection of candidates for new heroes was formerly under the National Emulation Committee and the Ministry of Labour, it now fell to the various branches of activity under the direction of their ministry. The third national conference produced 45 future labour heroes and 985 emulation fighters, to spearhead the

[23] *Tờ trình về việc đề nghị tặng Danh hiệu Anh hùng và Khen thưởng các đơn vị tiên tiến, các Anh hùng, Chiến sĩ thi đua đi dự đại hội liên hoan công nông binh lần thứ ba* (Report on propositions for nominating heroes and decorating vanguard units, heroes and emulation fighters at the third national conference for workers, peasants, and soldiers), in AVN3, Coll. QH, file no. 367, document no. 1034-HC, 1 May 1962.

[24] Andrew Hardy. *Red Hills. Migrants and the State in the Highlands of Vietnam.*

reorientation of the nation's economy.[25] Almost half of the titles went to figures from the cooperative movement and outstanding workers from heavy and light industry (11 and 10, respectively). In addition, the government wanted to promote the integration of southern migrants, and so awarded nine people from South Vietnam. They also demonstrated their goodwill towards the Chinese minorities in the northeast (mostly in Hải Ninh) — an area which had always been a sensitive subject between the two nations[26] — and elected three "overseas Chinese" to show their internationalist spirit: Châu Hoà Mủn, a fisherman from the border region of Hải Ninh, Voòng Nải Hoài, a truck driver from the Cẩm Phả mine, and Mai Tinh Kang, a worker in a power tool factory in Hanoi. In the end, the government chose just a few individuals from minority ethnic groups (Bàn Văn Mình, an ethnic Man from the Thái Mèo autonomous zone, was the ideal spokesman) and focused instead on the majority Kinh who worked in the new economic zones established within predominantly ethnic provinces.

On the eve of the Gulf of Tonkin incident in August 1964, the DRV continued to produce its "great virtuous men". During the five election sessions of these new men, the government endowed all of its provinces — with the notable exception of Ninh Bình — with a contingent of new heroes. They were spread out evenly throughout the country, which reflects the determination of the DRV's policy on heroism. The geography of the new hero helped define a new political figure, whose genesis was intimately linked with the reconstruction of the national space.

Geography of the New Hero

The Propaganda Committee of the VWP now had a contingent of new heroes that spanned the 24 provinces of North Vietnam. The final decision

[25] Heavy industry: 6; light industry: 4; education: 1; health: 3; culture: 1; agricultural cooperatives: 10; businesses: 2; state-run provisions: 1; post and telecommunication: 1; artisanry: 1; forestry: 1; hydraulics: 1; defence industry: 2; architecture: 2; roadworks: 4; electric power: 1; geology: 1; farming: 3. See *Nhân dân*, Hanoi, 4–6 May 1962.

[26] "Les fidèles du nouveau régime comme ceux du Kuomintang d'antan ont la même tendance considérer le territoire de Hải Ninh, qu'ils étendent volontiers jusqu'aux riches charbonnages de Hồng Gay et même Hải Phòng, comme une terre chinoise" (Those loyal to the new regime, like those of the Kuomintang before them, tended to see Hải Ninh — which they willingly extend as far as the rich coal mines of Hồng Gay and even Hải Phòng — as part of China). In the 1950s, Chinese policy on this border region was a case for serious contention between the PRC and the DRV. An intensive study on the issue remains to be done. See CAOM, Coll. HCI, file no. 245/718, document no. 11162, 27 December 1951.

in the selection process rested with the government and its representatives, and the criteria were often based on some statistical objective (gender, ethnicity, social origin): "It was first a question of means and statistics. If a sector or a province already had a lot of heroes, the government would support another sector or province that had been overlooked."[27] Between 1952 and 1964, the only exception to this rule was the Catholic enclave of Ninh Bình province, which had still not seen a single new hero among their ranks. Elsewhere, the government respected a more localist orientation. The new hero personified the nation on the provincial level.

If we divide North Vietnam's 24 provinces into 3 sub-regions (the mountainous north, the Red River Delta and coast, and the southern provinces),[28] and consider the heroes selected from South Vietnam and mainland China, it is clear that the creation of the hero mainly boiled down to demographics. The more populous a region was, the greater its chances of producing a significant number of new heroes. The provinces of the Red River Delta alone produced a third of the new heroes elected between 1952 and 1964. But production of "great men" was by no means an urban affair: Hanoi only had ten heroes from 1955 to 1962, and Hải Phòng only had one in 1958.[29] The new heroism privileged the countryside. Rural provinces with a high population density played key roles in the organisation of the bureaucracy of heroism. Once again, the province of Nghệ Tĩnh (Nghệ An-Hà Tĩnh) was at the forefront of the national movement. Twenty of its citizens received a title, giving it the highest concentration of new heroes in the nation (13.5 per cent).[30] The Nghệ Tĩnh rural zone, a small

---

[27] Interview, Quynh Bàng commune (Quỳnh Lưu district, Nghê An province).

[28] Mountainous regions: Khu tự trị Việt Bắc, Khu tự trị Thái-Mèo; Red River Delta and coastal area: Hanoi, Hà Bắc, Hải Hưng, Vĩnh Phú, Nam Hà, Thái Nguyên, Yên Bái, Hòa Bình, Hải Phòng, Hà Tây, Quảng Ninh, Nam Định, Thái Bình; South of the DRV: Thanh Hóa, Nghệ An, Hà Tĩnh, Quảng Bình, khu vực Vĩnh Linh.

[29] Heroes from Hanoi: Nguyễn Phú Vị (1955), Nguyễn Văn Thành (1956), Nguyễn Phúc Đồng (1958), Lê Minh Đức (1958, from the South), Phạm Ngọc Thạch (1958, from the South), Phan Tính (1958, from the South), Đỗ Văn Tiết (1962), Mai Tinh Kang (1962, of Chinese descent), Nguyễn Văn Lợi (1962, from the South), and Nguyễn thị Hiếu (1962).

[30] Heroes from Nghệ Tĩnh: Cù Chính Lan (1952), Nguyễn Quốc Trị (1952), Hoàng Hanh (1952), Phan Đình Giót (1955), Đăng Quang Cầm (1955), Phan Tư (1955), Trần Can (1956), Phạm Minh Đức (1956), Đăng Đình Hồ (1956), Nguyễn Thái Nhự (1956), Nguyễn Đỗ Lương (1956), Nguyễn Xuân Lực (1956), Nguyễn Trung Thiếp (1958), Nguyễn Toàn (1958), Hoàng Mỹ (1958), Trương Sỹ (1958), Phan Văn Cường (1962), Trần Văn Giao (1962), Nguyễn Văn Lang (1962), and Cao Lục (1962).

industrialised urban centre (Vinh) with a high population density and a majority of ethnic Kinh, was exactly the type of geo-demographic area targeted by the government. Along the same lines, the provinces of Vĩnh Phú (7 per cent), Hà Bắc (5.5 per cent), Nam Định (4.8 per cent), and Quảng Ninh (4.8 per cent) were at the head of the national movement.

While the shift from military heroes to labour heroes should logically favour provinces with a heavy industrial base, this was not at all the case.[31] This could suggest that the shaping of the new hero was in fact determined by the socio-economic restructuring of society. Such an approach would support an intentionalist view of the emergence of the new heroic figure. As an example, Thái Bình province had over 70,000 workers but was granted no labour heroes between 1952 and 1964. The government seemed to think that it was already adequately represented by its two military heroes so did not really need one more (in terms of mobilising the masses).[32] Similarly, the region of Hải Phòng, the industrial heartland of North Vietnam with more than 20,000 workers in 1959, only saw one worker elected labour hero in 1958. In contrast, Nghệ Tĩnh had 20 times fewer workers than Thái Bình but garnered more than 13 per cent of the national total.

The uneven distribution of new heroes in North Vietnam sparked the emergence of a new geography of identity, with the province of Cao Bằng in the north (4.8 per cent of the national total), Vĩnh Phú in the Red River Delta (7 per cent), and Nghệ Tĩnh in the south (13 per cent) delineating this space. The DRV thus deliberately chose to create new heroes in the less ideologised areas, regardless of the outcome of the emulation campaign in the region. While the emulation fighter was a direct consequence of the emulation campaign, the new hero, on the other hand, was quite separate from the movement. Senior cadres in charge of emulation knew what they were doing, and the presence of heroes throughout the nation was indeed a result of careful organisation. The new outstanding citizen was then expected to concretise at the local level both national unification and ethnic homogenisation.

---

[31] In 1956–57, the DRV had 260,000 workers (2 per cent of the total population). See *Danh sách các công ty trong các Tỉnh năm 1959* (List of businesses from all provinces in 1959), in AVN3, Coll. BLD, file no. 449, unnumbered document, 1959.

[32] Nguyễn Thị Chiên was born in 1930 in the commune of Tán Thuật (Kiến Xương district), and Vũ Mạnh (or Đỗ Văn Đoàn) in 1924 in the village of Hữu Bằng (Thái Thụy district). The former was elected in 1952 and the latter in 1956. See *Anh hùng lực lượng vũ trang nhân dân* (Heroes of the people's armed forces). Hanoi: nxb quân đội nhân dân, 1978, pp. 13–5 and pp. 164–6.

The New Hero's Professional Career

The new hero of Sino-Soviet extraction posed a challenge to Vietnamese society: how does one confer national prestige on a heroic figure who is still in activity (from 1952–1964, 87 per cent of the heroes were elected while they were still alive)? What does one do with these model citizens once the flamboyant tale of their exploits has been utilised? "A hero is a person who does not age", they often say in the countryside. The hero of Tuyên Quang, however, grew increasingly bent over with the passing years. In reality, the title of hero heralded the moment when its recipient had to distance himself from his family. The government encouraged the hero's disappearance to better control how he was remembered and to strengthen the myth surrounding him in the countryside. The new hero left his village only to lose himself in a distant city, far from any connection to his bloodline. He began a second life: the life of a government cadre with honorary responsibilities. What real role did these heroes have within the government apparatus?

The title of "new hero" did in fact offer a means of social ascension. The government assigned its top heroes to carry out propaganda missions in their field, and stressed that the hero's professional rise was also due to his exceptional productivity and/or success in battle. For government leaders, the new hero had not only performed exceptional deeds, he now also required personalised administrative placement, which was an incredible idea for most people. Crowned "Hero of the Armed Forces" in 1952, the ethnic Tày La Văn Cầu was a boon for the propaganda department of the VWP. In the beginning he still had trouble writing in *quốc ngữ* (a transliteration of the Vietnamese language), but the young soldier was sent to give talks in the Tày language about his experiences to units of the PAVN stationed clandestinely in the Việt Bắc. With the return of peace, all labour heroes had to do the same, and several times a year they had to host lectures and conferences in production areas (factories, agricultural cooperatives, etc.) and within the government apparatus.[33] Once they were selected, the government reserved the right to terminate their propaganda activities if they did not achieve the desired results. The low cultural level of the new heroes often made further work in these areas impossible after

[33] *Chỉ thị về tăng cường công tác văn hoá trong quần chúng* (Directive on strengthening cultural activities for the masses), in AVN3, Coll. BVH, file no. 960, unnumbered document, 5 October 1961.

the first probationary year. When the results were satisfactory, however, the administration appointed the new hero to a position overseeing propaganda. Thus Phùng Văn Khẩu (1955), after receiving his title and additional training, left his job as a gunner in 1961 to become deputy political commissioner of an artillery regiment. Similarly, the military hero Chu Văn Mùi (1955) was assigned by the Ministry of Defence to be head of Ideological Affairs of his regiment and a few years later was appointed secretary of the Party cell.

Very few new heroes experienced this kind of career advancement, but their upward mobility was real and someone of humble origins could be propelled to the forefront of the local scene. But often the government did not want to proceed beyond that. It could be dangerous to promote someone to too high a level, given the presumed limitations of the candidates. Government leaders were afraid that the new hero's reputation would suffer if he was unable to perform duties at the national level. In the end, the issue of heroism remained primarily a peasant affair for the government. They had no intention of forming an elitist body within society out of the new heroes, aiming instead to reaffirm their identification with the people. The military hero and the labour hero symbolised a reworking of the hierarchy of honours. In no way were they to be confused with actual political leaders, as this could have had a negative effect on the masses. The new model citizen gave the people the hope of upward mobility based on merit. If the emulation fighter was living proof of a tangible ideal, the new hero brought together both the accessible and the wondrous. The government contrived to position the heroic figure on this scale of political perception. Official propaganda stressed that the new hero was not only higher in the hierarchy than the emulation fighter, he also enjoyed greater political authority. Showing the new heroes flanked by portraits of Hồ Chí Minh was insufficient — the government wanted to give the hero the illusion of a political reality, albeit through subterfuge.

In the late 1950s, the government was thus trying to integrate the carefully selected heroic figures into leadership positions within its administration. Already in 1954, "new men" were assigned important positions in the communal people's assemblies.[34] In 1959, their presence in the local

---

[34] *Thống kê kết quả bầu cử Hội đồng nhân dân và Ủy ban nhân dân các tỉnh Thanh Hóa, Nghệ An, Hà Tĩnh năm 1962* (Results from the 1962 elections of people's commissions and committees in the provinces of Thanh Hóa, Nghệ An, and Hà Tĩnh), in AVN3, Coll. BNV, file no. 1778, 1962.

decision-making apparatus was increased during elections of the people's assemblies and committees at the communal, district, and provincial levels. In 1959 seats for the National Assembly were also up for re-election. The provincial People's Committees were told to include the new heroes from their constituency in their electoral lists.[35] In the end, only 7 of 32 provinces in North Vietnam did so, actually electing a "hero" to represent them in the National Assembly.[36] The province of Cao Bằng put the soldier La Văn Cầu (1952) first on their list, and Hà Đông chose to be represented by the labour hero Cao Viết Bảo (1958). Elsewhere, local People's Committees generated a mix of new heroes and political figures. The proposed list in the first electoral district of Hanoi included ten names (the capital was then divided into three electoral units): Hồ Chí Minh, Nguyễn Quảng Du, and Phạm Hùng (Deputy Prime Minister) were the first three, then came the disabled labour hero Ngô Gia Khảm (1952) and the national emulation fighter and future labour hero, Đỗ Văn Tiết (1962). In Hanoi, heroes made up 10 per cent of the delegates sent to the National Assembly.[37] Elsewhere, the percentage of outstanding figures was sometimes higher: Phú Thọ had 18 per cent (2 of 11 delegates), Cao Bằng 16.5 per cent (1 of 6), Hải Dương 11 per cent (2 of 18), Hà Đông 11 per cent (1 of 9), or lower, as in Thanh Hóa (7.5 per cent, or 1 in 13) or Thái Bình (4.5 per cent, or 1 in 23). In 1960, the second legislative session of the National Assembly welcomed 11 new heroes: hardly more than 3 per cent of the 362 deputies of the new chamber.[38] Note, however, that only La Văn Cầu

---

[35] Election results published in the *Official Journal*. See *Công Báo*, Hanoi, no. 23, 8 June 1960: 389–95.

[36] Only 6 of 27 provinces (Cao Bằng, Phú Thọ, Hải Dương, Thái Bình, Hà Đông, and Thanh Hóa) did so, plus the city of Hanoi. The other administrative areas — autonomous zone (Khu tự trị Thái-Mèo), city (Hải Phòng), and administrative zone (Khu Hồng Quảng, khu vực Vĩnh Linh) — did not elect anyone in 1960.

[37] Thirty representatives were elected at this time, among whom were three official heroes: the workers Ngô Gia Khảm (1952), Lê Minh Đức (1958), and Đô Văn Tiết (1962). See *Công Báo*, Hanoi, no. 23, 8 June 1960: 389.

[38] The official breakdown was presented thus: 56 delegates from ethnic minorities; 49 women; 40 youth (21–30 years of age); 50 workers; 46 peasants; 20 soldiers; 65 intellectuals, artists, and scientists; 2 from the bourgeoisie; 3 Catholic priests; 2 ethnic Chinese; and 34 refugee cadres from South Vietnam. In 1960, 11 new heroes were elected deputy to the National Assembly: Ngô Gia Khảm (1952), Trần Đại Nghĩa (1952), Lê Minh Đức (1958), Phạm Ngọc Thạch (1958), Tôn Thất Tùng (1962), Nguyễn Công Thiệp (1958), Cao Viết Bảo (1958), Đinh Văn Xếp (1958), Đỗ Văn Tiết (1962), Đặng Đức Song (1956), and La Văn Cầu (1952). See *Công Báo*, Hanoi, no. 23, 8 June 1960: 389.

(1952) and Đặng Đức Song (1956) had been elected from among the military heroes; the others were all labour heroes. Being a deputy, of course, did not put the new hero at the centre of the political scene. "One must admit that since their appointment to the National Assembly, these deputy-heroes never really played any particular political role."[39] La Văn Cầu (1952), elected representative of minority peoples on the floor of the Assembly, never had many illusions: "As a member of the National Assembly, I was there in principle as delegate for the army and minority peoples. It was important for the country to have people who speak minority languages to spread the spirit of these ethnic groups in Vietnamese society. But in fact the government did not consult me often."[40]

Three figures had a different experience, however: Trần Đại Nghĩa (1952), Phạm Ngọc Thạch (1958), and Tôn Thất Tùng (1962). Respectively, Chairman of the State Committee for Science and Technology (1964–1971), Minister of Health (1958–1968), and Vice-Minister of Health (1947–1962), these three labour heroes — an engineer trained in France and two doctors — did not reflect the portrait of the hero we have sketched thus far. From a socially advantaged background, Tôn Thất Tùng was even a descendent of the royal family, and all three had been remarkable students during the old regime. Highly skilled and patriotic, they already held important positions in the government when they were named labour heroes. Trần Đại Nghĩa (1912–1997) invented the Vietnamese bazooka and was among the most gifted weapons designers of his generation.[41] Phạm Ngọc Thạch (1909–1968) was a renowned physician and tuberculosis specialist who became head of the Central Medical Institute in Hanoi in 1958.[42] And Tôn Thất Tùng (1912–1982) was a skilled surgeon who in 1962 ran the famous Việt Đức hospital in Hanoi.[43] Still, neither of them really occupied key positions, and their political role was actually rather limited. The government rewarded them more for their professional accomplishments and assigned them technical positions in accordance with their skills. Except in the case of these three men, the DRV was not ready to

[39] Interview, Hanoi.

[40] Interview with La Văn Cầu, Hanoi.

[41] *Anh hùng lao động Trần Đại Nghĩa* (The labour hero Trần Đại Nghĩa). Ban tuyên truyền và văn nghệ, 1952.

[42] Mai Văn Tạo. *Anh Tư Thạch* (Big brother Tư Thạch). Hanoi: nxb Y học, 1981.

[43] Tôn Thất Tùng. *Đường vào khoa học* (The path towards knowledge). Hanoi: nxb Y học và Thể thao, 1974.

Figure 15. Cover of the biography of the hero Trần Đại Nghĩa

grant too much visibility to these new heroes, so their positions in the government were primarily honorary.

The Status of the New Hero

At the end of the Franco-Viet Minh War, the DRV wanted to increase the number of new heroes without "consequently decreasing their value". In several reports, the Ministry of Labour was concerned about the possible loss of the title's prestige. The government had to find a way to permanently etch the phenomenon into the people's minds. One easy answer was to offer financial incentives to new patriotic honourees. If they could make these new awards pay off, the people would be much more interested. Lenin had already supported such a tactic for the Soviet Union in the 1920s. At the Tuyên Quang conference of 1952, the government gave out gifts to everyone who received an award. The Catholic Hoàng Hanh received a water buffalo, a set of towels, and photographs of his leaders; Nguyễn Quốc Trị received a Mao Zedong badge, a Parker fountain pen, and a set of towels and handkerchiefs; La Văn Cầu got a Stalin badge, a Canadian jacket, and a set of towels and handkerchiefs. Along with these small gifts, the government added money — rarely exceeding three months' pay — and other staples (sugar, tea, chocolate, potatoes, cigarettes, etc.). This practice was common in Vietnamese tradition and was repeated during each of the many meetings held in the hero's honour once he returned home.

Receiving this honour thus enabled the recipient to rise several steps on the government pay scale. Following her appointment as labour hero, the heroine Nguyễn Thị Mi's salary was increased by 225 per cent (from 27 to 61 *dông* monthly). Although the government tried to avoid putting a price tag on heroism, the hero's progress up the corporate ladder was always indirectly accompanied by a significant raise. On top of the increase in pay, authorities also gave the new hero a home in his new location. Official records stressed these important material benefits to convince the people of the hero's rise in society.[44] The title of new hero offered very real economic benefits to people struggling with poverty and the difficulties of everyday life.

[44] *Thông tri về việc quản lý anh hùng chiến sĩ thi đua* (Decision on the management of heroes and emulation fighters), in AVN3, Coll. BLD, file no. 561, document no. 1383, 28 August 1958.

The government also showed its thanks by sponsoring a "Journey to the West". Since 1952, the government routinely sent a few "new men" with its delegations to brother nations.[45] This journey undoubtedly increased the hero's prestige among the people. Serving as ambassador or spokesperson for the national cause was an unexpected turn for the average peasant and worker. The trip also gave the hero the opportunity to meet the supreme leader, Hồ Chí Minh. In one of the few memoirs published on the subject, the heroine Nguyễn Thị Khương (1958) sums up this new status:

> After the conference, I was invited by the Party and Uncle Hồ to visit China. After spending three days in our sister country we returned to Hanoi and met again with Uncle Hồ. He asked, 'So, did you enjoy the visit? What did you like there?' Comrade Hông Tiên, head of the delegation, rose to give his account, but our Uncle asked him to remain seated. 'We both know I would rather hear from the rest of you.' He looked at me and asked, 'So, how did it go, Madame Khương? Will you be able to do the same thing at home?' 'The Party, the government, and you yourself offered me the chance to visit a sister country, and my heart is full of enthusiasm. I think that Vietnam can do as well as China.'[46]

In the 1950s, foreign travel was a privilege of the powerful, so such a reward was a considerable step up for them in the eyes of their community.

Apart from these honours, what long-term benefits did the highest-ranking new heroes receive? A model citizen's virtue deserved some kind of government assistance in return. When Party leaders decided to increase the contingent of new heroes in 1954–55, health care was a prime concern, so the DRV proposed to take care of them throughout their lives. The government now paid for hospital fees, treatment, and the delivery of medication for heroes and their families — which sometimes sparked jealousy among the villagers. Not surprisingly, the DRV decided to describe in detail the dedicated care they were giving to their model subjects. Thus, when the labour hero Ngô Gia Khảm was seriously injured in a work accident at the clandestine weapons factory at Tuyên Quang in 1952,

---

[45] *Triệu tập Hội nghị bồi dưỡng Chiến sĩ thi đua toàn quốc và anh hùng* (Review of the conference on encouraging national emulation fighters and heroes), in AVN3, Coll. BLD, file no. 504, document no. 2233/LDTD, 26 September 1955.

[46] Nguyễn thị Khương and Hải Thoại. "Niềm vinh dự lớn nhất" (On the occasion of the greatest of honours), in *Avoóc Hồ, Hồi ký cách mạng* (Uncle Hồ, memoir of the revolution). Hanoi: nxb Kim Đồng, nxb Văn hóa-dân tộc, pp. 179–80.

he was sent with great fanfare to a hospital in Moscow for treatment by the "best Soviet surgeons" in recompense of his patriotic commitment.

Yet this did not suffice. Not everyone could expect medical care in foreign countries. In 1958, the government offered its ill or infirm new honourees a stay in a luxurious convalescent home. Anyone holding a national title (emulation fighter at the national level or new hero) was eligible. Local governments had to send the national administration a list of their candidates, not exceeding 30 per cent of the workforce. They had to be careful not to overdo it. An average stay at the home was not to exceed two weeks. The patient's parent organisation (company, cooperative, local government) took care of his living expenses (estimated at 2,500–3,000 *dông* per day). They were treated to rest, comfort, and relaxing activities "to fortify the spirit of these exemplary men". Upon their release, the government asked patients to hold talks in their workplace "describing the nature of their stay in these rest camps and showing how well the State had looked after them".[47] They had to spread the word. In the fall of 1958, the DRV had eight convalescent centres (in Hanoi, Thanh Hóa, Phú Thọ, Hải Phòng, Hồng Gai, Nam Định, Quảng Bình, and in the Thái-Mèo autonomous zone).[48] The treatment centre in Hanoi, located in the hamlet of Nghi Tàm (zone no. 6 of Yên Phụ), was the biggest. Its buildings were "quiet and clean, the rest home in Nghi Tàm offered patients the highest possible care thanks to the excellent quality of service and quality meals". When it was inaugurated in October 1958, however, the director was surprised that they had only 52 patients, including only 2 labour heroes: Lê Văn Hiến (1958), who was 68 years old, and Hồ Xây Dậu (1958), who was 38. In his first reports, he was pleased with the average length of stay: 42 of his patients (80 per cent) stayed at least 12.5 days of the 15 granted by the State. During these stays, the staff held lectures by cadres from the central government as well as touristic excursions, all "in an atmosphere of relaxation necessary for successful physical recovery." Other

[47] Nguyễn thị Khương and Hải Thoại. "Niềm vinh dự lớn nhất" (On the occasion of the greatest of honours).

[48] The two most important were in Hanoi (with 109 beds) and Sầm Sơn, in Thanh Hóa (80 beds). Six more smaller facilities were in the following provinces: Phú Thọ (20 beds), Hải Phòng (30), Hồng Gai (15), Nam Định (25), Quảng Bình (10), and the autonomous Thái-Mèo zone (5). See *Một số điểm bổ sung Thông tư số 25/TD-LD về việc anh hùng, chiến sĩ thi đua nghỉ dưỡng sức* (A few points for strengthening the health care measures for heroes and emulation fighters), in AVN3, unnumbered document, September 30, 1958.

rest homes in the country found themselves almost always full. Unfortunately, there are no official statistics on exactly how many new heroes actually took part in this programme between 1958 and 1964. It is also hard to know how often people went back for further treatment. Could someone return several times, and how soon after the previous visit? But this is all beside the point. These institutions, though few in number, allowed the government to show the extent of their concern. The DRV showed yet again that they would stand by anyone who made a commitment to the nation, and they would remain loyal to deserving citizens for the rest of their lives.

Lastly, the professional journey of the new hero sometimes involved punishment for those who deviated from the Party's collective discipline. The government tried to avoid any "degeneration of the new hero" (*anh hùng bị phản bội*), and I have not found any legal documents outlining the disciplinary measures that would have been enacted. The term "degenerate hero" first appeared in administrative reports of the early 1960s, but in any case, a breach of discipline was always dealt with behind closed doors. Vietnamese political culture has always dealt with its problems on two levels; the important thing was to keep it quiet. The myth of the unblemished patriotism of their finest citizens must not be tainted. When the punishment concerned a low-level hero (emulation fighter, exemplary worker, or outstanding cadre), the local Party cell suggested that the central government simply remove the title. The same was applied to new heroes charged with serious misconduct (corruption, ideological divergence, breach of discipline, etc.): "Generally, when confronted with such a problem, the Institute of Medals decided along with the Party to withdraw the title from the degenerate hero. But honestly, the title of hero was not a big deal. All you had to do was remove his biography from the new editions and make sure no one mentions his name during rallies and public discussions."[49] Time and the severity of the Party's collective discipline did the rest. It was considered unseemly, if not dangerous, to inquire about someone who had been suddenly erased by the DRV. In the early 1970s, the labour hero Đỗ Tiên Hảo (1962) found himself the object of the governmental disgrace. Accused of embezzlement and corruption in his management of the Yên Duyên cooperative in the outskirts of Hanoi, Hảo was dragged to court, expelled from the Party, stripped of his title of labour hero, and deprived of all of his "privileges". On the eve of the outbreak of war with the South,

[49] Interview, Hanoi.

however, cases of "degenerate heroes" were still rare in northern Vietnam. The State undoubtedly had its hands full with the emulation fighters and exemplary workers who were less rigorously selected.

The DRV's piety towards the nation's heroes was concretised in this need to take care of their daily needs. In the minds of the people, anyone with a title was part of an elite national body. The hero defined an ideal and thus deserved special treatment from the authorities. His accomplishments, whether fictionalised or real, placed him on a scale that was different from others. Official biographies, life stories, and heroic memoirs gave pride of place to the value of his great deeds. From soldiers under enemy fire to workers confronting production needs, cadre teachers, farmers, truck drivers, and engineers, everyone had to answer the demands of rising production standards in order to strengthen a nation in reconstruction and preparation for war. The greater a hero's productivist or military deeds, the more it confirmed his mission as model citizen for the nation. At the same time, the hero was also presented as the herald of a repositioning of North Vietnamese society within the community of socialist nations. And as more and more heroes were produced, the State had a harder time managing all of them. In 1964, the young soldier Nguyễn Văn Trỗi fell in the line of duty and was posthumously awarded the title of military hero. Through him, the government was finally able to connect two long-standing heroic traditions: the imported new man began to acquire the kind of power held by the traditional historical figure, announcing the inexorable transformation of *homo vietnamicus*.

CHAPTER 5

The Life of the Dead

We must give credit to man's talent and intelligence for success in the many acts of life, for if we attribute everything to spirits and ghosts we make a mockery of man himself. We believe that the only temples worth venerating are those of loyal subjects, the heroes and faithful servants of the country.

Phan Kế Binh[1]

"It has been a long time since anyone has seen a ghost near Mount Buddha. Now is the time of heroes; and ghosts — even invisible ones — no longer belong."

Nguyễn Khac Trường[2]

The living spirit of the dead tells of a continuity through time. The Sinologist Simon Leys writes that: "Permanence does not deny transformation, but informs it ... continuity is not guaranteed by the immutability of inanimate objects, but is achieved in the flow of successive generations."[3] In the sinicised world, the deceased or the ancestor becomes the object of a cult that creates a link to the living. The life of the dead is the essence of the national community. After 1945, the Vietnamese communist regime never challenged the foundations of popular belief. A number

[1] Phan Kế Bính. *Việt nam phong tục* (Mores and customs of Vietnam, 1915). Presentation and annotated translation by Nicole Louis-Hénard. Paris: PEFEO, 1975, pp. 84–5.
[2] Nguyễn Khắc Trường. *Des hommes et autant de fantômes et de sorciers* (Men and as many ghosts and sorcerers), p. 15. Taken from the French translation.
[3] Simon Leys. "*L'humeur, l'honneur, l'horreur. Essai sur la culture et la politique chinoise* (1991)" (Humor, honor, horror. Essay on Chinese culture and politics), in *Essais sur la Chine.* Paris: Laffont, 1998, pp. 739–56.

of directives did indeed alter the relationship between the new man and the spirits of his ancestors, but the aim was not to completely overturn traditional practices and beliefs.[4] In the late 1940s, the government wanted to simplify traditional rituals without altering the relationship to the deceased. The imported revolutionary praxis did not necessitate a deconstruction of the idea of life after death since no such transition exists in Vietnamese culture. Death is a past and future state. It is a permanence that orders the world of the living and gives it meaning. Any ruling power needed the support of its illustrious spirits to remain in power.

After 1954, ancestor cults held a key political role in the affirmation of the State. The dead were considered in much the same way as they had been during the Nguyễn dynasty, but in the nineteenth century the "cult of outstanding soldiers and citizens needed an official historiography; it was one of the most important parts of government activity."[5] The dead legitimised the power of the living and imposed order and cohesion on the collective "from the family to the village to the State", the traditional triptych. The life of the dead represented the hidden side of the reorganisation of society taking place in the 1950s. The DRV thus operated on two levels, overseeing basic human affairs as well of those of the Beyond. In Vietnam the hero or the tutelary spirit was not always chosen posthumously. Exemplary citizens, whether living or dead, had always been honoured by the community for services rendered to the "mother country". Thus, while the new hero was still alive and active, the world of the dead could not be ignored either. The national martyr (*liệt sỹ tổ quốc*) was a kind of cultural double of the new patriotic hero. Though stamped with proletarian internationalism, the national martyr also offered a traditional face to protect the "spirit and morals of an ancient people". DRV leaders wanted to define the title without reference to class, religion, or politics. A glorious death helped to strengthen cohesion in a country with a fractured identity. Unlike the heroes from Tuyên Quang, who were politicised but also culturally exogenous, the national martyr brought together and unified

[4] "After the revolution, new forms of ancestor worship did appear in North Vietnam. But they were pretty neglected during the war due to lack of money and time. We also had a very simple understanding of materialism, and often mixed up ancestor worship and superstition. So when they tore down the temples in Nghê An in the early 1950s, we raised up our ancestors who helped build the Party; it was a new source of pride for us but didn't really question anything." Interview, Vinh, Nghê An.

[5] Langlet. *L'ancienne historiographie d'Etat au Vietnam, tome I. Raisons d'être, conditions d'élaboration et caractères au siècle des Nguyên,* p. 35.

the people. In assuming exclusive control over devotional activities, Hồ Chí Minh's government claimed an unassailable legitimacy. Its policy on martyrs aimed to transform the Head of State into the sole intercessor between the realm of the living and that of the dead. This policy linked the valiant dead, who were both traditional and new heroes, with their doubles from Tuyên Quang in 1952. The life of the dead helped secure the victory of a new dynasty in power.

Ordering the Dead

"According to peasant tradition, we honour the men who died for their country, as well as soldiers and disabled veterans, since they exhibited great love for their country. They were the ones who drove out the French, puppet governments, and feudal landlords, and helped increase the mobilisation of the masses, lower land rents, and implement land reform."[6] The nation's martyrs generated enthusiasm for the resistance and helped educate the people. For centuries, the State kept guard over these "outstanding spirits" to establish political preeminence over its rivals. Classifying the dead was an ancient practice. The Ministry of Rites (a legacy of Chinese bureaucracy) had been in charge of classifying and ranking patriotic orders of merit since the fifteenth century. These decisions had a direct bearing on society since no death was anonymous, and descendants repositioned themselves socially in light of the ranking. From 1945 to 1956, the DRV simply distinguished between honourable deaths and dishonourable deaths — any soldier who died for a puppet army spread infamy upon his family. Honourable deaths, those who died for the just cause, were then divided into two categories: death on active duty or death in battle. The term *liệt sỹ* (martyr) was hardly used since it was too similar to *tử sĩ* (a soldier who fell in battle). In 1951, when the Ministry of Martyrs and Disabled Veterans issued posthumous certificates to soldiers and officials who had died for their country, all families of *tử sĩ* were included. This term covered anyone who died while on active duty, be it from an illness, an accident, or as a direct result of combat. Conversely, the term *tử trận* (killed at war) was more restrictive and referred to men and women who died on the battlefield.

---

[6] *Thông tri về ngày 27.7.1954* (Directive on the day of 27 July 1954), in AVN3, BTB, file no. 71a, document no. 48/TT-LVTQ, 2 June 1954.

Figure 16. Certificate of Posthumous Merit

Until 1955, the government used these terms indiscriminately to classify honourable deaths. They delayed classifying the dead before the summer of 1956, however, so as not to create problems with their influential allies. They tried a first tentative classification campaign within the context of agrarian reform, but the decisions of 1956 imposed a more comprehensive overhaul of the system. Ordering the dead was a cultural act which basically maintained the order of the living. The careful classification of the deceased was now an additional factor in the social positioning of the family and lineage. A new classification of deaths led the DRV to rethink its entire social policy with regards to the according of medals, pensions, and exemptions. They saw these reforms as a way to tighten their grip on the village communities that had been scarred by years of war and division. Their previous attempt to restructure the new society according to social class did not have the desired effect since people were not used to foreign concepts. In 1956, the government needed to consolidate its hold on a divided population, so the question of ordering the dead became a key matter for the its propaganda machine. Decree No. 980/Ttg (27 July 1956) and Directive No. 52 (26 October 1956) from the Ministry of Martyrs and Disabled Veterans created a new classification system: at the top of the ladder sat the figure of national martyr (*liệt sỹ tổ quốc*), then came the men who fell while on active duty (*quân nhân tử trận*), and lastly those missing in action (*quân mất tích*). After which came the martyr's family (*gia đình liệt sĩ*), families of those who died for their country (*gia đình tử trận*), and finally the families of those missing in action (*gia đình mất tích*).

The martyr (*liệt sỹ*) was "someone who had died gloriously in battle after 1925 while fighting imperialism and feudalism".[7] A glorious death was defined as "dying courageously at the front while defending the work of national revolution". They chose the date 1925 since that was the year Nguyễn Ai Quoc (Hồ Chí Minh) founded the *Thanh Niên* (Revolutionary Youth League) in Canton. They made an exception, however, and canonised the young Phạm Hồng Thái as "martyr of the national revolution", though he had died one year earlier (in 1924) after his assassination attempt on Governor-General Merlin in China. While the term *tử sĩ* had thus far been used to refer to all of the dead, the martyr of 1956 referred mainly to the "exemplary men" from the revolutionary parties (the ICP, Viêt Minh, and VWP). Although in principle the title of martyr was not strictly reserved for Party members — it could also be awarded posthumously to former members of the Nationalist Party of Nguyễn Thái Học who died during the repressions of 1930 — the text of 1956 stated that the nation's martyrs "must be Party members, members of associations and mass organisations of all revolutionary parties, and all patriotic mass organisations in neighbourhoods and villages".

Within the community of the dead, martyrs were a patriotic elite made up of exemplary men and women who died for the country's independence and the affirmation of the communist party. When asked about the criteria for earning this posthumous title, the government offered a tentative response. The death of a martyr resulted from a direct confrontation with the enemy (hand-to-hand combat, bombing, etc.), an attack, or imprisonment by the enemy. Official documents show that cadres and soldiers who had fought for the revolution and died later due to an accident or illness could not be classified as "martyrs". A document of 27 July 1956 established a list of all those eligible for the title: revolutionary cadres (including those in charge of reducing farm rents and agrarian reform); revolutionary soldiers of the PAVN; members of the Vietnamese

[7] *Giải thích về tiêu chuẩn liệt sĩ và gia đình liệt sĩ* (Explaining the defining criteria of martyrs and families of martyrs), in AVN3, BNV, file no. 2232, document no. 50/TT/LB, 1957.

Liberation Army and of the Army of National Salvation; organisations active during World War II in Bắc Sơn, Định Ca, Trang Xá, Lã Hiền, Đại Từ, Định Hoà, and Sơn Dương; combatants with local protection units; members of people's militia groups; deserving Việt Minh groups in existence before the revolution and guerrilla organisation; workers from the defence sector "who repaired or made weapons and fought to protect their plants during the resistance"; and finally, members of youth groups who fell defending their posts. The 1956 Act stated that in theory no distinction of class, religion, or politics should determine the status of "national martyr", but the criteria for "special cases" rendered this obsolete. Indeed, when it was time to classify deaths, cadres had to work on a case-by-case basis, carefully noting the deceased's "religion, ethnicity, activities against the enemy, activities involving the masses, and relationship with the local branch of the Party". Soldiers, officers, and policemen who did not fall into the category of martyr were granted the posthumous title of "war dead" (*tử trận*). A directive from the Ministry of Martyrs and Disabled Veterans of 26 October 1956 states that it was awarded to those who died of an illness or following an accident sustained while on duty.[8] The government played on the title's former prestige to mitigate the disgrace of this second-class posthumous rank. While it used to be reserved only for those who fell on the battlefield, the title's re-evaluation in 1956 was now so broad that it covered almost all deaths caused even indirectly by the war.[9] As a third step, the Ministry created a posthumous title for those missing in action. Unfortunately there are no reliable statistics on exactly how many went missing between 1925 and the early 1960s, but just as an example, the province of Hà Giang recorded 262 "martyr's families" in 1962, and 80 "families of the missing" who were granted an allowance by the government.

Classifying the dead gave the State an effective way to assert its dominance over the those left behind. It is generally estimated that more than 470,000 Vietnamese died during the Franco-Viet Minh War (1946–1954). In 1962, 11,290 "martyr's families" received a financial allowance from the Ministry of Martyrs and Disabled Veterans. Not all family

[8] *Về việc trợ cấp gia đình liệt sĩ, gia đình quân nhân, cán bộ công nhân, viên chức tử trận, hay mất tích gặp khó khăn trong đời sống* (On the support provided to families of martyrs, families of cadres, worker-cadres, and officials who died or disappeared while serving their country), in AVN3, BLD, file no. 886, document no. 1989, 2 April 1962.

[9] C.B. (Hồ Chi Minh). "Anh hùng giả và anh hùng thật" (Real and false heroes), *Nhân Dân,* no. 149, 21 November 1953.

members qualified for this rank, however. The title was restricted to the deceased's next-of-kin: spouse, immediate offspring (legitimate children), or parents. The government added a few explanatory paragraphs to the legislation in order to avoid an excessive number of beneficiaries, which could lead to political and budgetary ruin. Hence, when the wife of a martyr remarried, his family was no longer automatically entitled to retain the title; it depended on the financial situation of her new husband. Conversely, the former husband of a deceased female martyr could retain his title upon remarrying if he continued to raise the children from his first marriage. When the wife of a martyr lived with her in-laws, they were eligible for the title of "martyr's family" even though the title really belonged to the wife and children. In the absence of direct descendents, the paternal grandparents of the martyr could also receive the title. Lastly, when a child under 16 (or more if the child was disabled) lost both his parents and grandparents, the person or foster family who saw to the child's care could be classified as a "martyr's family".

The families of the "war dead" and the missing had even more limited access to the posthumous rank. The government took into account the family's standard of living and required that the deceased to have given at least three years of continuous service during the resistance or five years in peacetime.

Campaigns for Classifying the Dead

Posthumous awards or certificates were also a part of Vietnamese tradition. Since 1946, the Ministry of Martyrs and Disabled Veterans had established local branches (within the administrative committees of the military zones and provinces) that were placed in charge of these issues. In 1950, the arrival of Chinese advisers announced a partial reform of the Ministry's mission. In 1951, the government issued a "certificate from the grateful nation" to everyone who died for their country. In 1952, they added two additional certificates: one "for glorious families" and a "certificate of honour".[10] The distribution of posthumous certificates was supposed to accompany the campaigns of reclassifying the population, but it became common practice only later and was hardly used before the latter half of the 1950s.

[10] *Hồ Chí Minh Biên niên tiểu sử* (Hô Chi Minh, biographical accounts), vol. V, 1995, p. 283.

Posthumous awards situated a family within the new hierarchy of patriotic merit. They were based on lists drawn up by the various military and administrative levels, and validated by the Prime Minister's office, which officially announced the honours. The certificate was printed on a small rectangular piece of cardboard, 25 × 40 cm (10 × 16 in.), and contained the name of the martyr and his job title at the time of death, engraved in black letters on a tri-coloured background (white, red, and gold). The government asked its local branches to use all holidays as an occasion to solemnly distribute the certificate to the families concerned. Granted to all *tử sĩ* until 1956, the "certificate from the grateful nation" was later only awarded to those with the rank of martyr. The new distinction between the "war dead", the "missing", and "martyrs" changed the rules for obtaining the certificate. The "certificate in honour of glorious families" was created in 1952 and was awarded to families who had one member in the Resistance. It was no longer given to those who did not fully qualify as a "martyr's family". From 1956, families of the "war dead" or "missing" received second-class certificates, a "certificate in honour of glorious families", or a "certificate of honour". This new hierarchy of the dead echoed that of the living under the new regime.

Organising classification campaigns had become a priority, and the Ministry of Martyrs and Disabled Veterans gave special training to the cadres they sent out into the field. The movement took place over three distinct periods: 1954–56, 1956–59, and 1960–65. During the agrarian reform (1954–56), teams of cadres criss-crossed the nation to implement a reorganisation of society based on class (landless peasants, poor peasants, middle peasants, rich peasants, and landlords). According to official statistics, from 1952 to September 1956, 40 per cent of martyrs and "martyrs' families" within the PAVN were classified. The second period began in the fall of 1956 and lasted until the end of 1959. At the Ninth Plenum of the Central Committee of April 1956, the excesses of the agrarian reform were denounced. In September 1956, the Tenth Plenum of the Central Committee launched a campaign to rectify past mistakes.[11] Many communes accused the itinerant teams of misclassifying their dead. Local officials complained about the "errors and excesses committed by 'disabled veterans' who had been assigned key positions in the village administration by agrarian

[11] Võ Nguyên Giáp. "Bài phát biểu của đồng chí Võ Nguyên Giáp 29.10.1956" (Speech by comrade Võ Nguyên Giáp December 29, 1956), *Nhân Dân*. Hanoi, 31 December 1956.

reform teams", which of course had "a very bad influence on people".[12] While there have been several studies on the classification of the living, the registry of the dead remains largely unexamined. A certificate of martyrdom brought both prestige and advantage to its recipient, so a classification error could lead to serious problems within a community. Between 1956 and 1959, cadres from the Ministry of Martyrs and Disabled Veterans re-examined all records, and special cases were carefully reviewed. By 1959, the government had classified more than 60 per cent of the cases concerning martyrs and their families. And finally, the policy that had begun in 1956 was radicalised in 1960. The government confirmed the idea that a martyr was "first and foremost someone chosen for his revolutionary work, and his opposition to imperialism and feudalism, and who fell in battle with glory". The classification of bereaved families went hand-in-hand with the country's march towards a socialist economy. The propaganda department praised the families of martyrs, those who died for the nation, the missing, and the disabled "as the purest of all of us, of the Party and the government".[13]

At the village level, People's Committees were told to help integrate this new virtuous elite into local cooperatives and mass organisations. For provincial cadres, a list of martyrs' families became an indispensable political tool for training the people: "Since the return of peace, 350 disabled comrades or family members of martyrs in our province have joined the Party. Eighty per cent of them hold managerial positions in businesses and all of them have joined cooperatives."[14] By the early 1960s, these families had acquired such important roles in the ideologisation of the countryside and the management of local affairs that the classifying of the dead was no longer done by the local government but directly by the provincial branch of the Party.

---

[12] *Báo cáo công tác Thương binh liệt sĩ từ đầu năm 1962 đến nay và phương hướng nhiệm vụ thời gian tới (Nghệ An)* (Activity report on disabled veterans and martyrs from 1962 to today and a direction for the future [Nghệ An]), in AVN3, BNV, file no. 2267, December 1963.

[13] *Báo cáo công tác Thương binh liệt sĩ từ đầu năm 1962 đến nay và phương hướng nhiệm vụ thời gian tới (Nghệ An)* (Activity report on disabled veterans and martyrs from 1962 to today and a direction for the future [Nghệ An]), in AVN3, BNV, file no. 2267, December 1963.

[14] *Báo cáo tổng kết năm 1961 tỉnh Hải Phòng* (Account of the year 1961, Hải Phòng province), in AVN3, BNV, file no. 2248, unnumbered document, January 1961.

The Course of a Campaign

Let us now examine one of these campaigns in detail, that of Diễn Châu district (Nghệ An) in 1962.[15] In July 1962, the province sent a group of four officials to the district to oversee registration, under the direction of the Party committee.[16] The People's Committee of the district invited communal cadres from the area to a briefing to explain the procedure. The communes that were not represented (and there were many that day) would have to be visited without delay by the classifying team.[17] In the villages, the cadre in charge of cultural affairs had to ensure the proper implementation of these guidelines. The cost of organising informational meetings fell on the province. Provincial authorities drew up a calendar of operations: the registration of the population should take place between 26 October and early December, with the closing conference not later than 22 December — the anniversary of the founding of the PAVN.[18]

At the communal level, these campaigns relied heavily on their cooperatives.[19] As the lists were being finalised, the head of the cooperative called upon representatives from the various sectors involved: the Fatherland Front, the office of rural affairs, the youth organisation, and

---

[15] *Báo cáo công tác Thương binh liệt sĩ từ đầu năm 1962 đến nay* (Activity report on disabled veterans and martyrs from early 1962 to the present), in AVN3, BNV, file no. 2263, document no. 16776, 10 December 1962.

[16] In 1960, the report by the district of Tiên Lãng (Kiến An province) still showed that the district Party committe had greater decision-making power than the administrative branch. See *Báo cáo về việc thi hành công tác liệt sĩ của huyện Tiên Lãng* (Report on the activities in place for martyrs in the district of Tiên Lãng), in AVN3, BNV, file no. 2248, unnumbered document, 15 March 1960.

[17] They were briefed on the following questions: "What is a martyr? How can one tell a martyr (*liệt sĩ*) from someone who died for the country (*quân nhân tử trận*)?"; "Study of decree 14-CP and circular no. 38–41 on the policy regarding martyrs"; "Study of the principles and criteria for supporting the families and children of martyrs according to directive no. 1162 of June 20, 1961, by the Provincial Committee of Nghệ An"; "On the upkeep of martyrs' cemeteries"; etc., in *Báo cáo về việc thi hành công tác liệt sĩ của huyện Tiên Lãng,* 30 November 1962, p. 3.

[18] The People's Committee of Nghệ An gave the commune of Diễn Thịnh 50 *dông* to organise these meetings within the allotted time frame. See *Báo cáo về việc thi hành công tác liệt sĩ của huyện Tiên Lãn*, unnumbered document (UBND tinh Nghệ An for the district committee of Diễn Châu), 30 November 1962, p. 2.

[19] AVN3, BNV, file no. 2268, document no. 168 DC-LS, UBHC [administrative committee], Hà Nam province, 20 April 1964.

the provincial departments of health, disabled veterans, and education. In December 1963, cadres in charge of the registration process for Thanh Liêm district (Hà Nam) sent the following assessment to the People's Committee of the province:[20]

Number of "martyrs"	520
Number of "war dead" and "missing"	285
Number of martyr's families	512
Number of martyr's children	391
Number of disabled veterans	95
Number of special cases	75

Results of the Classification Campaign, Thanh Liêm (1963)

The report highlighted a number of weaknesses. In Thanh Liêm district, 7 villages still did not have a patriotic cemetery and 19 villages had not enacted special measures for the children and parents of martyrs. In addition, although the government recommended that all communes establish committees to implement these new policies, almost nothing had been done on the ground.

Thanks to reports from these classifying teams, DRV leaders were able to keep abreast of how well the government apparatus was taking hold in the provinces. Classifying a death allowed leaders to extend their reach into the village level. Already on 27 July 1951, the government had published a letter from Hồ Chí Minh encouraging disabled veterans to return to their villages and find work within the local economy.[21] The government obviously considered veterans a crucial part of the political and economic mobilisation of the country:

> We really must encourage disabled veterans to play a key role in their villages once they get home, in production, in campaigns to reduce land rents, and in land reform. Currently many disabled veterans have already demonstrated strong performance in production, and some of them also

[20] *Báo cáo công tác Thương binh liệt sĩ* (Activity report on disabled veterans and martyrs), in AVN3, BNV, file no. 2268, unnumbered document, 30 April 1964.

[21] *Báo cáo về việc thực hiện chủ trương đón Thương binh về xã và việc thực hiện chủ trương nay đến cuối năm* (Report on the treatment of groups of disabled veterans who returned to their communes, and continued treatment of the issue through the end of the year), in AVN3, BTB, file no. 22, document no. 770/TB, 3 June 1952.

> occupy key positions in the communal administration. This can surely have a powerful influence on the mobilisation of the people.[22]

The virtue and legitimacy of the DRV depended on its leaders having a firm grasp on the life of the dead. The policy on martyrs had three main components: establishing a system of financial support for the families of martyrs, combatants who died for their country, the missing, and disabled veterans; providing educational and professional benefits (government jobs) to these families on a quota basis; and granting them exemptions, which reinforced their priority status within society. Since Hồ Chí Minh's call of 1951, the government stepped up its measures regarding these families.[23] Agrarian reform cadres sped up the classification of deaths, sometimes committing errors in the process. Registering families helped identify those who were eligible for a posthumous certificate, and also allowed the government to determine the level of pension they were to receive, based on a national scale.

Classification of the dead was also essential for local cadres, who needed to accurately assess how much communal land should be reserved for the families of martyrs. The government's remuneration policy for its fallen patriots included the allocation of pensions, certificates, and medals. By classifying bereaved families, each province was able to identify the needy families in its jurisdiction. Since February 1947, the DRV had established a pay scale for both disability allowance and pensions for martyrs' families. The scale was updated in 1956 (Directive No. 980/Ttg of 27 July 1956) and again in 1959 (Directive No. 445/Ttg of 14 December 1959). The government granted pensions to families of: martyrs, those who died during the war, and cadres, workers and other patriots who had died or gone missing since 19 August 1945. The deceased had to have served a minimum number of years in service to the State (military, government, government-assisted organisations, etc.). The text specified that if the deceased had worked less than three years, the martyr's family could receive only a temporary pension. If he had worked for more than three years,

[22] *Báo cáo của Ban liên lạc Nông dân toàn quốc* (Report from the national peasant liaison bureau), in AVN3, BTB, file no. 71a, unnumbered document, 10 July 1954, p. 6.

[23] In 1952, a document by provincial authorities specified that they must "first bring disabled veterans back to their villages, especially those who could work or had special abilities". See *Báo cáo về việc ngày Thương binh liệt sĩ Tử sĩ từ đầu năm 1951 ở Quảng Trị* (Activity report on the day of disabled veterans and martyrs in 1951 in Quảng Trị), in AVN3, BTB, file no. 22, document no. 749, 2 April 1952.

the government support (pension or basic living expenses) would be more long-term (one year, renewable every year). The pension could not be paid until after the certificate of patriotism had been issued. How much support a family received depended on their economic circumstances, and government aid could last from three months to one year, and was renewable. The Ministry cautioned against monthly disbursements (often made directly in kind), and suggested that the aid be distributed three times per year. The distribution took place during Vietnamese holidays (traditional festivals and patriotic holidays).

Since the end of the war, pensions came out of the provincial budget, but authorities frequently had to ask the central government for help due to a lack of funds. Financial aid from multiple sources was not allowed (from both the commune and the province, for example), and families who lost more than one person were not allowed to receive more than a certain amount (set at thirty *dông* per month in 1962). For example, a peasant "father of a martyr" who was too old to work was paid 7.5 *dông* per month by the cooperative of his commune in 1962. In theory, he could not receive additional support from the State. In practice, however, if the communal authorities deemed it necessary, they could grant him additional aid "to help him get by". In this way, pensions were often accompanied by financial aid from the commune. Land reform had also authorised the redistribution of village land to exemplary citizens and their families. In 1963, land redistribution campaigns were carried out in Mỹ Hào district (Nghệ An province). Official documents refer to more than 1,000 *mẫu* (about 3,600 m^2, or slightly less than one acre) of arable land that was shared between the deserving families of the area. Local governments had been told to highlight these exemplary households back in 1957–59 during the creation of village cooperatives, and the cooperative's management committee played a key role in disseminating these policies. Families of the dead or disabled had to set an example for the rest of the village. The People's Committee gave extra points to families who joined cooperatives, and communal cadres came by in the winter to bring them warm clothes. Cooperatives were also responsible for feeding the children of martyrs and distributing extra rations of rice to needy families. This communal aid was in addition to the funds issued by the State two or three times a year. By funding pensions, the central government proved its filial devotion to the people, while aid on the communal level showed the local government's responsibility and duty toward its disadvantaged citizens.

After 1951, campaigns encouraged disabled veterans to return to their villages and promised aid for their reintegration into the economy and community in exchange for "good patriotic behaviour".[24] This basically meant preferential treatment by the local government. The People's Committee of Hải Thành (Quảng Trị province), for example, gave a six-*mẫu* rice paddy and a water buffalo to their returning veterans to help them get back to work, and their files were given priority during emulation campaigns. In 1953–54, the village of Hoàng Khai (Tuyên Quang province) only nominated disabled veterans for the title of agricultural emulation fighter. Positions within the local government were reserved for disabled veterans and members of "martyrs' families". The government encouraged these practices. They followed the track record of each family, their ranking in the hierarchy of bereaved homes, and what type of aid they had already received. The government read their medical records (the Ministry of Martyrs and Disabled Veterans had created an "injury scale" for this purpose) and then decided whether to promote them, send them to a convalescent home, or sign them up for further education. From 1950 to 1960, the DRV offered model citizens "who had special skills, a good outlook, and the desire to serve the people, the revolution and socialism" the chance to pursue higher education. The children of martyrs and disabled veterans were automatically exempted from paying tuition and received a stipend based on their financial situation.[25] In the countryside, the Party encouraged them to pursue further training and the Ministry of the Interior urged every level of the government to "help the children of martyrs find work".

The impact of this preferential treatment on the cohesion of the Vietnamese village was subject to numerous confidential reports. In 1958, a report by the Provincial People's Committee of Lào Cai criticised the excesses of the exemption policy at the village level: "If we continue this way, we risk creating serious rivalries between the cadres of the commune. Classification operations will then become a very delicate affair."[26] In Mỹ Lâm (Yên Sơn, Tuyên Quang), for example, 85 per cent of the village

---

[24] Hồ Chí Minh. "Thư gửi các thương binh tại mặt trận Trung du và Đông Bắc" (Letter to disabled veterans at the Central and Northern front), in *Toàn tập* (1951–54), vol. VI. Hanoi: nxb Sự thật, 1986, p. 46.

[25] In 1965–66, Minister of Education Tạ Quang Bửu (1910–1986) even proposed giving martyrs' children extra points on their university exams (1 to 2 *diêm*).

[26] *Báo cáo về phổ biến điều lệ huy động và sử dụng dân công hội nghị của tỉnh* (Report on spreading the rules of mobilisation and making use of the provincial conference on collective work sessions), in AVN3, BLD, file no. 414, document 939/DC (UBND Lao Cai), 7 June 1958.

(population of 1,185) was exempt from corvée obligations as a result of the "martyr policy".[27] Although the accusations were mainly against communal cadres who took advantage of the exemptions themselves, these reports primarily blamed excesses in the classification campaigns. Errors were committed during the campaign to rectify land reform in 1956–57, but mistakes like these were common in a rural society. Fighting the foreign invader was a good impetus to mobilise the population during the Franco-Viet Minh war, but the construction of socialism was far more abstract in the peasant mentality. The government ensured its presence and control over the people through the material encouragement of its most loyal citizens (honours, pensions, exemptions, etc.):

> Throughout history the Vietnamese people have been stimulated by self-interest. Material gain is a natural motivating force in a poor country. It was hard to satisfy the people so we had to try different things. We couldn't ask as much of them in peacetime (1955–1964) as we could during the war, since honour and patriotic selflessness were much weaker then, so material interest could help us enhance these moments.[28]

Socialism was no longer just an abstraction but offered a real improvement in the standard of living to those loyal to the nation.

The Day of Martyrs and Disabled Veterans

In June 1947, the DRV designated 27 July as a new holiday dedicated to martyrs and disabled veterans. Hồ Chí Minh made the symbolic gesture of giving one month's salary to disabled veterans. July 27 would be the image of a new national solidarity, as he explained: "You know I have no children. The Vietnamese nation is my family. All young Vietnamese are actually my children. When one of them dies, it's as if I have lost someone in my own family. They die so that our homeland can live forever;

---

[27] Among them were 50 ethnic Chinese (Hoa Kiều), 756 children/adolescents (below 17 years old) and the elderly, 164 disabled veterans, heads of martyrs' families, or working cadres. See *Tập tài liệu phổ biến học tập điều lệ dân công của khu, tỉnh năm 1958* (Documents on the adoption of the rules of collective work sessions in zones and provinces in 1958), in AVN3, BLD, file no. 414, document no. 343 (autonomous zone of Việt Bắc), 19 March 1958.

[28] Interview, Hanoi.

their souls will live forever in the spirit of Vietnam."[29] The martyr was the glue that held the nation together, and 27 July would keep the martyr's spirit alive in the minds of the people. Each level of government was to "encourage, praise the accomplishments of disabled veterans and martyrs' families, and applaud them whenever they take part in the movement". Through this patriotic fellowship honouring the dead, the government counted on winning people over to its political agenda.

In May 1947, the Ministry of Martyrs and Disabled Veterans sent information to all provincial People's Committees in the country on how to organise this new national day of remembrance. Provincial cadres "oversaw the district and communal committees to help them successfully carry out this highly important task".[30] In mid-June, communal People's Committees held talks with villagers to explain the nature of this new patriotic holiday. A collection was then taken up in each commune to buy gifts for needy families. Both the national and provincial press published special issues on the subject, the radio broadcast the central government's text on air, and provincial cultural departments created cultural shows and events.

In 1948, short patriotic emulation sessions were scheduled to bring the organisation to a close on time. Meanwhile, communal cadres and representatives of mass organisations had to study official documents after work. Provincial authorities prepared rewards and gifts for the participants, and local artists and performers were called upon to put on shows. In early July, plays, songs, and exhibits were presented to explain the importance of the new holiday. In July 1952, in Tuyên Quang, mass organisations from the province attracted more than 1,200 people for a painting exhibition held by the provincial artistic department. The Ministry of Martyrs and Disabled Veterans felt this was insufficient, however, and were afraid that the low turn-out "could potentially have a negative influence on

---

[29] Hồ Chí Minh. *Toàn tập* (1948–50) (Complete works), vol. IV. Hanoi: nxb Sự Thật, 1984, pp. 24–5.

[30] A document from the People's Committee of Thái Nguyên province shows that in 1951 four of the districts in the area had in fact established organisation committees in time: Phú Bình (26 June), Đại Từ (30 June), Minh Hóa (5 July), and Định Hóa (5 July), in AVN3, file no. 22, document no. 38, Thái Nguyên, 17 January 1952. As for the Việt Bắc, the provinces of Hải Ninh, Hồng Gai, Lào Cai, Sơn La, Tuyên Quang, and Vĩnh Phú still had not formed organisation committtees by 30 September 1951, in AVN3, file no. 22, document no. 38, Thái Nguyên, unnumbered document LK/VB, January 1952.

the masses". At the village level, mass organisations coordinated the activities.The children of *Thiếu Nhi* [Young Pioneers] sang songs honouring the nation's patriots in their hamlets, waving banners bearing the national campaign slogan: "Remember martyrs and be grateful to disabled veterans."[31] On 27 July they went around to every home to collect money, goods, or clothing to hand out to bereaved families.[32] Teen members of the *Thanh Niên* also took part in this patriotic remodelling of inter-generational solidarity. They were divided into groups and put in charge of maintaining cemeteries, memorials, and martyrs' graves. Communal leaders attached great importance to this maintenance and restoration. Women's Associations and the "Mothers of Combatants" were also mobilised to visit the families of martyrs and disabled veterans to "comfort them and show them that the State and the Party cared about them". These pioneering women encouraged the villagers to write — or, more often, to have someone write for them — letters to active-duty soldiers and sponsor soldiers who were far from home. Finally, the Peasants' Association urged its members to go to the rice paddies of those who had suffered a loss and help them with their work.[33] To thank the State for its help, bereaved families pledged their loyalty to the Party in return.

Martyrs and Disabled Veterans Day took root slowly in North Vietnam. Despite encouragement from government ministries, annual reports from local authorities reported delays. In the isolated and mountainous areas of the country, local officials "faced many difficulties in organising the

---

[31] The province provided them with posters, tracts, and banners. On 27 July 1951, for example, the province of Quảng Trị distributed 1,000 small posters bearing the campaign slogan, 7,600 tracts with songs for martyrs, 1,000 copies of official texts, 500 appeals from the province, and 20,000 patriotic tracts, in AVN3, BTB, file no. 22, document no. 749, 2 April 1952.

[32] For 27 July 1951, the amounts collected in the Việt Bắc varied by province: Cao Bằng: 4,479,774 *dông*; Lạng Sơn: 5,580,774; Phú Thọ: 1,350,982; Tuyên Quang: 1,558,401; Thái Nguyên: 7,581,152; Bắc Ninh: 1,762,450; Hồng Gai: 55,950; Lào Cai: 2,851,660; Quảng Yên: 2,825,790; Vĩnh Phú: 394,400; Yên Bái: 549,161; and Hà Giang: 1,798,098. *Báo cáo ngày 27.7.1951 Liên khu Việt Bắc* (Report on 27 July 1951 in the zone of the Việt Bắc) in AVN3, BTB, file no. 22, document no. 674 YB/5, 5 April 1952.

[33] Reports by the district People's Committees show the limits of the campaign. In the province of Hải Dương in 1954, for example, the mother of a newly decorated martyr found herself alone with eight *sâu* of rice paddy to cultivate. With no-one to help her, she had to hire a day-worker. The writer of the report implies that this was due to a lack of social support available to martyrs' families. See *Báo cáo về ngày 27.7.1961* (Report on 27 July 1961), in AVN3, BTH, file no. 71a, document no. 34/HD, 1954.

new movement of solidarity as per national guidelines".[34] In Bắc Giang, in 1954, provincial groups in charge of the holiday in the villages of Tân Hiên and Tân Hiệp were discouraged: "There still isn't any real awareness in these communes, and it's often hard to find people to help organise the structures we are trying to create."[35] But every June, each province selected representatives among the families of martyrs and disabled veterans and sent them to the national conference, organised and attended by members of the Politburo and the government.[36] In 1955, a newly created Provincial Committee for Reunification was tasked with choosing exemplary families and sending the list to the central government. These families were given financial support (to cover their transport costs, food, and accommodation) so that they could "bring their congratulations" to President Hồ and the government on behalf of their province.[37]

Come 27 July a conference was held in each provincial capital with central government officials, the executive committees of mass organisations, Party representatives, and several new "martyrs' families". In Kiến An in 1954, 64 disabled veterans, 5 bereaved families, and 5 people from "foster families of disabled orphans" were invited. The day began with a general overview of the nation's political and economic situation and continued with the reading of patriotic poems. At Kiến An, as in all provincial capitals that year, cadres shouted out poems written in honour of national martyrs by Hồ Chí Minh, Vũ Đình Tụng (Minister for Martyrs

---

[34] *Chương trình kế hoạch công tác liệt sĩ làm thí điểm ở Mộc Châu* (Provisional programme for activities regarding martyrs in Mộc Châu), in AVN3, BNV, file no. 2248, document no. 1537, 25 October 1960.

[35] *Báo cáo về việc Tổ chức ngày Thương binh tử sĩ ở Bắc Giang* (Activity report on the organisation of the day of disabled veterans and martyrs in Bắc Giang), in AVN3, BTB, file no. 71a, document no. 227 TB/G, 23 October 1954.

[36] Provincial committees did not always live up to the Ministry's expectations. The People's Committee of Cao Bằng, for example, announced to the central government in early June 1962 that they had only chosen one family. They chose Lý Việt Đàn (from the hamlet of Nà Chấu, Độc Lập commune, Quảng Uyên district), whose son Lý Văn Mưu had died at Đông Khê in 1950 and was awarded "hero of the armed forces" in 1956. See *Thông tri về Tổ chức hội nghị Thương binh liệt sĩ* (Directive on organising the commission on disabled veterans and martyrs), in AVN3, BNV, file no. 2253, document no. 11927, 20 August 1962.

[37] AVN3, BNV, file no. 2253, document no. 03 TB/NA, December 22, 1954. A document from 1961 states that the organisational committee gave 1.20 *dông* per day to each participant (for food and lodging), on top of their transport. See AVN3, BNV, file no. 2253, document no. 349, 19 January 1961.

and Disabled Veterans), leaders of the military zone, and scholars from the local people's militia. Representatives of disabled veterans and families of martyrs were then invited to share their experiences:

> They got up to talk about their lives, about their youth, courage, and the fatherland. Nguyễn Văn Uỷ from Hùng Thắng commune took the floor first. He explained to the audience how he had been awarded the title of exemplary cadre of the first rank in 1952. He was awarded the title a second time by the district due to his volunteer work in tax collection, and again by the provincial administration in 1953. He explained that he had done it all simply because it was his duty, the duty of every disabled veteran, to take part in the Vietnamese revolutionary movement with the greatest enthusiasm.[38]

The day was organised differently around the country. At Hải Dương, the conference hosted 78 delegates from 5 of its 6 districts. 52 communes had previously organised talks that were attended by almost 4,500 people, according to official statistics. Village debates attracted a record 40 to 100 people, and the commune held nearly 555 public meetings in memory of martyrs during the month, another record. In Hà Tĩnh, however, results were not as promising. The provincial committee noted with resignation that "the July 27 program was fully applied only in Đức Thọ".[39] Note, however, that in late 1954 the Ministry of Martyrs and Disabled Veterans had only fragmentary information about what had actually taken place. In North Vietnam, only the provinces of Phú Thọ, Tuyên Quang, Thanh Hóa, Hà Tĩnh, Bắc Giang, Thái Nguyên, Hải Dương, Kiến An, Thái Bình, and Nghệ An had submitted their report on the day's events.

Back in Hanoi, the Ministry of Martyrs and Disabled Veterans drew up a schedule of official visits. In July 1959, five groups were established, including a number of senior officials, plus Hồ Chí Minh, Lê Duẩn, Deputy Prime Minister Phạm Hùng, Defence Minister Vo Nguyễn Giap, and Tôn Đức Thắng, Chairman of the Reunification Committee. Hồ's delegation visited the imposing Mai Dịch martyrs' cemetery, located a few kilometres from the capital. The second group visited a camp for the blind, a typing

---

[38] *Báo về việc Tổ chức liên hoan Thương binh và gia đình quân nhân liệt sĩ trong dịp kỷ niệm Thương binh toàn quốc* (Report on the organisation of festivities for disabled veterans and families of martyrs for the national day of remembrance for disabled veterans), in AVN3, BTB, file no. 7, document no. 3587 vx/ka, 23 October 1954.

[39] AVN3, BTB, file no. 7, document no. 3587 vx/ka, document no. 14/HT, 13 October 1954.

school for the handicapped, a military field hospital, and a boarding school for the children of martyrs in Vĩnh Phú. The third team went further east into Hải Dương province, where they met with a group of disabled farmers from the village of Đông Triều and a "martyr's family" that had been pre-selected by local authorities. The fourth delegation visited a large camp for disabled veterans located two kilometres from the town of Bắc Ninh, followed by a "martyr's family" and the family of a disabled combatant. The fifth delegation had left Hanoi the day before to visit two camps for disabled veterans, one in Thanh Hóa province (two kilometres from the village of Thanh Hóa) and the other farther west, in Vinh (Nghệ An), before ending the day with a visit to the agricultural cooperative in Lý Thanh and to the families of a martyr and a disabled veteran. The government recommended that:

> its delegations have cordial discussions with all of the disabled veterans and families they meet during their visits. They should remind them that the government expects them to do serious work and be enthusiastic in their studies. Families of disabled veterans and the elderly must also be strongly encouraged to enthusiastically take part in work production. Finally, all delegations must remember to offer small gifts and have their picture taken with their hosts.[40]

Throughout the district and the commune, cadres organised personalised visits. At the village level, People's Committees asked the members of local mass organisations to form small delegations to visit the homes of the bereaved families. At all levels, these meetings had to retain a formal character while allowing for "frank and cordial discussions that would show the people how much the VWP and the government cared about the people".[41] During their visits, delegations handed out small gifts (food, medicine, clothing, or money) to show the government's concern for them. Village cadres then went to the town cemetery to lay a wreath of flowers.

---

[40] *Kế hoạch tổ chức Đoàn đại biểu Đảng, Chính phủ và các đoàn thể Trung ương đi viếng Nghĩa trang Mai Dịch và thăm thương binh, gia đình liệt ngày 27.7.1959* (Preparation by delegations from the Party, the government, and mass organisations from the central government for visits to the cemetery of Mai Dịch and meetings with the families of disabled veterans and martyrs, 27 July 1959), in AVN3, BNV, file no. 32/TB, 18 July 1959.

[41] *Thông tri về tổ chức Ngày thương binh liệt sĩ 27.7 1954* (Circular on the organisation of the day of disabled veterans and martyrs on 27 July 1954), in AVN3, BNV, file no. 2244, document no. 9132, 13 July 1959.

Invoking the spirits of the dead was a way to glorify the families that had lost a member. Official documents explained that "it was absolutely essential to show that a family could acquire real honour within their community".[42] A wreath was placed at the foot of the central stele, then discussions were held between veterans and the young pioneers and school children of the village.[43] The government encouraged people to spend the day, or even just the afternoon, helping disabled veterans and families of martyrs "without, however, unduly neglecting their own work". In some villages, "rice for solidarity" initiatives were organised for the needy, while processions were organised in others. According to official figures, 15,000 people took part in these celebrations in Hanoi in 1962, and 3,000 seats were reserved at the cinema for disabled veterans and the families of martyrs.

The DRV took advantage of the holiday to distribute medals and patriotic certificates. In 1950, the government had created a patriotic title destined solely for the disabled, and these decorations were handed out informally as cadres made their rounds among the families. Some communes, however, made the closing proceedings of 27 July into a more solemn event. It should be recalled that families attending these public meetings were traditionally given financial compensation from the government. The practice, both common and long-standing in Vietnam, played an important role in mobilising poor families who were unaccustomed to this type of attention. The compensation was not much, but its main purpose was to show the State's homage and gratitude.[44] In 1960, the People's Committee of Hải Ninh province granted the sum of 0.30 *dông* (often paid in kind: tea, cigarettes, cakes, etc.) to those who attended meetings at the communal, district, or provincial level. Beyond the desire to be politically associated with "the right crowd", were these naturally sceptical people enticed to ever more frequent meetings — what the historian Georges

---

[42] *Báo cáo về ngày 27.7 (tỉnh Hải Dương)* (Report on 27 July, Hai Duong province), in AVN3, BNV, file no. 2244, unnumbered document, 24 October 1954.

[43] *Chỉ thị về kỷ niệm 55 năm ngày Thương binh liệt sĩ 27.7.1960* (Instructions on the day of disabled veterans and martyrs, 27 July 1960), in AVN3, BNV, file no. 2253, document no. 30 NV/TBPV, 24 May 1960.

[44] In 1960, anyone who attended a government meeting received at least 0.20 *dông* (on top of food, lodging, and transport). See *Kế hoạch kỷ niệm Thương binh liệt sĩ ở Hà Nội* (Organisation of commemorations for disabled veterans and martyrs), in AVN3, DNV, file no. 2258, unnumbered document, 9 June 1960.

Boudarel dubbed "meetingitis"[45] — for material rather than ideological reasons? These financial benefits gave rise to dependency relationships, which did not cause any moral problems to either the State or the people. The government's genius was to have normalised the traditional relation of gift/counter-gift to its advantage. The new distribution of gifts was the revenge of those who had been overlooked by the old regime and showed in a good light the relatively modest payments of the current government compared to the excesses of the past.[46] For the common people, the meeting represented a moment of communion with the political authorities during which, dressed in their finest clothes, they showed their respect for the current government. In exchange, the government affixed its counter-signature on this symbolic transfer of power via the bestowing of gifts.

Patriotic Cemeteries

In 1954, 42 per cent of the DRV's social welfare budget was spent on benefits, pensions, and the building of rest camps and cemeteries, for a total of 4.8 billion *dông*. During the Franco-Vietminh war, the term *nghĩa địa* (literally "homage to the earth") was used to designate funeral plots on public communal land. In the early 1950s, the government adopted a new term, *nghĩa trang liệt sĩ*, specifically for "martyr's cemeteries": "The term *nghĩa địa* was replaced by *nghĩa trang liệt sĩ* due to the strong cultural connotation of the latter. A *nghĩa trang liệt sĩ* commanded even greater respect. The word implied a sense of elevation, and its use somehow evoked a greater sense of the beautiful."[47] Before the outbreak of war in 1964, the Ministry for Martyrs and Disabled Veterans counted a total of 1,975 communal cemeteries, 13 "intermediate" cemeteries, and 8 cemetery complexes dedicated to the great battles of the Franco-Vietminh war.

The creation of patriotic cemeteries created two types of problems. First, who could be buried there? Could they bury someone who had not performed any heroic acts? This was all up to the central government. The Ministries of Labour and of Martyrs and Disabled Veterans — taking over from the Ministry of Rites in the old regime — were responsible for making

---

[45] Georges Boudarel, ed. *La Bureaucratie au Viêt Nam* (Bureaucracy in Vietnam). Paris: L'Harmattan, 1983.

[46] It is interesting to note that the image of the corrupt mandarin reappears in a number of literary works published in North Vietnam in the 1950s.

[47] Interview, Hanoi.

Figure 17. Monument to the Martyred Dead, Vĩnh Phú province

Figure 18. Monument to the Martyred Dead, Cao Bằng province

Figure 19. Gates of the cemetery at the Tĩnh Túc mine

Figure 20. Tomb of the labour hero Cao Lục, Nghệ An province

the selection. To this end, cadres re-examined the death certificates issued by military units for the Department of Defence. Within the context of its "reform of society", the government took charge of funerary rituals.[48] It now covered the funeral expenses of those who died for their country, which was normally a heavy financial burden. Now these families only had to send a file to the provincial People's Committee and the burial ceremony was taken care of. The government established a file to classify the bereaved family and was thus able to decide where the deceased should be buried. The second issue raised by the new patriotic cemeteries stemmed from a confrontation between the political agenda and village customs. For centuries, funeral plots were strictly demarcated on public communal land. In the early 1950s, the central government made a unilateral decision to build the martyrs' cemeteries on collective land or on land confiscated from "traitors and landlords" during agrarian reform. However, creating these "gardens of heroism" meant physically moving existing graves. The village dead had to be classified, then exhumed and reburied in the patriotic cemetery. But Vietnamese tradition imposed strict rules on the removal of a body after burial. Luckily for the government, reburial was traditionally scheduled to be carried out three years after death, whereby the body was moved from its temporary location (determined by a geomancer) to the family plot within the commune. The DRV based the success of its cemetery programme on this ritual of the "second burial" (*cải táng*):

> If the family agrees to participate in the program to relocate graves before that date, then the local government may initiate the operation. However, if they are reluctant to do so, we cannot do anything. We have to show respect for local customs. Even if there are some things we cannot accept, and it would be better to rise above costly backward customs, all we can do is explain the benefits of Directive No. 252 (22/9/1958) on the relocation of graves.[49]

The government waited until the third anniversary of the end of the war against France in 1957 to begin building martyrs' cemeteries throughout the country. The traditional local custom made this an obvious choice.

---

[48] *Sur la modification des mœurs* (On the modification of customs), in CAOM, Coll. HCI, file no. 6/36, document no. 1376, 18 August 1948.

[49] *Chỉ thị về tích cực thực hiện những công tác còn lại trong mồ mả* (Instructions for organising the remaining work to do on tombs), in AVN3, BNV, file no. 2246, document no. 22/VG, 14 October 1959.

As war with the South approached, the DRV continued to mobilise the population using a mix of individual and collective interest. In September 1963, the Ministry of Martyrs and Disabled Veterans presented an initial assessment of its policy:

> The activities put into place for families of martyrs and disabled veterans contributed greatly to increased production in the cooperatives. They encouraged their children to do their military service and support Party and State policies. Many young and older people have enrolled in new training programs. The consequences of this policy are very important for the masses and for the love of the fatherland. It is a good way to honour the revolutionary spirit of the country.[50]

To gain popular support, the North Vietnamese press contrasted the DRV's policy of national solidarity to the negligence and anarchy of the Southern regime of Ngô Đình Diệm (1955–1963). The policy on martyrs played an important role in the "mobilisation of hearts". In Vietnam, a nation that took care of its dead fulfilled a divine duty, thereby earning an inalienable virtue. As the regime slowly freed itself from the sphere of Maoist influence and as war drew near, the central government sought the best way to assert its control over the people. In the early 1960s, the DRV fortified the resistance with regiments of men and ghosts, and hordes of peasants and vengeful spirits.

---

[50] *Tập tài liệu hội nghị thương binh liệt sĩ năm 1963 của Bộ Nội vụ* (Documents related to the Ministry of the Interior's conference on disabled veterans and martyrs in 1953), in AVN3, BNV, file no. 2269, single document, October 1963.

Chapter 6

The Cult of the New Hero

> A world cannot be fictional in itself, but depends on whether one believes in it or not; the difference between reality and fiction is not objective, it is not about the thing itself, but it is within us, whether we subjectively see it as a fiction or not. The object is never unbelievable in itself and its distance from reality cannot shock us because we do not even notice it, all truths being analogical.... How could people believe in all of these legends, and did they really believe them? The question is not subjective: the modalities of belief stem from modes of possessing truth; there have been many programs of truth throughout the centuries, with different distributions of knowledge, and these programs explain the subjective degrees of intensity of belief, bad faith, and contradictions within a single individual.
>
> Paul Veyne[1]

In August 1956, South Vietnam made it a crime to be a communist. In the North, DRV leaders were carefully re-opening the debate on how to reappropriate their historical patrimony. While Western historians often point to the 1956 Hundred Flowers Movement in China[2] as a great influence in the DRV's identitary construction, these historiographical debates were an even more radical shift. North Vietnam gradually (and discretely) re-established a generational parentage that distanced itself from Beijing. The reclassification of illustrious ancestors for the sake of the nation — not just of class, as China wished — helped the DRV develop a new geography of patriotic rituals throughout the country. The veneration

[1] Paul Veyne. *Les Grecs ont-ils cru à leurs mythes?* (Did the Greeks believe their myths?). Paris: Seuil, 1983, pp. 33–9.

[2] Georges Boudarel. *Cent fleurs éclosent dans la nuit du Vietnam* (One hundred flowers bloom in the Vietnamese night). Paris: Jacques Bertoin, 1991.

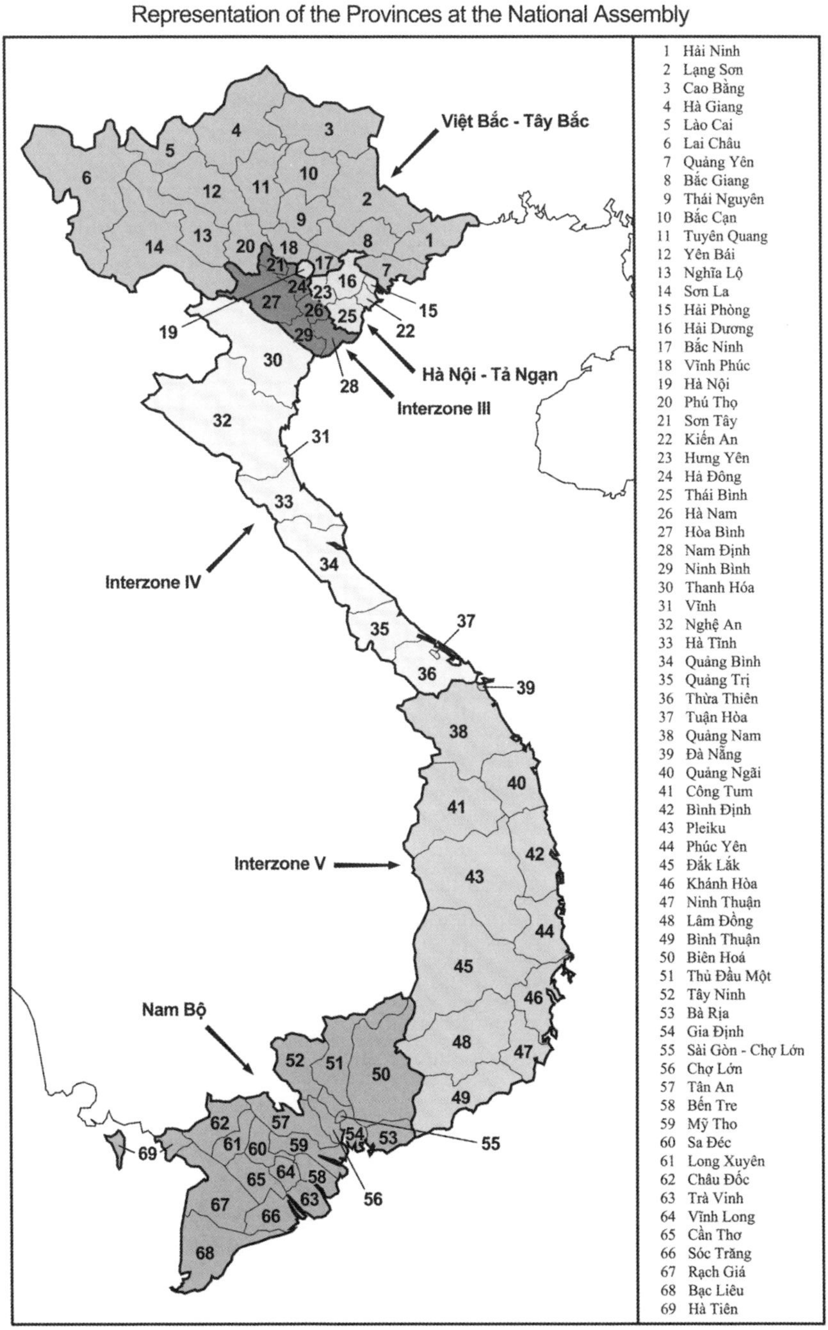

Figure 21. Map of the provinces

of "new heroes" helped strengthen the DRV's power at the village level. In the early 1960s, the State's forced march toward socialism was already faltering in some provinces. Some nervous cadres worried that these measures might divide the people in the push for patriotic mobilisation. In 1959, the guerrilla war against the South was being organised in Hanoi; in January, the fifteenth plenary session of the VWP began preparing resistance operations. With the war imminent, both the government and Party's top priority was to mobilise the population. The new hero's second career was about to begin.

Questioning National Heritage

On the eve of his army's return to Hanoi on 18 September 1954, Hồ Chí Minh assembled the soldiers from Division 308 of the PAVN in a temple dedicated to the Hùng kings not far from the capital. Under the auspices of these mythical ancestors, the president reminded his men: "The need to liberate, rebuild, and defend our country is still very strong and very important. The Hùng kings did great things for our country, but we have the same duty to protect our country together."[3] The Hùng kings, like the Trưng sisters (?–43), Mai Thúc Loan [Mai Hắc Đế] (?–722), Ngô Quyền (896–944), Lý Thái Tổ (1010–1028), Lý Thường Kiệt (1030–1105), Trần Hưng Đạo (1228–1300), Lê Lợi (1384–1433), Nguyễn Trãi (1380–1442), Nguyễn Huệ (1752–1792), and Phan Đình Phùng (1847–1895) were the glorious ancestors of the Vietnamese fatherland, a nation which had just defeated France in the muddy stronghold of Điện Biên Phủ in May 1954. With the return of peace, government ideologues reoriented official historiography toward the eternal principle of Vietnam's "tradition of resistance against the foreign aggressor". In the spring of 1955, the historian Trần Huy Liệu (1901–1969) wrote in the history journal *Văn Sử Địa* that historians had been told to valorise "the fighting spirit of the Vietnamese people in order to protect the nation's independence and peace".[4] The previous

[3] Dương Trung Quốc. "Bác ở Đền Hùng — đính chính một sai sót" (Uncle Ho in the temple of the Hùng kings — Corrections on some inaccuracies), *Xưa và Nay*, Hanoi, no. 27, May 1996: 4.

[4] Trần Huy Liệu. "Tinh thần đấu để bảo vệ v hoà bình của dân tộc Việt Nam" (The spirit of the struggle to defend and bring peace to the Vietnamese people), *Văn Sử Địa*, no. 6, March–April 1955: 1–8. See also Phạm Văn Đồng. *Our Struggle is in the Past and at Present*. Hanoi: FLPH, 1955.

year, Hồ Chí Minh had strongly opposed a campaign to destroy the historical sites and monuments in Nghệ An during a visit by the agrarian reform teams. The DRV was not to erase its past. For centuries, Vietnam had turned to its glorious past to combat the cultural, political, and military weight of its Chinese neighbour;[5] they had no intention of changing this tactic. Maoist China was still a delicate subject for the DRV, following the strategic disagreement between Võ Nguyên Giáp and his Chinese adviser, General Wei Guoqing, after the battle of Điện Biên Phủ. And in the spring of 1954, the DRV had very delicately negotiated with Beijing for the departure of several detachments of the Chinese Communist army stationed on the Vietnamese side of the border, from Hải Ninh province to the rich coal mines of Hồng Gai.[6] Evidently, relations between China and Vietnam was already showing signs of strain well before the Sino-Soviet rupture of 1959.

In his speech at Tuyên Quang in May 1952, Trường Chinh had already stressed Vietnam's deep commitment to its own national values before the Chinese advisors present.[7] DRV leaders gave assurances to their new allies but without much conviction. In December 1953, the Central Committee of the Party formed a "committee for literature, history, and geographical research"[8] to reinforce the continuity of Vietnamese history over the universality and historical discontinuity desired by Maoist ideologues. Leaders in Hanoi discussed and interpreted Chinese texts, while the intelligentsia spoke of this "new history with the age-old quest for unity and independence".[9] This new historiographical trend reinforced the

[5] Nguyễn Thành Hùng. "Der Mythos von den Hung-Köningen und das Nationale Selbsverstandnis der Vietnamesen" (The myth of the Hùng kings and national self-image in Vietnam), *Verfassung und Recht in Ubersee*, Hamburg, no. 3, Fall 1979: 250.

[6] CAOM, Coll. HCI, file no. 245/718, document no. 11162, 27 December 1951.

[7] Trường Chinh. *Thi đua ái quốc và chủ nghĩa anh hùng mới* (Patriotic emulation and the new heroism). Việt Bắc: Nha Tuyên truyền và Văn nghệ, 1953.

[8] Văn Tạo and Nguyễn Quang Ân, eds. *Ban Văn Sử Địa 1953–1959* (Committee of the journal *Văn Sử Địa,* 1953–1959). Hanoi: History Institute, 1993.

[9] In 1954, the journal *Văn Sử Địa* published an article by the Chinese theorist Tiễn Bá Tán entitled, "Một vài vấn đề trong việc bình luận nhân vật lịch sử" (Some problems in evaluating historic figures) (*Văn Sử Địa*, no. 3, 1954: 58–70). It was re-issued in 1961 by the journal *Nghiên cứu Lịch sử* in a slightly modified version as "Một vấn đề trong việc đánh giá nhân vật lịch sử" (*Nghiên cứu Lịch sử*, no. 25, April 1961: 34–40.). In 1962 the Ministry of Culture also published the essay by the Chinese writers Trân Hoang Môi and Lâm Sam on the construction of the new man in the arts (*Sáng tạo con người mới trong điện ảnh*, 1962).

myth of the "great Vietnamese family, united and indivisible". In 1958, a National Committee for the History of the Party was established along with branches on the local level, completing the framework. Intellectuals were asked to write local chronicles (at the provincial, district, and commune levels) linking the fate of the local to that of the nation. The committee wanted to show that the communist movement had spread spontaneously in all provinces since the 1930s, and that throughout the nation, local Party cadres and young heroic figures inspired by its ideals played a key role in the resistance against the French at the local level. The young age of the heroic figures reinforced the virtue of the Party's ideology. In 1961, Nguyễn Lam wrote in the journal *Học tập* (*Studies*): "The only examples for our youth are the [new] heroes Lý Tự Trọng, Hoàng Tôn, Võ Thị Sáu, Trần Văn Ơn, Bế Văn Đàn, Phan Đình Giót, Cù Chinh Lan and Mạc Thị Bưởi."[10]

But even the presence of these worthy individuals could not adequately address the increasing identity crisis caused by the partition of Vietnam in 1954. To gain the support of the 50,000 Party members scattered throughout the South, they had to put more emphasis on the sacrifice of these young heroes and encourage them to join "the progressive forces that had taken refuge in the North". The cult of heroic ancestors was an important part of the mobilisation of minds in the South, where people were less receptive to internationalist rhetoric. All Vietnamese, from the North to the South, from the plains to the remote mountainous areas, or even those living abroad, believed in the same founding myths.

In the inter-war years, "the history of resistance and/or the resistance of history" was key in the establishment of power in North Vietnam. A reinterpretation of national symbols did not necessarily mean a return to the nation's essence. Historians were reinterpreting the heroism of national figures within the context of a universal and collectivist approach that was "faithful to the principles of Marxism-Leninism".[11] A key text by the

[10] Nguyễn Lam. "Giáo dục chủ nghĩa Cộng sản cho thanh niên" (Teaching communism to our youth), *Học Tập*, Hanoi, no. 5, 1961: 38.

[11] From 1954–56 a number of articles were published: Trần Huy Liệu, "Vai trò lịch sử của Trần Quốc Tuấn" (The historical role of Trần Quốc Tuấn), *Văn Sử Địa*, no. 10, September 1955: 8–17; Trần Đức Thảo, "Tìm hiểu giá trị văn chương cũ" (Re-examining the value of our ancient culture), *Văn Sử Địa*, March 1954: 27–39; and Nguyễn Minh, "Ôn lại khởi nghĩa của Hai Bà Trưng" (Remember the uprising of the Trưng sisters), *Văn Sử Địa*, February 1955: 48–59.

Chinese ideologue Chen Boda[12] (translated by Văn Tạo) served as theoretical cover for the campaign to reinstate figures from their national heritage. Writing about China, Chen harshly criticised historians and ideologues who continued to judge "the personalities of yesterday with today's eyes".[13] The Vietnamese advocated a re-evaluation of past heroes using the historical conditions of their time. But could a progressivist society venerate a landowning hero from the feudal era in the same way as an internationalist one? Intellectuals of the DRV answered this question without hesitation: "Yes, because both helped to protect the country and that is objectively of higher importance." How did Maoist ideologues react to the nationalism of the DRV's new historiography? For the Chinese, according to Chen Boda, "the spirit is the same, but the model is different." Vietnam's relationship to the past did not exclude loyalty to the essence of the Chinese culture and race:

> Should we now study the example of Yue Fei and Zheng Chenggong? Of course. Yes, because in these men's work we find an old Chinese cultural tradition. But our time is no longer that of Yue Fei or Zheng Chenggong; the political conduct, actions, and creations that we demand of our writers today are not those of the time of Yue Fei, and the spirit of resistance is no longer that of Zheng Chenggong's time. Everything the writer of today needs to study can be found among the workers-farmers-soldiers because they possess an exemplary good political conduct and spirit of resistance.[14]

In Asia, the feudal hero was granted a reprieve due to his participation in the nation's glorious past. In China, however, his exemplary character did not give him the right to be a model for society.

The historical hero was portrayed as the essence of a people or a race, but Maoists believed that Marxism-Leninism, while not denying a particular historical patrimony, implied a rupture. This approach was not as

---

[12] Chen Boda (1904–1989) was an intellectual from the Chinese Communist Party, private secretary to Mao Zedong during the campaign of rectification in the early 1940s, and member of the Propaganda Department of the Central Committee of the CCP. He played a key role during the first years of the revolution but was later accused of leftism and lost his position in 1969.

[13] Nguyễn Đổng Chi. "Ý nghĩa truyện Chử Đồng Tử" (The meaning of the story of Chử Đồng Tử), *Văn Sử Địa*, May 1956: 53.

[14] Tiễn Bá Tán. "Một vài vấn đề trong việc bình luận nhân vật lịch sử" (Some problems in evaluating historic figures), *Văn Sử Địa*, no. 3, 1954: 68.

easily accepted in Vietnam, where "the new heroes are direct descendants of ancient figures, as they too transmit the glorious spirit of our people. We cherish today's heroes as a way of paying respect to the great figures of the past."[15] The position taken here by Trần Huy Liệu, the most influential North Vietnamese historian and ideologue of the new historiographical approach, differed from that of Chen Boda. According to the latter, the break with the past was the result of a "superiority of the social logic of the toiling masses". Trần Huy Liệu would never go that far. When he wondered, in October 1955, how the Vietnam of the 1950s could use the heroic example of Trần Quốc Tuấn (thirteenth century), Liệu chose historic analogy rather than the logic of rupture. Trần Quốc Tuấn was a profoundly Vietnamese figure, he wrote, which gave the DRV the certainty "to free itself from the yoke of American imperialism, from enemies and present dangers in order to achieve the reunification of the country".[16] The reinterpretation of the Trưng sisters' revolt by the historian Nguyễn Minh in February 1955 reaffirmed the independence of this Vietnamese approach from the principles of Chen Boda. He first denied any Chinese involvement in the rebellion, then wrote that:

> The revolt of the Trưng sisters ultimately teaches us many lessons for the patriotic struggle of today. In other words, history tells us clearly that we want to liberate our country and we want to strengthen society in order to provide the means to fight against invaders. Remembering the actions of our two popular heroines, Trưng Trắc and Trưng Nhị, strengthens our genuine patriotism and spirit of internationalism.[17]

In the 1950s in North Vietnam, intellectuals agreed to follow the approach of Chen Boda in which a historical figure was judged according to an anachronic ideological grid (class origin), but they refused to adopt the Maoist principle of a hierarchy of the heroic figures of the past and the new proletarian or peasant hero of today. The hero kept his place as intercessor between the people and the State; he was the regime's spokesman for "celestial legitimacy". His reinterpretation facilitated a dynastic change. Rather than representing the popular masses, the Vietnamese hero was

---

[15] Trần Huy Liệu. "Vai trò lịch sử của Trần Quốc Tuấn" (Trần Quốc Tuấn's role in history), *Văn Sử Địa*, no. 10, September 1955: 16.

[16] Ibid., p. 17.

[17] Nguyễn Minh. "Ôn lại khởi nghĩa của Hai Bà Trưng" (Remember the uprising of the Trưng sisters), *Văn Sử Địa*, February 1955: 50.

positioned as their teacher. The rupture desired by the new internationalist framework was diverted in favour of a cultural logic. The re-evaluation of the historical figure helped displace the heroes of Tuyên Quang in favour of those issued from a long historical tradition.

The Patriotic Calendar

Creating new patriotic holidays was an important step for the DRV in reclaiming its patriotic imaginary. Propaganda and the mobilisation of the masses also made it an urgent matter. A cult of the nation was established throughout the country via ceremonies dedicated to a united and common past. The DRV had entered a new era, however, and the imprint of internationalism was impossible to ignore. A fifteenth-century uprising lent the government a valuable source of legitimacy for launching socialism across the country. Similarly, commemorating the thirteenth-century hero Trần Quốc Tuấn became a way for leaders to warn people against the dangers posed by the Southern regime to territorial unity:

> Trần Quốc Tuấn is no longer with us, but his name lives on. The generation of Lê Lợi and Nguyễn Trãi in the fifteenth century, of Nguyễn Huệ in the eighteenth century, and of Hồ Chí Minh today continue the glorious deeds of Trần Quốc Tuấn. On this day in remembrance of Trần Quốc Tuấn, as the people of our nation prepare to fight for the reunification of the fatherland, they raise their eyes from the map of the country and wonder why we don't follow the footsteps of Trần Thiêm Bình and Lê Chiêu Thống to liberate the South, which is being oppressed by American imperialism and the clique of Ngô Đình Diệm.[18]

The new patriotic calendar was supposed to promote the continuity of the DRV's historical patrimony. Following the Geneva Accords of 1954, the government established three types of holidays: for the nation's history, for historic and patriotic national heroes, and for the holidays of brother nations. The dates were listed in order of importance. There were initially four days of remembrance "of the first order": 1 May (International Workers' Day), 19 August (the anniversary of the August Revolution of 1945), 2 September (National Independence Day), and 22 December (the founding of the PAVN in 1944). There were eight holidays "of the second

[18] *Speech for the commemorative ceremony in honor of Trần Quốc Tuấn*, in AVN3, BVH, file no. 936, document no. 2021, vh/vt, 26 December 1959.

order": 3 March (founding of the VWP, 1951), 7 May (victory of Điện Biên Phủ, 1954), 20 July (Geneva Agreement, 1954), 27 July (Day of Martyrs and Disabled Veterans), 23 September (the Nam Bộ revolt, 1945), 23 November (the Nam Kỳ uprising, 1940), and 19 December (beginning of the Resistance, 1946). The Ministry of Culture added a few days dedicated to the great figures of the "defence against foreign aggressors" but did not, however, grant them the status of second order. They organised the anniversary of Quang Trung's victory at Đống Đa (1789) on 12 February, the memory of Đề Thám (a.k.a. Hoàng Hoa Thám, 1913) on 10 February, the Trưng sisters on 14 March, the Hùng kings on 17 April, Ngô Quyền on 17 September , Trần Quốc Tuấn on 22 October, Lê Lợi on 24 October, Phan Đình Phùng (1894) on 26 October, and Nguyễn Tri Phương (1873) on 20 November.

The DRV then decided to add some more contemporary figures who were directly tied to the history of the Indochinese Communist Party. From then on, every 24 May the country would commemorate the memory of Hoàng Văn Thụ (1906–1944), the resistant fighter from Lạng Sơn, and 5 September was dedicated to Trần Phú (1904–1931), first secretary of the ICP. Unlike the holidays for historical heroes, the latter came directly under the propaganda section of the VWP, not the Ministry of Culture. Assigning responsibility for these various holidays was an important matter. In 1957, a Ministry directive decided who was to be in charge. The VWP was assigned its own commemoration (initially 3 March, then 3 February) and holidays in honour of Karl Marx (5 May), Hoàng Văn Thụ, and Trần Phú. The government was responsible for Labour Day (1 May), the anniversary of the August Revolution (19 August), and Independence Day (2 September); the Fatherland Front for the anniversary of the start of the anti-French resistance (19 December), as well as the revolts of Nam Bộ and Nam Kỳ; the Department of Defence took over the commemoration of the Geneva Accords and the anniversary of the founding of the PAVN (22 December); the Committee for Scientific Studies took on the celebrations of Hoàng Hoa Thám and Phan Đình Phùng; ceremonies conducted in the memory of all historical figures (Lê Lợi, Hai Bà Trưng, and Trần Hưng Đạo) were entrusted to the Ministry of Culture; and finally, the Vietnamese Committee for World Peace was put in charge of days honouring foreign dignitaries.

Established right after the end of the war, the new patriotic calendar reunified the national imaginary by linking the major stages of the nation's historical heritage. According to the historian John Kleinen, this juxtaposition allowed the Marxist government to "reinvent a tradition for its own ends".[19] The reinterpretation of the role and nature of the nation's ancestors announced a reappropriation by the new regime of its historical heritage. With the return of peace, the government enacted legislation that banned the sale of antiquities without government authorisation and encouraged the protection of national heritage: "Our patrimony belongs to the people. It is vital that we protect these monuments for science, society, history and the culture of the nation."[20] Provincial committees were endowed with departments of cultural affairs, responsible for the registration of all historical relics in the country. The Franco-Vietminh war had provided the framework for a new local politics of commemoration.

In January 1956, the new cultural department of Lang Son province conducted a survey of the area and added a series of propositions for new memorials from its "new history". Local cadres suggested that they erect a statue of the revolutionary Hoàng Văn Thụ in the centre of Lạng Sơn prefecture. Thụ was important because he was a local man who had fought to defend his land; the fact that he was a Party member and fought for his country was of secondary importance. The VWP played upon these intersecting imaginaries in order to better control them. Despite the many demands coming in from the provinces, the central government preferred not to get involved. Vietnamese communist leaders had, after all, chosen the path of socialism along with their brother nations, so had to adhere to a particular binary reading of history. By 1960, the rupture between Moscow and Beijing was complete. The DRV took advantage of China's unstable domestic political situation to accelerate its subtle ideological emancipation from the PRC. Throughout Vietnam's history, periods of reform had always come about in times of weakness of the tutelary power. The DRV carried out a delicate balancing act between the two great socialist powers while cautiously reintegrating a nationalist strain at the heart of its discourse.

As the war approached, educating and training the masses became a top priority. By placing themselves at the head of a glorious genealogy, North Vietnamese leaders were better able to discuss foreign concepts with peasants unused to ideas from abroad. They waited until April 1963, however, to finally endorse the policy that they had been secretly pursuing for years: the government formally took control of the historical patrimony of

[19] J. Kleinen. "Facing the Future, Reviving the Past: Village and Ritual in Northern Vietnam", in Bernhard Dahm and Naimah Talib, eds, *Religious Revival in Contemporary Southeast Asia*. Singapore: ISEAS, 1997.

[20] AVN3, BVH, file no. 959, document no. 165 VH/VD, 2 February 1960.

a unified Vietnam in the name of the VWP. They drew up a list of figures who could be used in new street names, squares, parks, towns, and villages throughout the country. Public figures from the past and the present, as endorsed by the Party and the State, were now on equal footing. The directive recommended removing the names of "colonialists, imperialists, traitors to the nation of Vietnam, representatives of the exploiting class, and mandarins"[21] and replacing them with those of Party leaders, revolutionary martyrs, and reformist heroes. Provinces were given lists of suitable names and events generated jointly by the Departments of the Interior and Culture along with the Historical Institute. If any events directly linked to the local heritage of the province were missing, provincial authorities had to immediately inform the central government to look into the missing information. Cadres had to utilise local figures while also including a balanced representation from Southerners, ethnic minorities, and women. At the communal, district, and provincial levels, lists were prepared by local cadres who were asked to explain "in simple terms" the central government's reasons behind their choices. In 1963, historical continuity was achieved between the 45 "historic" figures (from Bà Triệu to Lý Thường Kiệt, Phạm Hồng Thái, and Nguyễn Thái Học) and the small band of heroes plucked from the progressivist or communist resistance (Trần Phú, Lý Tự Trọng, Kim Đồng, and Mạc Thị Bưởi, for example). In some cases, the Ministry of the Interior authorised a name change in honour of new heroes, sometimes while they were still alive. There was a fusion between the ruling power and geographical space. Place names such as Quốc Trị (hero, 1952), Trường Chinh (Deputy Prime Minister), and Quốc Việt (Attorney General of the DRV), and neighbourhoods such as La Văn Cầu (hero, 1952) and Nguyễn Thị Chien (hero, 1952) sprang up throughout the nation. In the early 1960s, however, the movement only affected a limited number of communes, but it confirmed the villagers' belief in the protective power of a heroic spirit. In the past, Vietnamese peasants worshipped a god of the earth who brought good fortune to the whole community. Implicitly, the directive of April 1963 occupied the space left vacant since the years of agrarian reform. The land of the nation's ancestors and martyrs ensured as before the protection of its souls and spirits; the North Vietnamese

---

[21] *Quy định chi tiết thi hành Chỉ thị số 23 Tlg ngày 15.4.1963 của PTT về việc sửa đổi và đặt tên vườn hoa, quân trường, tên xã, thôn và thị trấn* (On the renaming of public spaces and parks, factories, communes, hamlets, and towns), in AVN3, Coll. du BNV, file no. 1886, document no. 17 LB/NV-VH, 1963.

commune clung to its new "guardian spirits" to confront the tense times leading up to the resumption of war. This State approval slowly gave birth to a patriotic cultural geography.

Types of "New Spirits"

The new geography of patriotic rituals included three types of heroes: early leaders of the ICP, heroic figures from the anti-colonialist era (1925–1952), and the imported "new hero".

Most new ritual sites were dedicated to ICP leaders (or of the *Thanh Niên* before that) who were active from 1920 to 1940. Provincial cadres chose figures of national import (Ngô Gia Tự, Nguyễn Văn Cừ, Trần Phú, Lê Hồng Phong, Hà Huy Tập, Hoàng Văn Thụ, and Hồ Tùng Mậu) and others from the local scene (Phạm Quang Lịch in Thái Bình, Nguyễn Đức Cảnh in Hải Phòng, and Hoàng Đình Dong in Cao Bằng). Thái Bình province inaugurated a House of Remembrance to Phạm Quang Lịch in the town of Đình Phùng (Kiến Xương district) in an effort to symbolically link local history to that of the State, with its victory over "foreign invaders". Phạm Quang Lịch (1901–1937) had served as secretary of the ICP in Thái Bình in 1935–36 and was a key figure in the provincial revolutionary movement, so the day took on special significance as part of the the Party's "glorious resistance nationwide". Further north in the area of Lạng Sơn-Cao Bằng, local authorities took similar steps. The provinces of Lạng Sơn and Cao Bằng were home to the first revolutionary groups in the 1920s–1930s and gave birth to a host of revolutionary figures. Cadres from the two provinces followed the Party's propaganda recommendations to the letter, matching a national figure with a local one. The illustrious Hoàng Văn Thụ (1906–1944) was honoured with two memorials by the province (one built in his hometown, which now bore his name, and the other in the centre of the village of Sơn La). He was paired with the cadre Lương Văn Chi, former resistance fighter from the Bắc Sơn uprising of 1940, who was celebrated in his home commune of Văn Quan (Bắc Sơn). Cao Bằng commemorated Hoàng Đình Dong, the province's first major revolutionary, born in the commune of Đề Thám (Hòa An district),[22] and

[22] Trần Phượng. "đc Hoàng Đình Dong với Đảng bộ Cao Bằng" (Comrade Hoàng Đình Dong and the Party section of Cao Bằng), *Tạp chí Kiểm tra*. Hanoi, no. 2, April 1996: 33–4.

allied him with the young Kim Đồng (1928–1943), a symbol of patriotic youth, active member of the *Thanh Niên*, and central figure of the new patriotic pantheon.

The VWP increased its visibility in the countryside through these images of the nation's glorious children. Their aim was not so much to get the villagers to join the Party, but rather to offer them a unified vision of the nation's diversity. In Vietnam, the land itself created meaning and a sense of belonging, so a government's legitimacy depended on its visibility and material presence on national soil. The DRV praised the patriotic initiatives of the common man, stressing that one need not be a cadre, let alone from the central government, to challenge the colonial power. The heroic lives of the first mythical figures of the Resistance were in fact the easiest to transpose into the popular imagination. The ideal of the innocent young hero (from Phạm Hồng Thái to Lý Tự Trọng, Kim Đồng, and Lê Hồng Phong) had a broad appeal since they emulated their ancestors with simple acts of bravery when faced with the "loss of the fatherland". As the war approached, the Party's propaganda department tried to make the history of the movement more personal.

Meanwhile, the new hero was forging a place at the centre of the new system of patriotic veneration. Cù Chính Lan (1930–1951), hero of the Battle of Hòa Bình; Nguyễn Viết Xuân (1934–1964), the first martyr of Quảng Bình province; Mạc Thị Bưởi (1927–1951), the guerrilla fighter from Hải Hưng; Cao Lục (1929–1974); and Ngô Gia Khảm (1912–1990) all joined the ranks of the DRV's "army of shadows".[23] Far from the glare of the press and welcomed in villages, the proletarian hero integrated fairly easily into the patriotic network — he was basically an ancestor who happened to have intersected with the destiny of the nation. He profited from the government's cult of continuity and his spirit deserved the government's care. Foreigners, especially those from brother nations, had to take into account the cultural framework inherent in the political life of Vietnam.

[23] The living were not generally worshipped in Vietnam. I did, however, find two religious sites dedicated to people who were still alive: a House of Remembrance for General Võ Nguyên Giáp built in 1986 in the commune of Lộc Thuỷ (Lệ Thuỷ district, Quảng Bình), and in 1995 a commune near Hanoi had to clamp down on a cult honouring Nguyễn Thị Bình (then Vice-President of the Socialist Republic of Vietnam) in a temple dedicated to the Trưng sisters.

A New Geography of Ritual

With the approach of war, the establishment of the new patriotic geography was a key part of the DRV's mobilisation efforts. The Ministry of Culture advised its provincial cadres to "build Houses of Remembrance for every hero, outstanding person, and great revolutionary in their jurisdiction".[24] The movement was launched in 1963–64 and was kept a high priority for decades — it was even stepped up during the period of *Đổi mới* (1986) to counter a weakening of national identity due to the policy of openness. The DRV wanted to mark its territory with the seal of this new patriotic imaginary. The decline of Chinese influence and rising tensions with the South shaped the new context: both feudal heroes and reformists now accompanied the people on their way to victory and national unification.

The creation of this new political and ritual topography was not widely publicised. As the nation continued its march towards socialism, with speeches advocating the end of archaic customs and beliefs, how did Party cadres react to the new campaign's deployment in the field? Officially, the VWP continued to condemn traditional acts of worship that smacked of feudalism. As a result, any confusion between the two practices had to be avoided. A new terminology was adopted to distinguish the new ritual sites from the old.[25] The government thus created a new semantics, a modern way to pay tribute to the nation's illustrious ancestors. These new practices were apparently accepted in the countryside without the slightest problem. Provincial cadres stressed that the new memorials were needed to strengthen the patriotic education of the nation's youth at the approach of war: "We must erect altars to honour our Party's heroes. They help educate the new generation. Children know about these heroes, of course, but the cultural level in rural areas is low. The altars let us sustain a memory

[24] The text cites as example the commune of Đức Lac (Làp Thach, Vĩnh Phú), which built a House of Remembrance in honor of the local war hero Trần Cừ so that "the people learn from his example". *Đề án tổ chức cơ quan Văn hóa các địa phương năm 1960 và năm năm 1961–65 của Bộ Văn Hóa* (Project of the Ministry of Culture to create a cultural bureau on the provincial level in 1960 and for 1961–65), in AVN3, BVH, file no. 752, single document, 1961.

[25] The distinction between the two was subsequently adopted, more or less. I will return to this with the example of the patriotic cult dedicated to the heroine Mạc Thị Bưởi in Hải Hưng province. The term *Khu di tích*, which in theory had no religious or ceremonial connotation, was often replaced by the more traditional *Khu vực thờ* or even *Đền thờ* in the areas where I did my research.

and a veneration that are useful in our daily lives."[26] Communal cadres encouraged people to get together in these new places of worship during patriotic holidays. At Nam Tân (Hải Hưng), the memorial dedicated to Mạc Thị Bưởi was integrated into a former religious structure. A 25-year-old soldier from a neighbouring village recounts: "I had never been there before I became a soldier, I didn't even know where it was. Then I went there with my unit. It's okay to go there as a group, but I wouldn't go by myself. It's part of local culture, and the commune had great respect for keeping the memory of difficult times alive."[27] The success of the campaign was immediate. The people asked the government for money to build and organise rituals in honour of their illustrious children. The veneration of heroic figures within the commune was "a part of Vietnamese tradition", but its use was now a privilege of the central government: "If the commune built a memorial in honour of a local figure, I would feel I had to go and pay homage, to venerate the spirit of the illustrious dead, for the sake of our people and our Party."[28] When a venerable person died, the decision to commemorate his or her memory fell to the State.

These new political rituals found no resistance from the people. Within the ranks of the Party, however, the issue continued to be divisive. The more orthodox among them criticised the move away from the internationalist ideals and the continuation of popular beliefs and practices from a feudal time, which they saw as anachronistic. A high Party official declared thus, "I think our country should not build altars or monuments in honour of individual people. It is understandable, of course, that the State sometimes needs to erect statues for particular heroes. But in my opinion, it is better to build collective memorials."[29] Some blamed the government for promoting the worship of low-level figures: "We don't have any altars dedicated to official heroes in our district. You have to be very great, a great leader, to merit your own altar. A hero is just a normal person, which isn't really enough. When La Văn Cầu dies we could build him a statue, but not an altar. An altar is for people like Uncle Hồ or Trần Hưng Đạo."[30]

Officially, then, DRV leaders chose to keep a certain distance, insisting that the government had nothing to do with the indigenisation of the new hero. These practices came from below, from the people, they alleged,

[26] Interview, Quỳnh Xuân commune (Quỳnh Lưu, Nghệ An).
[27] Interview, Nam Tân commune (Nam Thanh, Hải Hưng).
[28] Interview, Nguyên Bình town (Nguyên Bình, Cao Bằng).
[29] Interview, Quỳnh Ngọc commune (Quỳnh Lưu, Nghệ An).
[30] Interview, Trùng Khánh town (Cao Bằng).

spreading beyond the control of the State, which was only going along with them. This was the official line, and it suited the VWP agenda perfectly. It keenly maintained the idea that it was not involved when, in reality, the Party's propaganda and political education sections were seriously dedicated to this project from 1962 onwards.

The New Memorials

Ritual ceremonies were a link between the living and the illustrious dead. On the family level, the veneration of heroes was the culmination of all ancestor worship: "The hero is the ancestor *par excellence*, whom we always invoke individually, while the worship of other deceased family members, as a cult of individual spirits, becomes optional after a while."[31] The ritual was different from those for family ancestors, however, because it was public and usually held throughout the territory. The collective nature of the patriotic ritual necessitated a place where the communicants could come together. Four new forms of patriotic ritual architecture were established: Houses of Remembrance (*Nhà lưu niệm*), commemorative statuary sites (*Đài tưởng niệm*), funerary monuments (*Khu mộ*), and ritual sites (*Khu vực thờ*).

The House of Remembrance was the most common type of building dedicated to the memory of a model citizen of the new regime. In the 19 provinces in North Vietnam where I found patriotic memorials, they had become the ideal type of new patriotic structure.[32] They depicted the major phases of the honouree's life, in which a "reformist" or proletarian iconography is intersected with a traditional aesthetic, incorporating an ancestral altar, a bust of the hero, incense holders, and "parallel sentences" written in his memory. Campaigns for building Houses of Remembrance were organised in two consecutive stages. During the first half of the 1960s, communes financed the renovation of a village house, often the repossessed house of a former landlord, into a memorial for the heroic dead or his lineage. From 1975 onwards, the central government chipped in to allow the construction of more impressive sites.

The second type of commemorative space featured a statuary, which was obviously a more foreign concept. A new phenomenon in Vietnamese

[31] Stefan Czarnowski. *Le culte des héros et ses conditions sociales* (The cult of heroes and their social conditions). New York: Arno Press, 1975, p. 11 (1st edition, 1919).
[32] Four of these provinces (Hoà Binh, Hải Phòng, Hà Giang, and Yên Bái) chose to use a different term for the structure.

Figure 22. House of Remembrance for Lê Hồng Phong, Nghệ An province

Figure 23. Commemorative statuary sites for Hoàng Đình Giong, Cao Bằng province

Figure 24. Funerary monuments for Phan Đình Giót, Hòa Bình province

Figure 25. Ritual sites for Trần Phú, Hà Tĩnh province

tradition, the *Khu Di Tích* (literally "place of relics") consisted of a statue or monument dedicated to a key figure in the nation's recent past, to which the government added a biographical plaque summarising the main stages of the hero's life, as well as an ancestral altar so visitors could keep his memory alive. The DRV's statuary programme was begun in tandem with its policy on martyrs. In Hoà Binh, a monument dedicated to Cù Chính Lan (military hero, 1952) was built at the site where he died (Bình Thành, in Kỳ Sơn district); in Hà Tĩnh, in the village of Cẩm Quan (Cẩm Xuyên district), a statue was dedicated to the soldier and hero Phan Đình Giót who fell in the battle of Điện Biên Phủ; and in Cao Bằng, on the road to Pắc Bó, a monument was erected in honour of the young minority hero Kim Đồng and his family. The village community and mass organisations rallied around these grand, monumental architectural sites designed to bring people together and celebrate a shared heritage. The statues, which were common in urban areas, were thus also part of the emergence of a new political ritual in the country. Since the resumption of war with the South, the pioneers and youth groups of Hanoi filed past the bust of Nguyễn Văn Trỗi in the middle of Lenin Park in a show of piety, respect, and admiration for the exemplary life of their heroic elder. The cost of building these sites, however, and the novelty of the phenomenon, made it initially difficult for provinces to acquire this type of commemorative space.

The third type of patriotic ritual architecture was the funerary space. Unlike the martyrs' cemeteries mentioned above, these were smaller constructions built around the tomb of an accomplished person. The monumental aspect of the site evoked the deceased's power vis-à-vis his contemporaries. Whether outside of the commune (at the hero's place of death, for example) or within the village limits, funerary spaces were physical proof of the government's piety towards its illustrious spirits. Funerary spaces were found in most provinces. In Đa Lộc (Hậu Lộc district, Thanh Hóa province), a monument to the resistance heroine Tơm ("Mother Tơm" or Mẹ Tơm) was erected behind the communal People's Committee building. In the district of Hưng Nguyên (Nghệ An province), a small funerary monument was built in honour of Hoàng Hanh, the first Catholic hero of the DRV, amidst the graves of the martyrs' cemetery.[33] The largest of this type was dedicated to Hồ Chí Minh's parents. It was built in 1975 by

[33] Hoàng Hanh never had the influence amongst Catholics that the government had hoped for. When he died (1963), his family asked provincial authorities for help in building a monument to him, but the authorities declined. Interview, Nam Đàn, Nghệ An.

the provincial government in Nam Đàn (Nghệ An) on a hill overlooking the town of Kim Liên, Hồ's birthplace. The government made an effort to embellish all of the graves of its model citizens, regardless of size, as proof of their piety and virtue. In short, the DRV financed and decorated the funerary spaces of its heroic dead, thereby situating them within a reworked hierarchy of patriotic merit.

The final type of patriotic architecture, the temple or ritual site, most clearly resembled the religious space of former times. Fewer in number, they were often built later than the other structures mentioned above. Called *Nhà thờ* (literally "church") or *khu vực thờ* (ritual site), these commemorative structures maintained a direct link with traditional religious practices, with the altars and small temples of the past.[34] Their construction or renovation was financed by the government. Traditional temples were not as common as Houses of Remembrance, which made sense given the DRV's political situation, as the latter were more in line with internationalist ideology. Many communes wanted something with a bit more permanence, however, that did not conflict with the new government's political agenda. Since the 1970s, a whole host of small temples were built in honour of Hồ Chí Minh, but some were also dedicated to new heroes. In Thạch Minh (Hà Tĩnh), for example, a temple was built for the pioneer Lý Tự Trọng, who was sentenced to death by the French in 1931 at the age of 16. An altar had been built just after his death, and the government decided to renovate it in 1978 respecting Sino-Vietnamese architectural traditions. From the outside it resembled a *Đền thờ* (temple) from the past. Inside, the composition and arrangement of religious objects honouring the young communist and his parents re-establish the traditional relationship with the sacred; the "parallel sentences" commissioned by the district government of Thạch Hà, meanwhile, confirm the site's ritual function. Lý Tự Trọng became the new tutelary spirit of the village.

Houses of Remembrance, commemorative monument complexes, patriotic funerary sites, and new temples helped redefine the new patriotic ritual geography. By the late 1960s, 13 of the 23 provinces in North Vietnam already had patriotic ritual sites. Before examining this space in detail, we turn to the provinces that were apparently excluded from the movement.

The excluded provinces fall into three geographical areas: the mountainous northwest (the provinces of Lai Châu, Lào Cai, and Hà Giang); the

[34] Nguyên Van Khoan. "Essai sur le Dinh et le culte du génie tutélaire des villages au Tonkin" (Essay on the Dinh and the cult of the tutelary spirit in the villages of Tonkin), *BEFEO*, Paris, no.s 1–2, 1–6, 1930, pp. 107–139.

Figure 26. Ritual sites for Lý Tự Trọng, Hà Tĩnh province

Figure 27. Ritual sites for Phạm Quang Lịch, Thái Bình province

populous and industrialised provinces (Hà Tây, Bắc Thái, Hanoi, Nam Hà, and Quảng Ninh); and Ninh Binh province, the Christian enclave in the North. The sparsely populated northwest was initially overlooked by the Party's propaganda department, which preferred to focus on more populated areas. The northwest also had very few Kinh, who were the government's main target for recruitment.[35] Lai Châu, Lào Cai, and Hà Giang were mostly populated by ethnic Thái, Hmong, Yáo, Giày, and Khơ Mú minorities before the government's campaigns for economic resettlement, who had different rites and beliefs from that of the Kinh. Despite all the talk of unification, the minority peoples were always on the margins of national events. The DRV had a hard time ideologising them, and as the war approached, cadres from the propaganda department had other priorities. For example, all patriotic ritual structures in Nghệ An province were built in the lowland districts, inhabited predominantly by Kinh, or in districts that had been occupied by refugees from the South in the late 1950s. In the western part of the province, the mountainous districts of Quế Phong, Kỳ Sơn, Tương Dương, Quỳ Hợp, Quỳ Châu, Con Cuông, and Anh Sơn, inhabited by ethnic Thổ, Thái, Hmong, Khơ Mú, Chứt, and Ơ Đu, had no memorials to honour the heroes of the DRV. Thus, demographics and ethnicity were two main factors in the construction of memorials. There were also fewer memorials in highly populated urban and industrial areas such as Hanoi, Hà Tây, Nam Hà, Thái Nguyên, and Quảng Ninh. It appears that the DRV's propaganda machine turned its sights from the centres of power (both political and intellectual) and production to focus on the poorly ideologised countryside. Finally, the third sub-group to be left behind had its own strong religious identity. Located 180 kilometres south of the Hanoi, Ninh Bình is the heart of Vietnamese Christendom (Phát Diệm diocese), and its inhabitants were mostly Catholic, a cause of worry for the DRV.

Patriotic rituals existed, thus, in 13 of the nation's 23 provinces. For convenience, I have divided the ritual structures into two sub-groups: ritual sites dedicated to heroes of the Party and the Resistance, and those dedicated to new internationalist heroes. To avoid oversimplifying, however, I take a more detailed look at the structures of Nghệ Tĩnh (Nghệ An and Hà Tĩnh province) below.

The provinces north of the Red River Delta had been the heart of the nationalist and communist resistance against the French since the 1930s.

[35] Nguyễn Văn Thắng. *Ambiguity of Identity: The Mieu in North Vietnam*. Chiang Mai: Silkworm Books, 2007.

When Hồ Chí Minh returned to Vietnam in February 1941 after decades abroad, he established his camp along the Chinese border at Pắc Bó in Cao Bằng province. The government built a commemorative monument and a museum there, and later placed nearby a statue of the young Nùng resistance fighter, Kim Đồng, who was shot by the French in 1943. A few kilometres to the south, the provincial branch of the Party built a House of Remembrance for the revolutionary Hoàng Đình Dong in his hometown of Đề Thám (Hòa An district). In Lạng Sơn, they honoured two heroic figures from the province: Hoàng Văn Thụ and Lương Văn Chi. The government financed the reconstruction of Hoàng Văn Thụ's original house on stilts in his village. The commune was renamed after him (Hoàng Văn Thụ commune, in Văn Lãng district), and an imposing memorial (100 m^2/1,000 sq.ft.), a stele, and a small statue were erected. The city of Lạng Sơn erected a memorial stele and a small altar to him in the former Franco-Vietnamese school where he had studied. The commune of Văn Quan (Bắc Sơn district), on the other hand, built a monument in honour of a very local figure, Lương Văn Chi, the guerrilla hero of the Bắc Sơn revolt. Further south, in the Red River Delta, Hà Bac province had had memorials since the 1940s in honour of Ngô Gia Tự (1908–1935) and Nguyễn Văn Cừ (1912–1941), the first ICP leaders born in the area. In 1942, authorities built an altar near the Tự family home in Tam Sơn (Tiên Sơn district), which they later turned into a spacious House of Remembrance across from another building dedicated to his parents. Not far from there, in Phù Khê (Sơn Tiên district), there is another memorial in honour of Nguyễn Văn Cừ.

In the coastal province of Thái Bình, in Đình Phùng (Kiến Xương district), the former home of Party Secretary Phạm Quang Lịch (1901–1937) was rebuilt and transformed into a House of Remembrance, as well as that of the former party secretary of the province, Nguyễn Đức Cảnh, in the centre of Diêm Điền (Thái Thụy district). The construction of monuments was more sporadic in the remote western provinces of Lai Châu, Lào Cai, Sơn La, and Yên Bái. In 1980, Sơn La province only had a small commemorative space in its provincial seat, at the site of the old French prison, dedicated to the cadre Tô Hiệu, who died in prison in 1944. In Yên Bái, provincial authorities had established a memorial in the late 1940s to the Nationalist party leader Nguyễn Thái Học (1904–1930), who was executed by the French after the revolt of 1930. The new government paid homage to the former leader of the VNQDD at his tomb, located in a neighbourhood of Nghĩa Lô bearing his name.

Figure 28. Commemorative statuary sites for Kim Đồng, Cao Bằng province

Figure 29. Commemorative statuary sites for Nguyễn Văn Trỗi, Hanoi

Starting in the 1960s, North Vietnam also built ritual sites honouring its new heroes, though slightly fewer in number. In the north of Tuyên Quang province, Đức Xuan commune (Nà Hang district) had a memorial space honouring the labour hero Ngô Gia Khảm, who earned a title in 1952 for his record-setting productivity in an underground arms factory. In Vĩnh Phú, the artilleryman Nguyễn Viết Xuân was venerated in his village of Ngũ Kiên (Vĩnh Tường district). In Hải Hưng, in the heart of the Red River delta, the commune of Nam Tân (Nam Thanh district) built a patriotic memorial for the young guerrilla fighter Mạc Thị Bưởi. Further south, a few kilometres from the town of Hoà Bình, the village of Binh Thanh (Kỳ Sơn district) honoured the martyr-hero Cù Chính Lan (1952). Finally, in Thanh Hoá and Quảng Bình, there were two ritual sites built in honour of the heroic women who died in the struggle against France: "Mother Tơm" in Đa Lộc (Hậu Lộc, Thanh Hoá) and "Mother Suốt" in Bảo Ninh (in the provincial seat of Quảng Ninh).

These new patriotic ritual sites were part of a complex network of commemorative sites. In 1962, in the former province of Nghệ Tinh, the propaganda department of the People's Committee asked the Party to erect an altar in memory of Trần Phú (1904–1931), First Secretary of the ICP, who was sentenced to death by the French at age 27 in his native village of Tùng Ảnh (Đức Thọ district). At the same time, district authorities inaugurated a small temple to Phan Đình Phùng, a nineteenth-century scholar and instigator of the rebellion of Vietnamese scholars known as *Cần Vương* (Loyalists). Not far from there, in Nam Đàn, a ritual site was built in honour of the patriot-scholar Phan Bội Châu (1867–1940). A few kilometres away, authorities built a cenotaph (without the actual body[36]) for Lê Hồng Phong, the charismatic former Secretary-General of the ICP from 1935–36, and an important funerary monument in honour of Cao Lục, labour hero of 1962 and president of the cooperative of Hưng Thái commune. In August 1975, the district of Nam Đàn also inaugurated an impressive memorial dedicated to Nguyễn Sinh Sắc and Hoàng Thị Loan, Hồ Chí Minh's parents. In Thạch Hà (Hà Tĩnh) in 1978, the temple dedicated to the young patriot Lý Tự Trọng who died in 1934, was expanded. In 1980, the village of Tùng Ảnh (Hà Tĩnh) added a House of Remembrance to the altar in honour of Trần Phú; and Hưng Nguyễn district did the same in 1989 for Lê Hồng Phong, and then in the 1990s rebuilt the memorial to the young Phạm Hồng Thái. Also in Hà Tĩnh, the small town of Cẩm Xuyên celebrated the life of the 1930s revolutionary Hà Huy Giáp and the military hero Phan Đình Giót, honoured posthumously in 1955. Finally, Quỳnh Lưu district (Nghệ An) chose to remember Hồ Tùng Mậu, the revolutionary and friend of Hồ Chí Minh.

The real art of the VWP's propaganda section and political education was their ability to express the difference between the old and new. The new ritual structures of the DRV were rooted firmly in secular ground,[37]

[36] Lê Hồng Phong, first-generation revolutionary and husband of Nguyễn Thị Minh Khai, is buried at Côn Đảo (Poulo Condor), where he died in 1941.

[37] "One day, one of Confucius's disciples asked him: What if a king granted you a land that you could rule over as you wished; what would be your first act? 'The first thing I would do,' said Confucius, 'would be to correct all names.' The disciple was stunned: correct all names? This would be your first priority? Are you serious? Confucius explained to him: 'If names are not correct, if they don't correspond to reality, then language has no object. When language has no object, action is impossible, and as a result, all human efforts fall apart. It would be impossible and fruitless to try and control anything. This is why the first job of a real statesman is to correct all names'." In Simon Leys. *L'Ange et le cachalot*. Paris: Seuil, 1998, p. 26. Available in English as *The Angel and the Octopus: Collected Essays, 1983–1998*. Sydney: Duffy & Snellgrove, 1999.

though commemorating the great men of the new regime was an obvious continuation of customary traditional practices. The government officially broke the relationship to the sacred, but retained a traditional relationship with the heroic act.

Mạc Thị Bưởi, a Patriotic Rite

To better understand the interpenetration of cultural and political legitimacy, I examine the case of Mạc Thị Bưởi (1927–1951), a young North Vietnamese woman whose life echoed that of the Soviet heroine Zoya Kosmodemyanskaya (a Russian partisan killed at the age of 18 by the Nazis in 1941). Martyr of the national resistance against France, Bưởi was posthumously elevated to hero of the DRV in May 1955. A ritual was dedicated to her in the village of Nam Tân (Nam Thanh district, Hải Hưng province), 80 kilometres from Hanoi, where she was born in 1927 to a family of poor peasants.[38] She was a descendent of the sixteenth-century scholar, Mạc Đĩnh Chi, tutelary spirit of his village (Long Động). At the time of the insurrection of August 1945, she was a 18-year-old liaison officer. In 1946 she was chosen as representative of the Women's Association of her village, and the following year was elected to its executive committee at the communal level while continuing her activities as the liaison with district authorities. In 1948 she joined the Party, where she learned to read and write. She distinguished herself in the Resistance and was recognised for her courage in slipping into enemy territory. The revolutionary government placed great hopes in her. In April 1951 she was stopped by a French army unit as she was going to the district prefecture for further training. She was tortured but never broke her silence, as her biographers proudly report. Hoping to die on her native soil, she told her captors that she had secret documents, which she would surrender if she were brought home. Once back in the village of Long Động, she rebelled and was struck down, swearing her loyalty to the Party and Hồ Chí Minh with her last breath.

On 31 August 1955, the National Assembly awarded her the posthumous title of "Hero of the People's Armed Forces". For the new regime,

[38] This date is from the official biography in the first volume of *Anh hùng lực lượng vũ trang nhân dân* (Heroes of the people's armed forces), published in Hanoi in 1978 and 1994. It also appears in Trần Cẩn's *Mạc Thị Bưởi* (Hanoi, 1957). The poet Trần Đăng Khoa, however, has 1929 in his *Khúc hát người anh hùng* (Hanoi, 1974).

Anh hùng quân đội
MẠC-THỊ-BƯỞI
Huân chương quân công hạng hai

Figure 30. Portrait of Mạc Thị Bưởi

Mạc Thị Bưởi embodied the indomitable character of Vietnamese women. Her short biography, written in 1955 by the editorial board of the propaganda department, has never been rewritten.[39] It was included in the series "Follow the Example of Communist Combatants", published serially by the national press. It served as a backdrop for theatrical adaptations, screenplays, poems, and formal speeches that commemorated her memory. Over time, this official biography has taken precedence over oral memory, determining the type and meaning of the memories of those who knew her.

The commemorative and ritual apparatus dedicated to Mạc Thị Bưởi developed in the years following her appointment. She received her posthumous award in August 1955, which was a huge honour for her family. In

[39] In the final years of the war with France, the editorial committee was made up of the following members (as well as some anonymous high Party officials): Nguyễn Đình Thi, Nguyễn Huy Tưởng, Xuân Diệu, Nguyễn Xuân Sanh, Kim Lân, Tô Hoài, Vũ Cao, Tú Nam, Từ Bích Hoàng, Lê Đạt, and Nguyễn Hồng.

Figure 31. Cover of the biography of Mạc Thị Bưởi

July 1954, her sister, Mạc Thị Thành, became secretary of the communal Women's Association. Shunted aside in December 1955 and August 1956 by the agrarian reform team carrying out the regeneration of Party cadres, and subsequently rehabilitated, Mạc Thị Thành served as party secretary and president of the commune until her death in the early 1990s. Mạc Thị Bưởi's title lent her family a moral authority that underlay these new responsibilities. In return, however, as per the established custom, Mạc Thị Thành had to pay tribute to her illustrious sister. As far as anyone in the village remembers, Thành never neglected her responsibility in 30 years as head of the commune. The State showed the same piety to the heroine's family. Every year they sent a car to the village to fetch Bưởi's mother to ceremonies honouring her daughter.[40] They offered Mạc Thị Thành's husband, Nguyễn Công Hùng, a job with the local government; their children's future was also taken care of. The cult of Mạc Thị Bưởi is basically a relic of the notion of filial piety, which was the pillar of family morality with a political dimension, and which continued within the new ideological framework of the North Vietnamese regime. From the village to the district, Mạc Thị Bưởi was one part of a national project still in construction. She was the only national hero from Nam Thanh. She lent district authorities a strong political legitimacy and enhanced the region's visibility. To its inhabitants, Bưởi gave a human face to an official discourse that was often far removed from daily village life. This native daughter served as a springboard to launch the government's policies. Emulation campaigns held every year bore her name, alongside production groups, women's associations, and cooperatives.

Although there is no archival proof, Mạc Thị Thành's position in the government played a very specific financial and political role in the management of her sister's memory. There were four main phases in the development of the ritual apparatus dedicated to Mạc Thị Bưởi. From 1955 to 1974, the district had three separate sites in her honour: a large funerary monument in the district seat, an ancestral altar in her family home that drew both family members and political pilgrims, and a cenotaph in the middle of the communal cemetery. In 1973, there were more visitors than

[40] In early November 1956, for example, the government sent a car to drive her to a ceremony in Hanoi celebrating the issuing of a commemorative stamp for her daughter (there were four stamps in the series designed by Bùi Trang Chước: for 1,000, 2,000, 4,000 and 5,000 *dông*). According to everyone I interviewed, the appearance of this car made an indelible mark on the collective memory of the hamlet of Long Động.

these structures could accommodate, so the district decided to build a bigger house called the "Mạc Thị Bưởi Friendship House" in honour of her family: Mạc Thị Thành, her husband, their six children, and Bưởi's mother. The government also built a tomb in the courtyard in honour of her father, who had died before 1945, and eventually her mother, who died in 1988. In 1983, the province funded the construction of an impressive, six-metre-high statue in Nam Thanh cemetery, depicting the heroine in full Socialist Realist style. But they did not stop there. In the early 1990s, the Party's communal committee suggested they build a "Mạc Thị Bưởi House of Remembrance" near the "Friendship House", to match the newly renovated small temple dedicated to the tutelary spirit Mạc Đĩnh Chi. The renovation of this temple relied on funds collected within the town,[41] as opposed to the House of Remembrance, which came entirely out of the communal and district budget. The local government, probably afraid that the myth of the young revolutionary was not sufficiently rooted in people's minds, wanted to retain control of the national cult. They tried to recuperate some of their financial investment, however, by keeping the money and gifts offered by each delegation at the building's inauguration.

In September 1995, the town of Nam Tân had what was literally called a "ritual site", divided equally between the altar of Mạc Đĩnh Chi on one side and the Mạc Thị Bưởi "House of Remembrance" on the other. Communal cadres preferred the term *Khu di tích* (patrimonial space), which excluded any religious or ceremonial connotations, but the villagers did not care for it and kept the more traditional term *Khu vực thờ* (ritual site). Village elders from the Bureau of Patrimony decided to compromise and called it the *Khu di tích Đền thờ Mạc Đĩnh Chi, Mạc Thị Bưởi* (Patrimonial space and temple for Mạc Đĩnh Chi and Mạc Thị Bưởi). The communal government invented this superposition of the two cults. The secretary of the local Party cell of Long Động summed up the pairing simply: "Mạc Đĩnh Chi is an illustrious person, Mạc Thị Bưởi is a heroine of the revolution; one was very learned, the other fought valiantly. In the end there is not much difference."[42]

The devotional house dedicated to Mạc Thị Bưởi is 5.5 metres wide and 6.5 metres long (18 × 21 feet). It has a simple construction and is

---

[41] The building was not yet classified "historic monument" (*di tích lịch sử*) and in fact did not qualify for any public financial aid. See Interview (Nam Thành commune, Hải Hưng).

[42] Interview, Nam Tân commune (Nam Thành, Hải Hưng).

divided into two separate areas. A short flight of stairs leads to a large outdoor terrace, which wraps around the main part of the building. A central doorway opens onto a single room, 4 × 6.5 metres (12 × 20 feet), with two side windows. Furnishing is kept very simple. To the right of the entrance there is a low table and four chairs for visitors. Lining the walls are a dozen or so photos of the inauguration ceremony of 10 September 1995 and of events organised at the house. The altar to Mạc Thị Bưởi is in the centre, in a small niche 2 metres high and 1 metre wide. A large plaster bust of the heroine, painted yellow, sits in the middle, with a red cloth draped in the background. There are offerings around the altar (fruits, banknotes, etc.), as well as flowers and an incense holder filled with glowing sticks. To the right, at the foot of the altar, stands a stele inscribed with the names of the 31 martyrs of Long Động village from the Franco-Vietminh war (1946–1954). On the left, a second stele honours the victims of the war with America (1964–1975), with fewer names this time. Between the two stands a red wooden box for offerings. The building and its interior decoration were entirely functional and austere. And the choice of location, between the Friendship House devoted to her family and the temple to her ancestor, the village tutelary spirit, gave it greater representative power. The sacred quality of the building was enhanced by its very structure, architectural style, location, and geomantic properties.

A visit to the ritual site of Nam Tân now entails two separate sites for a population that no longer distinguishes between the two figures:

> The difference between Mạc Thị Bưởi and Mạc Đĩnh Chi lies in their roles, one was a war hero, the other an intellectual from the old system. But they are both important, I don't want to separate them, it's the same thing. I will burn incense in both places. Our country is this way, this is the traditional system in Vietnam.[43]

This architectural continuum allowed the DRV to reaffirm the continuity of the nation's history. The ceremonies held for Mạc Thị Bưởi juxtaposed the two national calendars: the traditional lunar calendar and the new patriotic-revolutionary one. They intersected and complemented each other without overlapping, except during the new lunar year.

These two parallel religious cults did not come under the same authority, however. Moreover, followers of both sides were fairly intransigent

[43] Interview, Nam Tân commune (Nam Thanh, Hải Hưng).

about the temporal organisation of their ceremonies. In theory, the village[44] of Long Động observed dates only from the traditional calendar. A committee for the management of patrimony was created, consisting of 24 members (2 or 3 communal cadres, 7 or 8 representatives of various sectors, and a dozen village elders — both scholars and cadres) presided over by a president who was appointed head of the commune and delegate of cultural affairs. Within the hamlet itself, ritual sites came under the secretary of the Party cell.[45] As a result, celebrations were held in two different places. Traditional rituals began in the temple dedicated to Mạc Đĩnh Chi and ended with a visit to the altar of his distant relative Mạc Thị Bưởi. While ceremonies honouring the Trân dynasty scholar were quite popular, those for Mạc Thị Bưởi took a while to gain momentum. Cadres from the province, district (usually from the cultural department or from the bureau of disabled veterans), and the commune attended the ceremony each year, and brought her family gifts. The village administration, made up of groups of five to ten people from each neighbourhood,[46] would go in the morning, usually from 8–10 a.m., to burn incense at her altar and place offerings. Villagers took the opportunity to stop by her family's Friendship House to show their piety and gratitude. At other times, the family, neighbours, and devotees of the heroine got together for commemorative services based on the traditional (lunar) calendar, which had been simplified by the new regime. Everyone still celebrated the first and fifteenth of each month, the spring and fall festivals,[47] the fifteenth day of the first month, and the day of peaceful souls, but many holidays had been abandoned. For example, they no longer celebrated the beginning or end of the transplanting of rice,

[44] I am aware of the distinction between a *làng* (village), a *thôn* (hamlet), and a *xã*, (commune, in the administrative sense), but in this particular case I use *thôn* to indicate the lowest level of village organisation.

[45] He sometimes took on the ancient title of *cụ thủ từ* (ritual guardian) to define his role, as did a certain Mr. Mùi in the village of Thổ Hà (Vân Hà commune in Hà Bắc province), who was in charge of a small temple dedicated to former president Hồ Chí Minh (Đền thờ Hồ Chủ tịch).

[46] The *thôn* of Long Động had 250 families, divided into 3 neighbourhoods (*xóm*). On the anniversary of Mạc Thị Bưởi's death, 30 to 40 groups were organised and involved most of the villagers.

[47] *Trung thu* is traditionally a festival honouring children. For the occasion, national and local authorities organised a variety of activities (carnival rides, games, parades, etc.) in their continued effort to win over the nation's youth. This was the only traditional festival outside of Têt that came under the direct responsibility of the central government.

the new rice of the ninth month, or the opening of the seals on the seventh day of the first month. Other holidays only concerned the immediate family so did not involve a collective ritual. On these occasions, individual families paid homage to the village's two glorious ancestors or asked for help with their troubles. Holidays of this type are: the day of seeking tranquillity (the fifteenth day of the seventh month), the day of the deliverance of souls, Tết, the third day of the third month, the fifth day of the fifth month, and ceremonies at the end of the year (the second day of the twelfth month). Other holidays related to daily events from the village (marriage, death, special accomplishments, etc.) also required people to honour the memory of the two village heroes. But the most important ritual element took place outside of the traditional holidays. Mạc Thị Bưởi received special attention during the important dates in the new patriotic calendar. Invariably, the year began with the anniversary of the founding of the Party (3 February), then came Women's Day (8 March), the anniversary of the liberation of Saigon (30 April), Hồ Chí Minh's birthday (19 May), the Day of Martyrs and Disabled Veterans (27 July), the commemoration of the August Revolution (19 August), Independence Day (2 September), and ended with the anniversary of the founding of the PAVN (22 December).

The ritual around Mạc Thị Bưởi was thus intended as a tribute to the exemplary nature of this village ancestor. The authorities wished to encourage the population — usually via local government representatives — to emulate the virtue of their fellow citizen. It was not exactly a question of veneration but of creating a direct link between the actions of this peasant girl at the height of the war with France and the daily struggles of a farming village (increasing production, fighting illiteracy and social evils, etc.). This political veneration was essentially a local one. A provincial cadre, civil servant, or army officer was always on hand to represent the government. The delegations first met at the People's Committee building of the commune and then went to the heroine's House of Remembrance accompanied by a representative of the group in charge that day (the president of the Women's Association for Women's Day, etc.). A speech was given extolling the deeds of Mạc Thị Bưởi and encouraging everyone to follow her example. Then, one after another, the delegations gathered before her altar to lay offerings and burn incense. The second phase took place at the Friendship House dedicated to her family and the tomb of her parents, where the delegations repeated the gestures they had made at the devotional house. They sat and drank tea, and smoked the *thuốc lào* (a water pipe, usually made of bamboo) with a representative of the family. Some offerings and gifts were left in tribute to the deceased. After leaving the house, some delegates went to the town cemetery to pay their respects at the symbolic grave of the heroine. Finally, to close the half-day's events, and when finances permitted, a reception was sometimes organised by the commune.

The simplicity of this political ritual only had meaning when juxtaposed with those of the past. The life of the young heroine Mạc Thị Bưởi embodied the evolution of post-colonial Vietnam. A valiant combatant, she was chosen among all others to satisfy the requirements of internationalist recognition. She had also been modelled on a foreign concept, so in order to gain legitimacy she had to assimilate into a cultural context that could be easily understood by her peers. Lastly, she was a symbol of identity transformation to those abroad, but an expression of continuity for her own community. She was both a daughter of the village and a child of the nation, and helped the State penetrate into the heart of village tradition behind the "bamboo hedge". The land of the ancestors now had a remarkably effective tool for loosening the grip of its atavistic ethno-geographic beliefs. Martyr for a patriotic cause and mouthpiece for its political legitimacy, the new hero became rooted in the local and helped create a new imaginary for the reunified nation.

Chapter 7

Mass Culture and the Patriotic Pantheon

> It is not very important to know what few things myths can tell us about the future; they are not astrological almanacs.... Myths must be seen as a way of acting on the present.... The myth [is] an organisation of images that can instinctively evoke all of the feelings related to the various manifestations of the war against modern society.
>
> Georges Sorel[1]

The new hero had indeed become a reality, but his true nature lay in his political role. The new man in a Marxist-Leninist society was primarily an object of political propaganda. He was more appearance than essence. He gained influence within society only as an object of representation, and as a link between the government and the people, he had to accept a certain immateriality. The hero was at the centre of an imagined community in which politics was defined by ethics and collective morality. The assent of the people depended on how well he established the course of a new virtuous path. Government leaders thus sought obedience through moral and spiritual values, not only through force.[2] The new heroic figure was the personification of a general idea. He was not only an example and a model for DRV leaders, but a "constantly active source in [their] lives, for [their] power, success, and the continuation of the dynasty for the good of the people".[3] The hero's role in society cannot be understood outside

[1] Georges Sorel. *Réflexions sur la violence* (Reflections on Violence). Paris: Seuil, 1990, pp. 83–4 (1st edition, 1908).
[2] Nguyễn Thế Anh. "La conception de monarchie divine dans le Viêt Nam traditionnel", *BEFEO*, Paris, no. 84, 1997: 151.
[3] Ibid.: 157.

Figure 32. "Avant-Garde Youth" (*thiếu nhi*)

of this relationship with the government. By recognising the new man, the DRV continued its mission to provide a moral education to its people without, however, trespassing against a popular consciousness that was not easily moved.

The official new morality sanctified a cultural relationship with virtuous ancestors — only the frame of reference had changed. Government leaders mastered the art of double-talk and adapted themselves to a foreign institutional framework without renouncing the characteristics of their own cultural environment. The new hero began as a propagandistic tool, as the final aim of patriotic emulation, and gradually took on a cultural role within the community, ushering in a sense of political permanence. Without this transformation, the new regime would never have gained political prominence. A dynastic change depended on it. The emergence of a new historical pantheon provided the cultural ballast necessary for the communists to retain power over their "merely Nationalist" opponents. The genesis of the new man sprang from the national emulation movement as it spread throughout the country, but his acceptance within the popular mentality depended on the success of the mass culture campaign.

Mass Culture and the New Hero

A few months before the thirtieth anniversary of the Party (3 February 1960), Hồ Chí Minh gave a lengthy speech on national radio on 15 December 1959. A few days prior to the event he had criticised the weaknesses of several cadres in an informal talk, and he now returned to the question of the virtue of the new man: "The heroes of the Party and the people are collective heroes who are deeply imbued with the revolutionary virtues of the Party. Only such revolutionary virtue will allow us to lead the working class, organise and unify the masses, and make the revolution a success."[4] He declared that the heroes and heroines of the present day were the leaders of the emulation movement in North Vietnam and the sworn enemies of the "U.S.-Diêm regime" in the South. The new hero was part of the government's reorganisation efforts. The country was torn apart by the end of the war in 1954, so new and dedicated cadres were desperately needed to rebuild the country.

The government was determined to increase its ideological visibility throughout the country. The challenge now was to develop a real mass culture. They had seven main objectives: to disseminate Marxist-Leninist theory and the policies of the Party and the government, spread the scientific advancements necessary for the development of society, continue to enrich people's minds, produce quality literary and artistic works, organise cultural events, implement a new morality to build the new man, and eradicate old habits to build a new life. The DRV placed the new man at the heart of its educational efforts and put forth this model of revolutionary virtue as the only way to acquire the "New Spirit".[5] The "policy of mass culture" was to "help workers understand advances in politics, science, and mass culture in order to fully carry out the plan".[6]

---

[4] Report from the Vietnamese Information Agency, 15 December 1959, BBC 212, 19 December 1959, p. B/6.

[5] Hồ Chí Minh. *Về xây dựng con người mới* (On building the new man). Hanoi: nxb Chính Trị Quốc Gia, 1995.

[6] *Đề án công tác Văn hóa đối với công nhân* (Project for cultural activities aimed at workers), in AVN3, Coll. BVH, file no. 880, document 234 HC/VH, 1956.

To implement this policy, the government relied on the new exemplary men selected during the patriotic, and later socialist, emulation campaigns. Artists and intellectuals were mobilised and put to work. The patriotic crusade for the liberation of South Vietnam was stepped up. Prime Minister Phạm Văn Đồng gave talks on how art must serve the people, drawing upon the principles of Lenin and Mao.[7] All types of artistic expression were harnessed for patriotic propaganda, from film to theatre, literature, music, poetry, and painting. The hero was displayed everywhere — he was sung about, painted, sculpted, told in stories, performed, danced, portrayed in verse, prose, images, or illuminations, and was a key part of the government's mobilisation policy. In the autumn of 1964, the Ministry of Culture started making more movies about the lives of new heroes.[8] Since 1959, when the first full-length movie by a domestic studio was produced, films had been made about Kim Đồng, the young combatant from Cao Bằng (1964, directed by Nông Ích Đạt and Vũ Phạm Lan), and Cù Chính Lan, the martyr of the battle of Hòa Binh.[9] Two new projects were underway in 1964: a movie about the life of the young Lý Tự Trọng[10] and one about the last hours of Nguyễn Văn Trỗi, the new martyr and symbol of the struggle in South Vietnam (*Nguyễn Văn Trỗi sống mãi*, directed by Bùi Đình Hạc and Lý Thái Bảo).[11] Studios also produced short films and documentaries about exemplary emulation fighters and new heroes that itinerant cultural groups screened around the country. The people could thus admire the valiant teacher Trần thị Đào (*Cô Trần thị Đào*, 1962), the student Ngô

[7] Phạm Văn Đồng. *Sur quelques problèmes culturels. Causeries* (Discussing some cultural issues). Hanoi: ELE, 1980 (re-issue). Hồ Chí Minh. *Văn hoá Nghệ thuật cũng là một mặt trận* (Culture and art are part of the same front). Nxb Sự thật, 1980 (re-issue).

[8] Bành Bảo, Hữu Ngọc. *L'itinéraire du film de fiction vietnamien* (The evolution of the Vietnamese fictional film). Hanoi: ELE., 1984. Phạm Ngọc Trương, Hữu Ngọc, *et. al. Le film documentaire vietnamien* (The Vietnamese film documentary). Hanoi: ELE, 1987.

[9] AVN3, Coll. BVH, file no. 278, unnumbered document, January 1965.

[10] *Đề tài kịch bản phim truyện 1965 của Xưởng phim Hà Nội* (Screenplay subjects from Hanoi film studios in 1965), in AVN3, Coll. BVH, file no. 275, document no. 162/BVH, 30 January 1965.

[11] The original screenplay for the movie changed over time. In 1965, a new version based on the hero's life, called *Sống như Anh* (To live like you), was distributed by the Propaganda Department of the Party's Central Committee and Cultural Department: "Between 4 July 1965 and 25 February 1966, the screenplay was enriched by the ideas of Tố Hữu, Comrade Quân Trương, and people from the Department of Reunification". See *Công tác của Xưởng phim Hà Nội* (Activities of the Hanoi movie studios), in AVN3, Coll. BVH, file no. 275, document no. 56/BVH, 23 February 1966.

Đắc Kha (*Học Sinh Ngô Đắc Kha*, 1962), and the labour hero Nguyễn Văn Thuyên (*Anh hùng Nguyễn Văn Thuyên*, 1962).[12]

Cultural cadres were asked to think about how to improve the "look" of the new hero. In 1962, cultural publishing houses put out a translation of the essay by the Chinese Culture Minister Trần Hoàng Môi on the new hero in the visual media:[13]

> Depicting the revolutionary hero in a human and realistic way is crucial to audiovisual creation — in the past as in the present, and is in fact the responsibility of all who create. We have to continuously and resolutely create the image of the new revolutionary hero based on the principle that we are at the service of workers, peasants, and soldiers, so as to serve the political aims of the working class and work seriously for the construction of socialism.[14]

Literature and the arts were dedicated to defining the new man. The transmutation of the "spirit" was carried out using the full arsenal of Leninist propaganda. Government leaders wanted to offer the Vietnamese people a "good morality". They began their socialisation of North Vietnamese society and presented a virtuous model to follow. Technical advancements had only modernised an ancient principle except now the DRV had more propaganda tools at its disposal, making it easier to transmit information throughout the country. Without this complex system of disseminating knowledge, the government would not have been able to establish the new national heroic figure within the popular imagination.

Talking about the Hero in the Commune

In the fall of 1956, the Ministry of Culture sent a group of cadres to the small mining town of Cẩm Phả (in the zone of Hồng Quảng) to study the initial results of its mass culture efforts. On the ground, the three local

---

[12] *Báo cáo tổng kết đèn chiếu năm 1962 và phương hướng nhiệm vụ công tác năm 1963* (Summary of screening activities for 1962 and plan of action for 1963), in AVN3, Coll. DVH, file no. 107, unnumbered document, December 1962.

[13] In 1962, Trần Hoàng Môi was the head of the Cinema Department at the PRC's Ministry of Culture.

[14] Trần Hoàng Môi. "Sáng tạo nhân vật mới xứng đáng với thời đại" (Create avant-garde figures in accordance with the times), in Trần Hoàng Môi, Lâm Sam, *Sáng tạo con người mới trong điện ảnh* (Creating the new man in cinema). Hanoi: nxb Văn hoá Nghệ thuật, 1962, p. 3.

organisational entities (Party, government, and mass organisations) were responsible for disseminating ministerial directives. One cadre was assigned to the Party cell to oversee propaganda matters. A new department of cultural affairs was created within the village People's Committee to serve as relay with mass organisations. It consisted of a small team of three cadres: the department head, an official in charge of artistic propaganda (movies/performing arts), and another in charge of literacy. Finally, the trade union of Cẩm Phả had two specialised cadres, one in charge of propaganda and one for cultural affairs.

Cẩm Phả was classified as a high-priority industrial development zone (mining). In 1956, the small town had 15,000 inhabitants: 2,000 were of Chinese origin (out of whom 40 per cent were miners) and another 2,000 were from various ethnic backgrounds (out of whom only 7 per cent worked in the mine). The rest of the population consisted mainly of Kinh, most of whom were either miners or local government officials.[15] In 1955–56, only 5 per cent of the 4,000 workers in Cẩm Phả could read and write properly. This figure soon changed, however, as 980 people and 1,535 workers signed up for literacy classes, an educational coup that lowered the illiteracy rate to below 32 per cent, according to official statistics. Note that a great many of the ethnic Chinese (*Hoa Kiều*) in the town spoke no, or very little, Vietnamese.

The Ministry of Culture's goal was to establish "a dense infrastructure of cultural activities to improve work in the mine and in the daily lives of workers and their families in the neighbourhood".[16] Propaganda facilities were set up on the neighbourhood, business, and communal levels to make use of the government's new propaganda tools (books, films, photographs, cartoons, plays, etc.) in an effort to mobilise a population with little cultural education. Within the mine itself, the inspection team reported that "cultural activities remained quite underdeveloped because of difficult working conditions". The union's delegate for cultural affairs merely distributed daily newspapers (*Nhân dân*, *Tiền Phong*, etc.) and posted them on the wall for workers. Every day, a cadre read the news aloud for 10–15 minutes during the lunch break or sometimes before the start of the workday. News about production levels and exemplary workers from the factory,

[15] *Đoàn nghiên cứu tình hình khu Hồng Quang. Báo cáo nghiên cứu tại thị xã Cẩm Phả* (Study group on the situation in the zone of Hồng Quang. Report on the town of Cẩm Phả), in AVN3, Coll. BVH, document no. 12/VH, November 25, 1956.

[16] *Đoàn nghiên cứu tình hình khu Hồng Quang. Báo cáo nghiên cứu tại thị xã Cẩm Phả* (Study group on the situation in the zone of Hồng Quang. Report on the town of Cẩm Phả).

Figure 33. Communal cultural centre

or about other industrial operations across the country was broadcasted. Lastly, there was a small social club that in late 1956 had nearly 100 books, a few chess sets, and newspaper boards. The inspection team from the Ministry of Culture noted, however, that very few workers actually went there and that the activities offered were inadequate.

Outside of the mine, cultural activities took place in the communal cultural centre and its neighbourhood branches, the cultural clubs.[17] The government proclaimed nationwide that "cultural centres were the hope of the people". A directive from the Ministry of Culture exhorted its cadres "to spread propaganda to the people through cultural centres and clubs, which were the heart of cultural activities for workers".[18] Cultural centres

---

[17] In 1956, the Ministry of Culture announced that "communal clubs" would thenceforth be called "communal cultural centres". The difference lay in the size of the institution. At the neighborhood level, they could still be called clubs. A cultural centre provided a variety of services (theatre, sports facilities, library, etc.) while a club was smaller. In reality, however, communes made decisions on a case-by-case basis and did not always respect the central government's distinctions, such that both clubs and centres could be found throughout the communes. See *Thông tri bổ sung về công tác xây dựng Nhà văn hóa* (Directives for strengthening the programme to build Cultural Centres), in AVN3. Coll. BVH, file no. 888, document 1369NH (UBKC Khu IV).

[18] *Đề án công tac văn hoá đối với công nhân* (Project for cultural activities aimed at workers), 16 April 1956.

and neighbourhood clubs developed their activities in tandem.[19] An inspector from the Ministry of Culture suggested that they offer more picture books to the public. Biographies of heroes were the most commonly borrowed books, with *Mạc Thị Bưởi* (1955) and *The Exemplary Struggle of Heroic Combatants* (*Gương chiến sĩ đấu của anh hùng chiến sĩ*, 1955) at the top of the list. The book distribution department had a smiliar experience: the lives of heroes were selling well in the area of Hồng Gai and were frequently re-ordered by cultural centres. The town of Cẩm Phả not only had a cultural centre but also an entertainment hall (for theatre, song performances, etc.), a 400-seat movie theatre, a radio broadcasting facility, and a people's bookstore. These new cultural facilities allowed mass organisations to organise local arts projects in their villages and neighbourhoods. With each new propaganda tool, the government got closer to imprinting the image of the new hero in the popular imagination.

The town of Cẩm Phả was a perfect example of this. It had been equipped early on with some of the best cultural facilities since it was considered a priority zone, and the government's main goal was mobilising the working class. But Cẩm Phả was not the only city to be privileged. In 1956, other areas with a large working-class population were outfitted with similar facilities.[20] In the district of Nguyên Bình (Cao Bằng), the tin-mining town of Tĩnh Túc was endowed with a library and a small cultural centre in 1955–56, while no such facilities were built in the district seat of Nguyên Bình until 1961. Industrial cities were priority propaganda targets for the State, followed by the administrative centres (provincial and district seats). Hà Giang province, for example, did not have an industrial

[19] In the city of Cẩm Phả, only two neighborhoods had a functioning club in 1956. The club in neighbourhood no. 9 had 120 books, 5 newspapers, and a few games, but only 30–40 people went there per day. On the communal level, the reading room at the cultural centre in Cẩm Phả was much better stocked (1,200 books), but it also attracted relatively few people (50–70 people per day). What kinds of books were people reading? We know, for example, that "most of the books were never checked out, especially the ones on politics and economics".

[20] Outside of Hồng Quang, the highest concentration of workers was in the cities of Hanoi and Hải Phòng, the provinces of Việt Trì, Thái Nguyên, and Nam Định, and the provincial capitals of Thanh Hoá (Thanh Hoá) and Nghệ An (Vinh). See *Tổng kết công tác phát hành phim và chiếu bóng năm 1962 và phương hướng nhiệm vụ công tác năm 1963* (Summary of movie screenings and "magic lantern" shows in 1962 and plan for the following year), in AVN3, Coll. BVII, file no. 107, document no. 379/VH, 1 February 1963.

base in 1956,[21] but the provincial committee already had a department of cultural affairs that built a public library, a cultural centre, and neighbourhood clubs. An inspection team from the Ministry of Culture was not impressed, however, and regretted that "the people still weren't prepared enough ideologically, despite all of the assistance provided by the central government. Of the 32 artistic cells that had been created, only 11 of them were up and running a few months later."[22] The situation was different in the neighbouring province of Lào Cai. In addition to the cultural facilities provided by the provincial committee, there were several factories and industrial sites that were under direct ministerial supervision. Production units gave rise to public libraries, clubs, and cultural centres that sprang up and thrived in the far reaches of the province. Thus, the process of ideologising the population varied between the rural and industrial provinces of the country.

Ideologisation in Remote Areas

Ideologisation was more sporadic in the remote towns and villages that lacked an industrial infrastructure. The Ministry of Culture published a handbook for cadres assigned to these regions to help them adapt the "policies of mass culture to the environment of remote regions". Ethnic minorities still did not speak much Vietnamese and funds were sorely lacking. The establishment of a cultural facility in these communes was unthinkable given the estimated costs, so the government could only send itinerant cultural groups. They were trained and organised by the department of cultural affairs of each provincial People's Committee. Some were even sent directly from the district. Experts from the Ministry of Culture suggested they put on more "magic lantern" shows, show more films (full-length movies, documentaries, and shorts), organise theatre evenings and recitals of patriotic songs, and hold exhibits of "colourful images exalting the solidarity, production, and great heroes of national culture".[23] The itinerant groups distributed books, organised talks, and trained rural cadres.

---

[21] *Thống kê số lượng công nhân các ngành năm 1955–59 của Sở Lao động* (Statistics from the Labour Department on the number of workers per sector in 1955–59), in AVN3, Coll. BLD, file no. 449, single document, 1959.

[22] *Báo cáo về văn hóa đại chúng* (Report on mass culture), in AVN3, Coll. BVH, file no. 888, document no. 194/VH (Ty văn hóa, UBHC tỉnh Hà Giang), 1956, p. 3.

[23] *Kế hoạch báo cáo của Bộ Văn hóa ở các khu tự trị* (Provisional report by the Ministry of Culture aimed at autonomous zones), in AVN3, Coll. BVH, file no. 888, unnumbered document, p. 5.

In the 1950s and 60s, most of the ideologisation of North Vietnam took place through the occasional visits by itinerant cultural cadres. Official statistics do not show clearly just how many communes were actually affected by or excluded from these tours. For example, the table below shows reports by cadres from Cao Bằng to the Ministry of Culture on the activities of its mobile units in charge of "magic lantern" shows for 1956 (when the first two groups were created) to the end of 1963.[24] It unfortunately does not provide any clear indication of the number of communes actually visited, but if we look at the data for 1962, we see that there were only two groups running the 816 projections for the year, or 408 showings per group, which seems rather unrealistic. Given the distances and the conditions of the roads and paths between the villages, which were often steep, it would seem that several projections were held in a small number of communes.[25] It plumps up the statistics but in reality, numerous communities across the province, such as the village of Vũ Nông (Nguyên Bình district, Cao Bằng), were never visited by an itinerant cultural group between 1956 and 1965. In 1962, barely one-fifth of the 48,000 inhabitants of Nguyên Bình district saw these shows in 1962.

Year	*Number of showings*	*Number of groups*	*Number of spectators*
1956	66	2	8,278
1958	217	1	13,710
1958	568	5	45,115
1960	699	5	50,861
1961	842	4	60,968
1962	816	2	40,809
1963	133	1	7,500

Activities of itinerant teams of "magic lantern" shows, Cao Bằng province (1956–1963)

[24] *Báo cáo thống kê tình hình phát triển sự nghiệp văn hóa thông tin Cao Bằng* (Statistical report on the development of cultural and information enterprises in Cao Bằng province), in AVN3, Coll. BVH, file no. 302, document no. 12/ CB, 12 December 1964.
[25] In 1956, the province of Yên Bái sent an itinerant cultural group into the mountainous areas. In the course of the year, 120 (out of 215) screenings were shown in 16 communes. The team states in their activity report that eight screenings were shown in each commune. See *Tóm tắt thành tích của đội chiếu bóng lưu động số 9 Chi nhánh 4 năm 1956* (Review of performance of itinerant projection groups, no. 9, session no. 4, 1956), in AVN3, Coll. BVH, file no. 61, document no. 40/VH, January 1957.

The lack of statistical evidence makes any estimate at the national level impossible. Even at the height of the movement (1959–1961), it seems difficult, if not unthinkable, that such a limited number of cultural teams could cover such a large area, reaching communes that were far apart and often quite isolated.

These campaigns had a dual objective: to aid in the construction of socialism and reinforce the struggle for national reunification. In 1963, a cadre from the Ministry of Culture explained that:

> Movies had a great impact on the villagers, many of whom had never seen such technology before. Itinerant cadres showed them the example of Lý Tự Trọng, Kim Đồng, Võ Thị Sáu and other heroes and emulation fighters. Through the lives of the nation's exemplary martyrs, the villagers understood how to adopt such heroic behaviour in their daily lives and improve their lives.[26]

The Ministry strongly advised its cadres to respect the manners and customs of ethnic minorities. A beautiful account of the propaganda group's work among minority peoples was written by Nguyễn Tuân.[27] The Ministry advised provincial departments of cultural affairs to create their own shows and documentaries, or write patriotic songs directly inspired by local revolutionary heritage (*Lạng Sơn anh dũng*, *Sơn La anh dũng*, etc.).

The ideologisation of the communes from the Red River delta and remote towns in the plains or coastal villages proved equally uneven. From 1959–1960, the ideologisation of the peasant masses was left to production groups and cooperatives[28] in charge of setting up the basic structures of mass culture,[29] notably the first people's bookstores. A cultural centre was

---

[26] *Báo cáo công tác đèn chiếu năm 1962 và phương hướng nhiệm vụ công tác năm 1963* (Report on projection activities for 1962 and plan for the following year), in AVN3, Coll. BVH, file no. 107, document no. x/vh, January 1963.

[27] Nguyễn Tuân. *Nhật ký* (Journal). Hanoi: nxb văn học, 1976.

[28] For more on this, see Martin Grossheim's interesting chapter on the collectivisation of the commune between 1960 and 1975 (Ch. III, "Das Dorf in der Phase der Kollektivierung"), in *Nordvietnamesische Dorfgemeinschaften: Kontinuität und Wandel*. Hamburg: Mitteilungen des Instituts für Asienkunde, 1997, pp. 222–55.

[29] In the springtime of 1962, the Việt Bắc zone organised a cultural conference for the area. Many cooperatives were criticised for their lack of cultural activities. In conclusion, one cadre admitted that "the movement had developed very slowly" in the zone. See *Báo cáo tổng kết công tác Văn hóa quần chúng 1961 và tháng đầu năm 1962 ở miền núi* (Account of mass culture activities in the mountainous regions from 1961 to early 1962), in AVN3, Coll. BVH, file no. 1104, single document, 4 June 1962.

created in Thái Binh in 1956, and shortly after, the People's Committee started 87 such institutions among its 301 communes. On average, these bookstores had 25–50 books and a selection of newspapers (*Nhân dân*, *Tiền Phong*, *Nông nghiệp và Khoa Thường Thức*, *Thời sự Phổ thông*). In the village of Hữu Bằng (Sơn Tây), the president of the commune said: "We still haven't held any discussions because none of our cadres feel competent to do so. We haven't established a cultural cell either, nor a newspaper reading group; in short, we haven't really done anything yet but we do have the building."[30] In 1961 in Quỳnh Lưu (Nghệ An), most communal cooperatives and production groups had a small people's bookstore. The Ministry was of course disappointed that many of them were under-staffed and under-utilised by the people. There were some good tricks, however, for beefing up the weak numbers. The provincial government of Vinh (Nghệ An), carried away by the game of statistics, awarded a certificate of exemplarity to the commune of Nghĩa Đàn for its "record number of books": they had 8,446 books in all, which makes 25 books per family, or 6–7 books per person. In actual fact, a small group of exemplary families had 150–200 books each, a disparity that would have tempered the optimism of the official in question.

The neighbourhood library (or people's bookstore in the larger towns) thus played a key role in the ideologisation of the North Vietnamese village. In theory, every new book published was to be discussed among the villagers, but documents show that in 1964–65 very few communes actually did so. In Quảng Trạch (Quảng Bình), the head of the village library was decorated for having organised 34 lectures in 1965, including 9 dedicated solely to the hero Nguyễn Văn Trỗi (*Sống Như Anh* [Living like you]). Elsewhere, however, many communes did not have a cultural director, so had no way to acquire books. From time to time a cultural cadre from the district would come to the village, but usually people would have to go to the district bookstore. Despite these various problems, the people's library/bookstore was instrumental in popularising the new hero and emulation fighter in the countryside.

The local museum, or communal museum space, was another important part of the ideologisation of society. Although they did not become widespread until the war with the South (1965–1975), the Ministry of

[30] *Báo cáo tình hình kiểm tra một số xã ở Sơn Tây về nhà văn hóa, tủ sách* (Inspection report on some communes from Sơn Tây regarding cultural centres and bookstores), in AVN3, Coll. BVH, file no. 888, document no. 12/vh (UBHC liên khu III, Phòng Văn hóa), 18 August 1956.

Culture had suggested since 1961 that provinces build "Houses of Remembrance in honour of every hero, important person, and great leader from their area".[31] The new museum situated the local revolutionary heritage within a global perspective. In 1963, there were only four museums in the whole of North Vietnam: at Hồng Quảng, Hưng Yên, Hải Phòng, and Điện Biên Phủ. The one in Điện Biên Phủ opened its doors in December 1961 to mark the anniversary of the founding of the PAVN.[32] In Hanoi, the three national museums (of the Revolution, of History, and of the Army) designed and sent exhibitions to the provinces.[33] Elsewhere, provincial departments of cultural affairs encouraged communal authorities to open "small museum spaces" (*cơ sở bảo tàng*) to aggrandise local figures and key events in the visual arts. We do not know how many of these museums were actually built since there are no reliable statistics on the matter. During the interwar period, these clubs, cultural centres, libraries, itinerant cultural groups, people's libraries/bookstores, and basic village museums made up the DRV's ideological network. The nation's new heroes relied on these channels to begin their gradual penetration into the communal level.

A New Historical Pantheon

DRV leaders cleverly situated themselves within a virtuous genealogical heritage. The new identitary references were not gods and demigods, but they wove together various periods of the nation's revolutionary struggle. The State was anchored in the past and asserted itself through the heroism of its exemplary men. Individuals were often presented as a generic type (the Catholic peasant, the minority worker, etc.), symbols of the progress-ivist legitimacy of the new government. No spiritual references (gods, demigods, spirits, etc.) were allowed, of course, given its internationalist framework, and I use the term "patriotic pantheon" as a way to examine how the political imaginary was recreated to suit the times. This new referential world is a system of relations, and each figure exists only

[31] *Đề án tổ chức cơ quan văn hoá các địa phương năm năm 1961–1965 của Bộ Văn hóa* (Project of the Ministry of Culture for organizing cultural bureaus at the provincial level from 1961–1965), in AVN3, BVH, file no. 752, single document, 1961.

[32] AVN3, Coll. BVH, file no. 107, document no. x/bt, 17 January 1963.

[33] In 1965, the history museum sent an exhibition to the provinces of Hải Dương, Hải Phòng, Kiến An, and Hồng Quảng. The Museum of the Revolution and that of the Army prepared a show to be sent to the provinces of Tuyên Quang, Thái Nguyên, and Hà Giang. AVN3, Coll. BVH, file no. 107, document no. x/bt, 17 January 1963, p. 5.

through the network binding them together, defined by his relationship to the others. This relationship both dominates and explains him. It creates the overall plan wherein the hero is but one part and his role is understood only in light of the final aim. The classification of gods was a political issue in the sinicised world. The agnostic and modernist position of the new government in Vietnam did not imply a rupture with the past; on the contrary, the legitimacy of its short history depended on it.

The system of relationships linking the figures of the new patriotic pantheon incorporated four frames of reference: historical, geographical, ethnic, and functional. The government was basically honouring the model citizens of the new regime by venerating the glorious spirits of a new dynasty. While the nationalists merely appropriated the political imaginary stained with the blood of the collaborationist Nguyễn dynasty, Hồ Chí Minh and his followers rearranged the realm of their ancestors. They offered the people a patriotic pantheon made up of "pure beings" who reflected the legitimacy of their rule. The moral excellence of the revolutionary hero was the main source of political legitimacy. Of course, a nineteenth-century patriot had a harder time fitting into the new revolutionary morality given his links with the old system.[34]

The Patriotic Pantheon of the Democratic Republic of Vietnam[35]

1st row (18 figures)		
Nguyễn Thị Minh Khai	1930–1952	Quảng Ninh
Cù Chính Lan	1930–1952	Nghệ An
Hoàng Hanh	1888–1963	Nghệ An
Hoàng Văn Thụ	1906–1944	Lạng Sơn
Kim Đồng	1928–1943	Cao Bằng
La Văn Cầu	1932–	Cao Bằng
Lê Hồng Phong	1902–1942	Nghệ An
Lý Tự Trọng	1914–1931	Hà Tĩnh
Mạc Thị Bưởi	1927–1951	Hải Hưng
Ngô Gia Khảm	1912–1990	Hà Bắc

[34] Đặng Huy Vận. "Những năm đầu của phong trào chống Pháp ở Nghệ Tĩnh và quá trình hình thành thành cuộc khởi nghĩa Phan Đình Phùng" (The early years of the movement against the French in Nghệ Tĩnh and the evolution of the Phan Đình Phùng insurrection), *Nghiên cứu Lịch sử*, Hanoi, 1970, no. 133: 37–42.

[35] The figures were listed alphabetically within each rank.

Nguyễn Thị Chiên	1930–	Thái Bình
Nguyễn Thị Minh Khai	1910–1941	Nghệ An
Nguyễn Văn Trỗi	1940–1964	Đà Nẵng
Núp	1919–1999	Gia Lai
Phan Đình Giót	1920–1954	Hà Tĩnh
Phạm Ngọc Thạch	1909–1968	Sa Đéc
Trần Đại Nghĩa	1913–1997	Vĩnh Long
Trần Phú	1904–1931	Hà Tĩnh
Võ Thị Sáu	1935–1953	Bà Ria
2nd row (7 figures)		
Bế Văn Đàn	1931–1954	Cao Bằng
Ngô Gia Tự	1908–1935	Hà Bắc
Nguyễn Quốc Trị	1921–1967	Nghệ An
Nguyễn Thị Suốt	1902–1966	Quảng Ninh
Nguyễn Văn Cừ	1912–1941	Hà Bắc
Nguyễn Viết Xuân	1934–1964	Vĩnh Phú
Phạm Hồng Thái	1893–1924	Nghệ An
3rd row (7 figures)		
Cao Lục	1929–1974	Nghệ An
Cao Viết Bảo	1932–1985	Nam Định
Lê Minh Đức	1923–	Sa Đéc
Lê Văn Tám	1931–1945	Saigon
Trần Cừ	1920–1950	Vĩnh Yên
Trần Văn Ơn	1932–1950	Saigon
Vừ A Dính	19??–19??	Lai Châu

The new patriotic pantheon decided the course of the nation's history as determined by those in power, who needed to establish a monopoly on memory with the help of a few key figures. The boundaries of legitimacy were drawn by Hồ Chí Minh and, by extension, the various organisations in power (*Thanh Niên*, the ICP, the VWP).

A History in Four Acts

The official new timeline was divided into four main periods: the "Golden Age" of the early resistance against colonial rule (1924–1945), the Franco-Vietminh War (1946–1954), the struggle for socialist production (1955–1964), and the war against the South (1965–1975). It followed the outlines presented by the heroic figures of the new patriotic pantheon.

Phạm Hồng Thái (1893–1924) inaugurated the "Golden Age" of the first legitimate resistance against colonial rule (1924–1945) with his attempt to assassinate Governor Merlin in Canton in June 1924, thus becoming the first martyr of the "new history". He predated the creation of the *Thanh Niên* but was already in good company when he visited China in 1922 with Lê Hồng Phong and Lê Thiết Hùng to join the Resistance.[36] He was a great influence on the movement. The 1920s–30s were formative years for the Vietnamese Resistance. The ICP (and later the VWP) first created the myth of the indomitable cadre-militant at the height of the colonialist repression of 1930–33. The Sûreté came down hard on the first militants, all of whom met exemplary deaths during the two major waves of repression (1931–33 and 1939–1941). Trần Phú (1904–1931), elected first General Secretary of the ICP November 1930,[37] was arrested in Saigon in April 1931; he was tortured and died in September. Ngô Gia Tự (1908–1935), one of the founders of the ICP and its first cell in Hanoi on Hàm Long Street,[38] was arrested in 1930 and sent to Poulo Condor, where he drowned while trying to escape. Nguyễn Văn Cừ (1912–1941), founding member of the ICP and Party General Secretary at the age of 26 in 1938,[39] died in Poulo Condor in 1941. Lastly, the couple Lê Hồng Phong (1902–1942) and Nguyễn Thị Minh Khai (1910–1941)[40] both died at Poulo Condor, lending a tragic and romantic air to the self-sacrifice of the first generation of revolutionaries.[41]

---

[36] Phạm Thị Kim, ed. *Phạm Hồng Thái*. Hô Chi Minh City: nxb Văn Nghệ, 1994. Bách Hào. *Phạm Hồng Thái*. Nxb Nghệ Tĩnh, 1977.

[37] *Cái chết của Trần Phú, một chiến sĩ cộng sản* (The death of Trần Phú, a communist combatant). Ninh Bình: Phân Hội Mác, 1950. *Gương liệt sĩ* (Exemplary martyrs). Hanoi: nxb Kim Đồng, 1984, pp. 5–7.

[38] Lê Quốc Sử. *Ngô Gia Tự*. Hanoi: nxb Kim Đồng, 1979. *Gương liệt sĩ*, pp. 8–10.

[39] Đào Phiếu. *Nguyễn Văn Cừ, một lãnh đạo xuất sắc của Đảng* (Nguyễn Văn Cừ, an exemplary leader of the Party). Hanoi: nxb Sự thật, 1987.

[40] Đồng Thế. *Kể chuyện Lê Hồng Phong* (The storyteller Lê Hồng Phong). Hanoi: nxb Kim Đồng, 1970. *Nữ chiến sĩ cách mạng chị Minh Khai* (The revolutionary combatant Minh Khai). Nha Tuyên truyền và Văn nghệ, 1951; Nguyễn Tú. *Chị Minh Khai*. Hanoi: nxb Phụ Nữ, 1976.

[41] Sophie Quinn-Judge partially questions this myth in an article that was passed around secretly. She implied that Nguyễn Thị Minh Khai and Nguyễn Ái Quốc were married, a hypothesis that casts further doubt on the nature of her relationship with Lê Hồng Phong. See S. Quinn-Judge, "Hô Chi Minh: New Perspectives from the Comintern Files", in *Viêt Nam Forum*, New Haven, no. 14, 1993: 61–81.

In 1941, with Hồ Chí Minh's return to Pắc Bó (Hà Quảng, Cao Bằng), the Party's propaganda department wanted to scale back the heroisation of early patriots in favour of the still little-known figure of Hồ Chí Minh. During the Franco-Japanese occupation (1941–45), only the ethnic Tày Hoàng Văn Thụ (1906–1944) assumed a prominent place in official history, though less than those mentioned above.[42] Head of military propaganda for the Việt Bắc region, Thụ was arrested during a mission in 1943 and executed a year later. The hero of Lạng Sơn heralded a shift in the make-up of the Việt Minh's patriotic pantheon. The trend was now toward figures from outside of the Party apparatus who had died while performing courageous acts. The tragic fate of two heroic adolescents, Lý Tự Trọng (1914–1931) and Kim Đồng (1928–1943), illustrates perfectly the DRV's approach towards this early period of the ICP and the Việt Minh.[43] Both symbolised the voluntary and patriotic engagement of youth within the Resistance. On the eve of the August insurrection of 1945, the new regime had a series of figures-reference points within its collective memory for every moment of its brief revolutionary past.

The war against France (1946–1954) also generated its share of heroic figures who symbolised the struggle of an entire nation. Early Party leaders gave way to new heroes and a whole string of teenaged martyrs. From 1950 onwards, more and more soldiers were honoured: Trần Cừ (1920–1950) and La Văn Cầu (1932), who distinguished themselves at the front at Đông Khê in the fall of 1950,[44] the former losing his life and the latter his arm; Nguyễn Quốc Trị (1921–1967), who led his company to victory during the taking of Gối Hạc in May 1951;[45] Cù Chính Lan (1930–1951) who died a martyr's death at the front in Hòa Bình in 1951;[46] and Phan Đình Giót (1920-1954) and Bế Văn Đàn (1931–1954), who died during the battle of Điện Biên Phủ in the spring of 1954.[47] Of course, these were all

[42] Trần Đức Cường. "Hoàng Văn Thụ, một chiến sĩ cách mạng kiên trung" (Hoàng Văn Thụ, a resolute and loyal combattant for the revolution), in *Nghiên cứu Lịch sử*. Hanoi, 1984, pp. 52–5.

[43] *Gương liệt sĩ.*, pp. 52–5.

[44] *Anh hùng lực lượng vũ trang nhân dân* (Heroes of the people's armed forces), pp. 28–30 (on Trần Cừ) and pp. 12–4 (on La Văn Cầu).

[45] Xuân Diệu. *Kể chuyện Cù Chính Lan, Nguyễn Quốc Trị, Hoàng Hanh*. Hanoi: 1954.

[46] *Anh hùng Quân đội Cù Chính Lan* (The military hero Cù Chính Lan). Nha Tuyên truyền và Văn nghệ, 1952; Nguyễn Giang, *Truyện anh hùng Quân đội Cù Chính Lan* (History of the military hero Cù Chính Lan). Hanoi: nxb Văn Nghệ, 1955.

[47] Phác Văn. *Phan Đình Giót lấy thân mình lấp lỗ châu mai* (Phan Đình Giót blocks a canon with his body). Hanoi: nxb Việt Nam, 1954.

victories by the Việt Minh over French Expeditionary Forces. A number of villagers were also fêted: Mạc Thị Bưởi (1927–1951), Nguyễn Thị Chiên (1930), Nguyễn Thị Suốt (1902–1966), and the Bahnar leader Núp (1919–1999) from the Central Highlands, who were chosen to illustrate the courage and perseverance of communal guerrilla organisations.[48] The vigour of the nation was also expressed through the bravery of its many teenaged martyrs, four of whom received special honours by the propaganda department. In the South, Lê Văn Tám (14-years-old) doused himself with gasoline and then threw himself, aflame, into an enemy munitions depot in 1945. Also in Saigon, during the anti-American demonstrations of 1950, the student Trần Văn Ơn (1932–1950) courageously resisted Southern police forces and was eventually shot at point-blank range. In Cochinchina, Võ Thị Sáu (1935–1953) was sent to Poulo Condor prison at the age of 15 for having participated in several resistance operations; she died 3 years later from ill-treatment. Finally, in the northwestern mountains near Lào Cai, the teenager Vừ A Dính lost his life one night after leading some resistants to the start of their mission.[49]

The DRV threw all of its propagandistic might behind these soldiers, communal militia members, patriotic children, and their war of resistance. After the victory of 1954, however, ideologues from the VWP shifted their attention from exemplary resistance fighters to the struggle for socialist production (1955–1964). While the average peasant could understand the concept of the "hero-martyr" who fell in battle, he had a harder time understanding the honour bestowed upon an exemplary worker. Of the many people elected labour hero from 1952 to 1964, few managed to successfully take root within the popular imagination. Propaganda authorities noted this weakness and were content to focus their efforts on a few key individuals, knowing that they could never match the force of the nation's distinguished warriors. This basic wariness explains why few figures from the labour or peasant movement are included in the national pantheon. Only three labour heroes entered into popular consciousness: Cao Lục (1929–1974), outstanding leader of the cooperative at Ba Tơ in Nghệ An; Cao Viết Bảo (1932), exemplary worker in the weapons industry; and

[48] Trần Cần. *Mạc Thị Bưởi, Truyện – Thơ* (Mạc Thị Bưởi, poems). Hanoi: nxb Phổ Thông, 1957; Vũ Cao and Mai Văn Hiến. *Nguyễn Thị Chiên*. Quân đội Nhân dân, 1952; Nguyên Ngọc. *Đất nước đứng lên* (The nation wakes up). Hanoi: nxb Văn học, 1956.

[49] *Những ngày kỷ niệm lớn trong nước* (The nation's important dates of remembrance). Hanoi: nxb Quân đội Nhân dân, 1972, p. 172.

Lê Minh Đức (1923), a railway worker. Together, they represented the entry of North Vietnam into the socialist era.

Finally, the last reference period was the resumption of hostilities with South Vietnam. In 1964–65, the propaganda department of the VWP focused its efforts on the extraordinary lives of two young martyrs: Nguyễn Văn Trỗi (1940–1964), who was sentenced to death in 1964 after attempting to assassinate U.S. Secretary of State McNamara, and Nguyễn Viết Xuân (1934–1964), a young soldier who died in battle during the first American bombings. At each new stage of its struggle for independence, the DRV sought to respond with new heroic and loyal myths adapted to the times and to the ideal of invincibility put forth by official history.

Territory and Control

The widespread establishment of new heroes gave rise to a new geography of power which even today defines political culture in Vietnam. In a study of the demigods of Soviet mythology, the historians Nikolai Kopossov and Dina Khapaeva showed how the redistribution of patriotic titles in the Soviet Union benefitted the local level.[50] In rural societies, localism has always been a critical tool for getting the people to accept the material reality of the central government. The emergence of the DRV as a national political force was built on the pretence of a village politics developed and adapted to the rules of democratic centralism. In helping to rewrite the history of the new regime, the hero suddenly redefined the contours of the geography of power. The construction of the DRV's political identity was adapted to the three parts of its cultural roots (the myth of the reunification of the three *Kỳ* [regions], the north, centre and south).[51]

From 1964–66, the advent of many heroic figures from the South answered this quest for geographical balance. There was no question in Hanoi, however, of the North and South being completely equal: the

---

[50] N. Kopossov and D. Khapaeva, "Les demi-dieux de la mythologie soviétique, étude sur les représentations collectives de l'histoire" (Demigods in Soviet mythology, a study on collective representations of history), in *Annales ESC,* Paris, no. 4–5, July–October 1992: 963–87.

[51] North: Cù Chính Lan, Hoàng Hanh, Hoàng Văn Thụ, Kim Đồng, Lê Hồng Phong, La Văn Cầu, Lý Tự Trọng, Mạc Thị Bưởi, Ngô Gia Khảm, Nguyễn Thị Chiên, Nguyễn Thị Minh Khai, Phan Đình Giót, Trần Phú, Bế Văn Đàn, Ngô Gia Tự, Nguyễn Quốc Trị, Phạm Hồng Thái, Nguyễn Văn Cử, Nguyễn Viết Xuân, Cao Lục, Cao Viết Bảo, and Vũ A Dính. Centre: Nguyễn Văn Trỗi, Núp, and Nguyễn Thị Suốt. South: Phạm Ngọc Thạch, Trần Đại Nghĩa, Võ Thị Sáu, Lê Minh Đức, Lê Văn Tám, Trần Cừ, and Trần Văn Ơn.

revolution was still in Northern hands. The reality of the newly drawn geography of power was that nearly 70 per cent of the new heroes in the pantheon were from the North. The revolution, in its incarnation as a relationship of power, was first and foremost a Northern creation. More precisely, the actual heart of political power was in the region of Nghệ An/Hà Tĩnh, which produced 10 of the 22 figures in the North Vietnamese pantheon. This was also the birthplace of Nguyễn Ái Quốc (Nguyễn Saviour of the Nation), aka Hồ Chí Minh (He Who Enlightens). He was born in the village of Kim Liên, 14 kilometres west of the city of Vinh, on 19 May 1890. Some might say that this was just a coincidence, for why would the government want to privilege one region over another? Is the myth of the new hero not supposed to reinforce the traditional and originary link to one's own native village? Obviously the government had its reasons for doing what they did.[52]

The political decision-making process in Vietnam today is still marked by this principle, and the grouping of interests based on geographical solidarity is ever-present in its political culture. This issue merits further study, but I will merely add here that the new hero, as a sort of cultural relay between the central government and the provincial level, had since the 1960s become a highly effective tool for the reintegration of the local within the history of the nation. His empowerment at the provincial level was part of the affirmation of political centralism within a geographical space that had long been vulnerable to rupture. The rebalancing of the centre/periphery testified to the emergence of a new geopolitics of decision-making power that has continued ever since. The political imaginary of the DRV reflected the diversity of the nation, and political power was always conceived of with reference to the organisation of the family unit. The myth of the "great Vietnamese family" conferred upon government representatives a patriarchal role in society. Confucianism in Vietnam, according to the linguist Phan Ngọc, was different from its Chinese counterpart in its more ardent sense of the nation:

[52] In some areas the advantages were quite obvious: "Many villagers occupy high positions within the central government. Five people from Quỳnh Đôi were members of the central committee, six others were elected deputy at the National Assembly, and three more were members of the steering committees for mass organisations — and we've lost track of how many people from the commune hold key positions in the government, at all levels, from ministries to district people's committees. We sent quite a lot of people [to Hanoi] in the 1950s–60s", from an interview (Quỳnh Đôi commune, Quỳnh Lưu district).

> All Confucian concepts have to be seen through a first prism: the Vietnamese Fatherland. A single concept in Chinese philosophy splits to give rise to two concepts. With filial piety, for example, we find the lesser filial piety relating to the duties of a child to his parents (i.e., Confucian piety) and then the greater filial piety towards one's country. This duality runs through Vietnamese Confucianism. The interpersonal is on a lower level, while anything which serves the nation or the people is higher. This differentiation has never been stated by any Chinese writer. It is a Vietnamese idea. And Nguyễn Trãi did not hesitate when he had to choose. He chose the higher piety, higher wisdom, and higher humanism. It is the choice of any Vietnamese in any era. Contemporary history in Vietnam is all the proof you need.[53]

The DRV's new patriotic pantheon reflected the heterogeneity of the great Vietnamese family, a rallying point for different generations, genders, and ethnicities. Like a mirror of the national reality, its structure was that of a large family carrying on under the watchful eye of their *pater familias*, Uncle Ho. Teenagers or young adults sat side-by-side with their older siblings or parents. Lê Văn Tám was 14 when he sacrificed his life for his country, Võ Thị Sáu was 15, Cù Chính Lan was 22, etc. In 1952, when Hoàng Hanh accepted his title of hero, it was an "old man" of 64 who mounted the podium at the conference of Tuyên Quang. For the people to identify with their heroic figures, a mix of genders and ethnicities was also required. Women held an important position even within ethnic communities.[54] A woman's act of bravery was more meaningful in the people's eyes — her choice to devote herself to the nation rather than to her traditional duties (children, housework, etc.) reinforced the extraordinary nature of her chosen path. The re-evaluation of a woman's place in society was certainly common to all countries in the communist bloc, but in Vietnam it grew out of an ancient principle that for centuries gave a prominent place to the glorious deeds of the nation's heroines (Hai Bà Trưng, Bà Triêu, Bùi Thị Xuân, etc.). The great Vietnamese family fulfilled the myth of the national ethnic melting pot. Government leaders pointed out that ethnic minorities — rallying around the Kinh of course — participated

---

[53] Phan Ngọc. "Le confucianisme dans l'environnement sud-est asiatique" (Confucianism in the Southeast Asian environment). Hanoi: Épreuves, 1996, p. 6.

[54] There were only five women, however, out of the thirty-two heroic figures: Võ Thị Sáu (1935–1952), Mạc Thị Bưởi (1927–1951), Nguyễn Thị Chiên (1930), Nguyễn Thị Minh Khai (1910–1941), and Nguyễn Thị Suốt (1906–1968).

fully in the modernisation of the country. The bureaucracy of heroism made sure to integrate a whole series of new heroes from various ethnicities. The biography of the hero Núp, a Bahnar combatant from Gia Lai province, was published in 1956 by the writer Nguyễn Ngọc and was tremendously popular.[55] Within the patriotic pantheon, a great many figures were from ethnic minorities: three Tày (La Văn Cầu, Bế Văn Đàn, Hoàng Văn Thụ), one Banhar (Núp), one Nùng (Kim Đồng), and one Mèo (Vừ A Dính). National cohesion depended on a show of solidarity in the community.[56]

The new political pantheon of the DRV created a sense of belonging: — men, women, young and old, Kinh and minority — they were all facets of the great Vietnamese family as imagined and reconstructed by ideologues of the propaganda department of the VWP. The new hero of Vietnam formally followed the lead of the Sino-Soviet Stakhanovist model, but the internationalist dimension does not paint the whole picture. Ideologues and intellectuals from the DRV were clever in that they were able to back him up with a genealogy. With the emergence of a revolutionary lineage, the government acquired a historical foundation, and by reinventing its illustrious ancestors, the State took charge of a collective memory that had been stricken with selective amnesia.

---

[55] Nguyên Ngọc. *Noup le héros des montagnes* (Đất nước đứng lên) (Núp, hero of the mountains). Hanoi: ELE, 1956, translated by Georges Boudarel.

[56] The collective work edited in 1995 by Bế Viết Đẳng includes a list of minority figures who were awarded the title of "military hero" from 1952 to 1985. Among the 117 figures, the ethnic division is as follows: Tày: 25 (21 per cent); Nùng: 14 (12 per cent); Thai: 14 (12 per cent); Muong: 10 (8.5 per cent); Hrê: 10 (8.5 per cent); Gia rai: 7 (6 per cent); Ta ôi: 5 (4 per cent); Hmông: 6 (5 per cent); Khmer: 4 (3.4 per cent); Raglai: 5 (5 per cent); Banhar: 3 (2.5 per cent); Giè Triêng: 2 (1.7 per cent); Cao Lan–San Chi: 2 (1.7 per cent); Cham: 2 (1.7 per cent); Xo dang: 1 (0.8 per cent); Co tu: 1 (0.8 per cent); Xtièng: 1 (0.8 per cent); Co: 1 (0.8 per cent); Cho ro: 1 (0.8 per cent); Dao: 1 (0.8 per cent); Kho mo: 1 (0.8 per cent); Bru-Van Kiêu: 1 (0.8 per cent). See Bế Viết Đẳng, ed., *50 năm các dân tộc thiểu số ở Việt Nam*, pp. 271–6.

Conclusion

> The vanquished always want to imitate the victor in his distinctive characteristics, his dress, his occupation, and all his other conditions and customs. The reason for this is that the soul always sees perfection in the person who is superior to it and to whom one is subservient. It considers him perfect, either because it is impressed by the respect we have for him, or because it erroneously assumes that its own subservience to him is not due to the nature of defeat but to the perfection of the victor. If that erroneous assumption fixes itself in the soul, it becomes a firm belief. The soul, then, adopts all the manners of the victor and assimilates itself to him. This, then, is imitation.... This goes so far that a nation dominated by another, neighbouring nation will show a great deal of assimilation and imitation.
>
> Ibn Khaldûn[1]

A history of the new man in Vietnam requires an examination of the ruptures, inconsistencies, and misunderstandings contained within the source materials and words of those involved, both past and present. This brings us back to the premise of this study. Nothing *a priori* is more familiar to the new Vietnamese hero than his Chinese or Soviet counterpart of the 1950s–60s. Yet, as the historian Carlo Ginzburg writes, "in the cross-section of any present are also encrusted many pasts, of varying temporal thickness, which can refer us to a much larger spatial context".[2] During the course of this work, I wanted to show that the development of the exemplary man in Vietnam depended deeply on the new government's need for legitimacy and identity. The question of heroism, through the lives of a few key figures, reveals the extent to which the DRV wanted to build a new nation, and in so doing sheds light on the many difficult choices that the government had to make in those uncertain times.

---

[1] Ibn Khaldûn. *The Muquddimah: An Introduction to History*. Princeton: Bollingen Series, 1967, p. 22. Edited and abridged by N.J. Dawood, translated by Franz Rosenthal.
[2] Carlo Ginzburg. *Ecstasies: Deciphering the Witches' Sabbath*. University of Minnesota: Pantheon, 1991, p. 21. Translated by Raymond Rosenthal.

At the close of the Second World War, Vietnam existed as a land of ancestors (*Tổ Quôc*) but not yet as a nation (*Quốc gia* or *Quốc dân*). Vietnamese nationalism had arisen fairly late, at the end of the nineteenth century with the movement of Vietnamese scholars called *Cần Vương* (Loyalists). The defeat of the Resistance, the division of the country, and its tutelage under the French led to a new understanding of the concept of a nation while weakening the relevance of Confucian ideas. "Words take on new meanings: like *dân*, which means child of the king, but became the word for citizen. Terms from modern Vietnamese enter the language: patriotism (*Ái Quốc*), nation (*quốc dân*), compatriot (*đồng bào*), national state (*quốc gia*), democratic republican revolution (*dân chủ cộng hòa*)."[3] Belatedly, the educated elite transferred their allegiance from the legitimacy of the king to that of the nation. But these concepts were still completely unknown to the majority of the people when the Viêt Minh appeared on the scene. With the rise to power in 1945 of an elite group that was mostly educated abroad,[4] the construction of a modern political identity became a priority for the DRV. The war, and the need to mobilise the population, forced the Resistance to seek the means for its own survival. It was no surprise that they would need heroes. The myth of the nation's saviour had never looked like this before. Traditionally there had always been some who wanted to "humanise" the hero by portraying him more like an ordinary person than an extraordinary one, since "heroes were only men, to whom credulity granted aspects of the marvellous".[5]

The new hero helped to build a new nation, but he also forced the government into deciding on a suitable model. When communism was imported into the Third World as an exogenous ideology, it had to be adapted to suit different cultures. I have chosen not to examine here the clash between Confucianism and Marxism in sinicised countries.[6] Vietnamese

[3] Brocheux, Pierre and Daniel Hémery. *Indochina, an Ambiguous Colonisation, 1858–1954*. Berkeley: University of California Press, 2009, p. 293.

[4] Anatoly Sokolov. *Kommintern i Vietnam*. Moscow: Institut Vostokovedeniia RAN, 1998. Published the following year in Vietnam as *Quốc tế Cộng sản và Việt Nam*. Hanoi: nxb Chính trị Quốc gia, 1999.

[5] Veyne. *Les Grecs ont-ils cru à leurs mythes*, p. 53.

[6] J. Chesnaux, G. Boudarel, and D. Hémery, eds. *Tradition et révolution au Viet-Nam* (Tradition and revolution in Vietnam). Paris: Anthropos, 1971; and Trinh Van Thao. *Viet Nam, du confucianisme au communisme* (Vietnam, from Confucianism to communism). Paris: L'Harmattan, 1990.

communism is pragmatic, so it was often resistant to the various outside influences that tried to shape it. Understanding the way in which a society copes with governmental decisions is a key part of political analysis. In Southeast Asia, Marxism-Leninism responded to the people's desire for independence and sovereignty through a brand of nationalism that aimed to anchor the revolution to the necessary and inevitable changes within each country. DRV leaders were torn between their dream of Soviet-style modernisation and the continued struggle for national liberation. The war legitimised the VWP in the eyes of the people and is key to understanding the foundations of a political regime that seemed indestructible. It also explains the regime's resistance to external change and influence. The rupture with traditional land-owning classes and the heroisation of the common man made this "popular" discourse much more appealing to the masses. The Maoism that took root in communist Vietnam began as a rural movement, and remained a tool that was introduced, represented, constructed, and defended by their longstanding and problematic neighbour to the north. As in China, communism in Vietnam stressed the modernity of the imported ideological model. The new Vietnamese elite was mostly fascinated by its success. They found its ideology to be "the very symbols of progress, as opposed to the traditional categories of Chinese thought, which privileged the countryside. Revolution and modernisation, as an indivisible whole, stand in opposition to counter-revolution and backwardness".[7] In the case of the DRV, the appearance of the new hero was initially a condition for obtaining legitimacy within the communist world. It is true, however, that the importation of *homo sovieticus* had to contend with the heroes of Tuyên Quang and were measured by their standard.

The question still remains as to how this imported model was put to use. In many ways, the new heroic figure fit into institutional categories common to the whole communist world. But the adoption of a foreign model in Vietnam suggests that it was not something fixed but would fluctuate, less due to changes within Vietnam than to the evolution of power relationships abroad. The new hero was an actor who was driven by certain necessities and followed a steady course. This is a key part of his adaptiveness, and it always seems to divide the field of historical research. Beyond the opposition Ideology/Culture, the image of the new man in Vietnam

[7] Yves Chevrier. "Mort et transfiguration: le modèle russe dans la révolution chinoise" (Death and transfiguration: the Russian model in the Chinese revolution), in *Extrême Orient-Extrême Occident*, Paris, no. 2, 1983: 71.

required a new sort of reasoning to be fully understood. Being neither completely foreign to traditional concepts, nor automatically similar to the Sino-Soviet model, and even less a blend of the two, he appears rather as the complex product of their similarities and differences.

Vietnamese communism must be understood in light of this double confrontation between the Soviet and Chinese models. China's strong influence on the creation of Vietnamese identity made it unlikely that they would simply transpose the Maoist model without question. And their reluctance to simply adopt a foreign concept reveals their constantly evolving state of analysis from one period to another. In Vietnam, political power had always progressed in relation to the position of its powerful neighbour. Understandably, Vietnamese leaders were eager to set themselves apart somehow. While Maoist China saw the adoption of an imported ideology as part of its historical confrontation with the West, Vietnam had to also take China into account. The entire governing structure of the DRV was developed with this dualism in mind. Hanoi had to honour this long-standing relationship while not showing too much allegiance.

This quest for impartiality undoubtedly destabilised the new North Vietnamese hero, but by limiting the hero's indigenisation to better reflect the Soviet canon, the government gained the desired distance from China. The history of communism in Vietnam should be seen in light of this principle of governance. It is true that after 1950 the DRV modelled itself greatly on Maoist China — land reform, accelerated collectivisation, and a similar desire to keep a tight grip on the masses — but the role played by Chinese advisers in the new emulation campaign that spawned the heroes of 1950–1952 was different from what they carried out in China. The version that prevailed following the Tuyên Quang conference was more the acceptance of a distant concept than a mere echo of the Chinese approach. In 1956, when the government condemned the "slavish imitation of foreign countries",[8] it pointed first at China, whose methods on the new man had thus far been faithfully applied.

In purely political terms, the new man was a key factor in the establishment of the North Vietnamese power base. The new hero was not only a symbol; he was very real both socially and politically. With the establishment of communist regimes in the sinicised world, countries had

[8] *Công tác thương binh liệt sĩ từ hòa bình lập lại đến này* (Activities for disabled veterans and martyrs from peacetime to today), in AVN3, BNV, file no. 2255, single document, 1961.

to redefine political loyalty, and thereby begin remodelling the virtuous man. The new ruling dynasty was obliged by the social reality to promulgate rules in accordance with the times. The government did not create the new man in opposition to society, but was instead aware of the rules and limits to social change within the community.

In Vietnam today, in towns and villages, in the newspaper, or in the government's words, one cannot but see this history in movement, a history in which the referents of yesterday intersect with those of today, one that is rich with allegories of a war of liberation that gave rise to the present. Despite the passing of time, the new hero is more than ever a reminder of the past, when the Vietnamese were victorious over a Western modernity ushered in by decades of French and then American presence on their soil. Exemplary workers, emulation fighters, and new heroes finally took hold with the express aim of forming an exemplary society, a stronger and more united community in which the belief in the future was deeply rooted in a nostalgia for the past.

Glossary

A

Anh hùng chân chính: legitimate hero
Anh hùng chủ nghĩa: heroism
Anh hùng hữu danh: renowned hero
Anh hùng lao động: labour hero
Anh hùng lịch sử: historical hero
Anh hùng lực lượng vũ trang: hero of the armed forces
Anh hùng mới: new hero
Anh hùng phản bội: treasonous hero
Anh hùng phong kiến: feudal hero
Anh hùng tập thể: collective hero
Anh hùng vô danh: anonymous hero

B

Ban canh nông: agricultural committee
Ban nghiên cứu lịch sử Đảng: study committee for Party history
Bần nông: poor peasant
Bàn thờ Tổ tiên: ancestral altar
Ban Thông Tin Tuyên Truyền: information and propaganda bureau
Ban Tổ chức Đại hội: committee for organising conferences
Ban Tuyên giáo Đảng Lao động: propaganda and political education section of the Party
Ban Vận Động thi đua: emulation committee or bureau
Bằng khen: certificate of merit
Bằng Tổ quốc ghi công: "the grateful nation" certificate
Bí thư xã: communal Party secretary
Bộ Canh nông: Ministry of Agriculture
Bộ Công nghiệp: Ministry of Industry
Bộ đội địa phương: communal forces of the PAVN
Bộ Giáo dục: Ministry of Education

Bộ Lao động: Ministry of Labour
Bộ Lễ: Ministry of Rites
Bộ nội vụ: Ministry of the Interior
Bộ Quốc phòng: Ministry of Defence
Bộ Thương binh — Cựu binh: Ministry of Disabled Veterans
Bồi dưỡng Anh hùng: training of heroes

C

Cá nhân xuất sắc: outstanding individual
Cải tạo tư tưởng: ideological reform
Cán bộ gương mẫu: exemplary cadre
Cán bộ lưu động Tỉnh: itinerant provincial cadres
Cán bộ sản xuất nông nghiệp: cadre for agricultural production
Cán bộ thi đua Tỉnh: provisional cadre in charge of emulation
Cán bộ văn hoá: cultural cadre
Cần, kiệm, liêm chính: thrift, diligence, integrity, honesty
Câu Lạc Bộ: club
Chi Bộ: Party cell
Chiến sĩ thi đua Công nghiệp: labour emulation fighter
Chiến sĩ thi đua Nông nghiệp: peasant emulation fighter
Chỉnh huấn: political rectification
Chính trị viên: political commissioner
Chủ nghĩa cá nhân: individualism
Chủ tịch xã: president of the commune
Chùa: pagoda
Cờ danh dự: patriotic banner
Cố nông: farm worker
Cơ quan Thông tấn xã Việt Nam: Information Bureau of Vietnam
Con người mới: new man
Công tác liệt sỹ: policy on martyrs
Công thần: cult of deserving officers

Đ

Đại diện Trung ương Đảng: representative of the Party's Central Committee
Đại gia đình việt nam: the "great Vietnamese family" (that is, the nation)
Đài tưởng niệm: commemorative statue
Dân công: civic worker
Dân quân: people's militia

Dân tộc anh hùng Việt Nam: the heroic Vietnamese people
Dân tộc thiểu số: ethnic minority
Đảng Lao Động: Vietnamese Worker's Party (VWP)
Đảng viên: Party member
Danh hiệu: title
Đất nước: the nation
Đất tổ tiên: the land of ancestors
Đền thờ: temple
Địa chủ: landlord
Đình: communal centre
Đoàn đánh cá: fishermen's group
Đội Bình dân học vụ: education group
Đội cải cách ruộng đất: agrarian reform team
Đội Chiến sĩ thi đua: emulation fighters' group
Đội dân quân văn hoá: cultural militia group
Đội lão quân: elderly militia group
Đời sống mới: new society
Đội trật tự: social control forces
Đội xung phong: vanguard group
Đơn vị du kích: guerrilla unit
Đức: virtue

G

Gia đình mất tích: family of one who is Missing in Action
Gia đình nuôi dưỡng thương binh: family taking care of a disabled veteran
Giải khuyến khích: encouragement prize
Giấy khen: proof of satisfaction, recompense

H

Hành động: action
Hiệu sách nhân dân: people's bookstore
Họ: family name, lineage
Hộ: home, hearth
Học sinh gương mẫu: exemplary student
Hội đồng Chính phủ: governmental commission
Hội đồng Huân chương Lao Động: information committee for awarding labour medals
Hội đồng Khen thưởng Trung ương: national awards commission
Hội đồng nhân dân: People's Assembly

Hội Liên hiệp Phụ nữ: Women's Association
Hội mẹ chiến sĩ: Association of Mothers of Combatants
Hội nghị thi đua toàn quốc: national emulation conference
Hội Nghiên cứu Chủ nghĩa Mác: Marxist study group
Hội Nông dân cứu quốc: association of peasants for national salvation
Hội trợ giúp giáo dục: association for the development of education
Hợp tác xã: cooperative
Huân chương Lao động: medal of labour
Huyện: district
Huyện uỷ: district Party committee

K

Khu: zone
Khu di tích: patrimonial space
Khu mộ: commemorative space built around the tomb of an illustrious person
Khu tự trị: autonomous zone
Khu vực thờ: ritual site

L

Làng: village
Lao động tiên tiến: vanguard worker
Lao động xuất sắc: outstanding worker
Lễ hội: festival
Liên hiệp Công đoàn: union organisation
Liên Khu: interzone
Liệt sĩ Tổ Quốc: national martyr
Lý lịch: biography

M

Mặt trận Tổ quốc: Fatherland Front
Miền Nam tập kết: South Vietnamese who took refuge in the North
Mộ giả: symbolic tomb

N

Nhà nghỉ dưỡng: rest home
Nhà Văn Hóa: cultural centre

Nhân cách cao thượng: exceptional person
Nhân thần: human spirit
Nhóm sản xuất: production group
Nềp nếp: order and discipline
Ngành: work sector
Ngày thương binh tử sĩ: day for disabled veterans and those who died for the country
Nghĩa trang: martyrs' cemetery
Nhà lưu niệm: House of Remembrance

P

Phái đoàn Chính phủ: government delegation
Phát động quần chúng: mobilisation of the masses
Phi nghĩa: unjust cause
Phòng Kế hoạch thi đua: emulation planning cell
Phong trào thi đua ái quốc: patriotic emulation movement
Phú Nông: rich peasant

Q

Quê hương: homeland

S

Sùng bái cá nhân: cult of personality

T

Tầng lớp dưới: lower class
Thanh niên: Revolutionary Youth League
Thị trấn: town
Thiên thần: heavenly spirit
Thiếu Nhi: children's organisation
Tiền tuất: pension
Tiểu sử anh hùng mới: biography of a new hero
Tỉnh: province
Tinh thần dân tộc: national spirit
Tỉnh uỷ: provincial Party committee
Tổ Đội Công: cell of mutual aid

Tổ Quốc: nation, fatherland
Tôn kính anh hùng: veneration of a hero
Tôn ti trật tự: social order
Trung nông: middle peasant
Tử sĩ: someone who died on duty
Tử trận: someone who died in battle
Tư tưởng tập thể: collectivist spirit
Tư tưởng xã hội chủ nghĩa: socialist spirit

U

Uỷ ban kháng chiến hành chính: resistance and administration committee
Uỷ ban Thống Nhất: committee for reunification

V

Vì Nghĩa: just cause
Việc bình thường hóa anh hùng: normalisation of the hero
Viện Huân chương: Institute of Medals
Vong quốc: loss of the nation

X

Xã: commune
Xã Hội mới: new society

Bibliography

Archives and Document Collections

National Archives of the Socialist Republic of Vietnam, centre no. 3, Hanoi, VN
Collection of the Ministry of Labour (Bộ Lao động), 1948–1964
Collection of the Ministry of the Interior (Bộ Nội vụ), 1948–1964
Collection of the Ministry of Disabled Veterans (Bộ Thương binh Xã hội), 1948–1964
Collection of the Ministry of Culture (Bộ Văn hóa), 1948–1964
Collection of the National Assembly (Quốc Hội), 1948–1964
Archives of the National Workers' Union (Tổng Công đoàn), Hanoi, VN
Archives of the Central Committee of the CPSU, Moscow, Russia
Archives of the Ministry of Soviet Foreign Affairs, Moscow, Russia
Southeast Asia Collection
Archives of the Cominform, Moscow, Russia
Centre des Archives d'Outre-Mer, Aix-en-Provence, France
Fonds du Conseiller diplomatique
Fonds du Conseiller politique
Fonds du Haut Commissariat pour l'Indochine
Fonds du service de protection du corps expéditionnaire
Guide to the Archival Collections are in Centre no. 3 of the National Archives, EFEO Hanoi, National Archives of Vietnam, 2006.

Secondary sources

Bakken, Borge. *The Exemplary Society. Human Improvement, Social Control and the Dangers of Modernity in China*. Oxford: Oxford University Press, 2000.

Benichou, Marcel. "Communisme et nationalisme", in *Hô Chi Minh: l'homme et son héritage*. Paris: Duong Moi/La voie nouvelle, 1990, pp. 117–50.

Beresford, Mary and Dang Phong. *Authority Relations and Economic Decision-Making in Viêt Nam. An Historical Perspective*. Copenhagen: NIAS, 1998.

Bodard, Lucien. *La guerre d'Indochine — l'enlisement (1963), l'humiliation (1965), l'aventure (1967)*. Paris: Grasset, 1997.

Boudarel, Georges. "Phan Bôi Châu et la société vietnamienne de son temps", *France-Asie*, Paris, no. 199, 4th trimester 1969: 355–433.

———. "Influences and Idiosyncrasies in the Line and Practice of the Vietnam Communist Party", in W.S. Turley, ed., *Vietnamese Communism in Comparative Perspective*. Boulder: Westview Press, 1980.

———. "L'insertion du pouvoir central dans les cultes villageois au Vietnam: esquisse des problèmes à partir des écrits de Ngô Tât Tô", in *Cultes populaires et sociétés asiatiques*. Paris: L'Harmattan, 1991, pp. 87–146.

Boudarel, Georges, ed. *La bureaucratie au Vietnam*. Paris: L'Harmattan, 1983.

Bourdeaux, Pierre. *Emergence et constitution de la communauté du Bouddhisme Hòa Hảo. Contributions à l'histoire sociale du delta du Mékong (1935–1955)*. Paris: Ecole Pratique des Hautes Etudes en Sciences Sociales. Unpublished thesis, 2003.

Brocheux, Pierre. *Hô Chi Minh. A Biography*. New York: Cambridge University Press , 2007.

Brocheux, Pierre and Daniel Hémery. *Indochina, an Ambiguous Colonisation, 1858–1954*. Berkeley: University of California Press, 2009.

Bui Quang Tung. "Le soulèvement des sœurs Trung dans les textes et le folklore vietnamien", *Bulletin de la société des études indochinoises*, Saigon, vol. 36, no. 1, 1961: 69–85.

Bui Tin. *Following Ho Chi Minh: Memoirs of a North Vietnamese Colonel*. Honolulu: University of Hawaii Press, 1995.

Cadière, Léopold. *Croyances et pratiques religieuse des Vietnamiens*. Paris: EFEO, 1992 (re-issue).

Chen Jian. "China and the first Indochina war, 1950–1954", *The China Quarterly*, no. 133, March 1993: 85–110.

Chen, K.C. *Vietnam and China, 1938–1954*. Princeton: Princeton University Press, 1969.

Chevrier, Yves. "Mort et transfiguration: le modèle russe dans la révolution chinoise", *Extrême-Orient*, Paris, no. 4, 1985: 81–139.

———. "De la révolution à l'État par le communisme", *Le Débat*, Paris, no. 117, November–December 2001: 92–113.

Chu Van Tan. *Reminiscences on the Army for National Liberation*. Ithaca: Cornell Univerity Southeast Asian Program, Data Paper no. 97, 1974.

Ci, Jiwei. *Dialectic of the Chinese Revolution, from Utopianism to Hedonism*. Stanford: Stanford University Press, 1994.

Clementin-Ojha, Catherine, ed. *Renouveaux religieux en Asie*. Paris: École française d'Extrême-Orient, 1997.

Condominas, Georges. *L'Espace social. A propos de l'Asie du Sud-Est*. Paris: Flammarion, 1980.

Culas, Christian. *Le messianisme hmong aux XIXe et XXe siècles. La dynamique religieuse comme instrument politique*. Paris: CNRS éditions-Editions de la MSH, 2005.

Devilliers, Philippe. *Histoire du Vietnam de 1940 à 1952*. Paris: Seuil, 1952.

Dror, Olga. *Cult, Culture, and Authority. Princess Liêu Hanh in Vietnamese History.* Honolulu: University of Hawaii Press, 2006.

Duiker, William J. "Hanoi Scrutinizes the Past: The Marxist Evaluation of Phan Boi Chau and Phan Chu Trinh", *Southeast Asia: An International Quarterly*, 1, no. 3, Summer 1971: 243–54.

———. *Vietnam: A Nation in Revolution*. Boulder: Westview press, 1983.

———. *Ho Chi Minh: A Life*. New York: Hyperion, 2000.

Dumoutier, Georges. *Les cultes annamites*. Hanoi: Schneider, 1907.

Fall, Bernard. *The Viet-Minh Regime*. Ithaca: Cornell University Press, 1954.

———. *Le Viêt Minh, la RDV 1945–60*. Paris: A. Colin, 1960.

Filtzer, Donald. *Soviet Workers and Stalinist Industrialisation: The Formation of Modern Soviet Production Relations, 1928–1941*. New York: M.E. Sharpe Inc., 1986.

Forest, Alain and Y. Ishizawa, eds. *Cultes populaires et sociétés asiatiques: appareils cultuels et appareils de pouvoir*. Paris: L'Harmattan-Sophia University (Tokyo), 1991.

Gaiduk, I.V. *The Soviet Union and the Vietnam War*. Chicago: Ivan R. Dee, 1996.

Gheddho, Piero. *Catholiques et Bouddhistes au Vietnam*. Paris: Alsatia, coll. Feux de l'histoire, 1970.

Giebel, Christopher. *Imagined Ancestries of Vietnamese Communism. Ton Duc Thang and the Politics of History and Memory*. University of Washington Press-NUS Press, 2004.

Ginsburgs, G. "Local Government and Administration in North Vietnam 1945–54", *The China Quarterly*, London, no. 10, April–June 1962: 174–204.

Goscha, Christopher. *Vietnam or Indochina? Contesting Concepts of Space in Vietnamese Nationalism, 1887–1954*. Copenhagen: NIAS, Reports Series no. 28, 1995.

———. *Thailand and the Southeast Asian Networks of the Vietnamese Revolution, 1885–1954*. London: Curzon Press, 1999.

———. *Historical Dictionary of the Indochina War: An International and Interdisciplinary Approach (1945–1954)*. Honolulu: University of Hawaii Press/ Copenhagen: Nordic Institute of Asian Studies, 2011.

Goscha, Christopher and Karine Laplante. *The Failure of Peace in Indochina*. Paris: Les Indes Savantes, 2010.

Goscha, Christopher and Thomas Engelbert. *Falling out of Touch: Study on Vietnamese Communist Policy towards an Emerging Cambodian Communist Movement, 1930–1975*. Centre for Southeast Asian Studies, Monash University, Clayton, 1995.

Gourou, Pierre. *Les Paysans du delta tonkinois*. Paris: Impr. de l'École française d'Extrême-Orient, 1966, (1st edition 1936).

Grossheim, Martin. *Nordvietnamesische Dorfgemeinschaften: Kontinuität und Wandel.* Hamburg: Mitteilungen des Instituts für Asienkunde, 1997.

Guérin, Matthieu *et al. Des montagnards aux minorités ethniques — Quelle intégration nationale pour les habitants des hautes terres du Vietnam et du Cambodge?* Bangkok-Paris: Irasec-L'Harmattan, 2003.

Guillemot, François. *Révolution nationale et lutte pour l'indépendance au Viêt-Nam (1938–1955): L'échec de la troisième voie Dai Viêt*. Paris: Les Indes Savantes, 2012.

Ha Van Thu and Tran Hông Duc. *Chronologie de l'histoire du Vietnam de la tradition orale à nos jours*. Hanoi: Éditions Thê Gioi, 2000.

Hardy, Andrew. *Red Hills. Migrants and the State in the Highlands of Vietnam*. Singapore: NIAS Press-ISEAS, 2005.

Hémery, Daniel. "Le communisme national au Viet Nam, L'investissement du marxisme par la pensée nationaliste", in René Galissot, ed., *Les aventures du marxisme*. Paris: Syros, 1984.

Hoang Van Chi. *From Colonialism to Communism: A Case History of North Vietnam*. New York: Praeger, 1964.

Huu Ngoc, ed. *À la découverte de la culture vietnamienne*. Hanoi: Éditions The Gioi, 2007 (4th edition).

Hy Van Luong. "Vietnamese Kinship: Structural Principles and the Socialist Transformation in Northern Vietnam", *Journal of Asian Studies*, Salt Lake City, vol. 48, no. 4, November 1989: 741–56.

———. *Revolution in the Village: Tradition and Transformation in North Vietnam, 1925–88*. Honolulu: University of Hawaii, 1992.

Jammes, Jérémy. *Les oracles du Cao Dai. Etudes d'un mouvement vietnamien et ses réseaux*. Paris: Les Indes Savantes, 2012.

Kerkvliet, Benedict J. *The Power of Everyday Politics — How Vietnamese Peasants Transformed National Politics*. Singapore: ISEAS, 2005.

Kerkvliet, Benedict J. and James Scott, eds. *Everyday Forms of Peasant Resistance in Southeast Asia*. London: Frank Cass, 1986.

Keyes, C., ed. *Asian Visions of Authority: Religion and the Modern States in East and Southeast Asia*. Honolulu: University of Hawaii Press, 1994.

Khapaeva, Dina and Nicolai Kopossov. "Les demi-dieux de la mythologie soviétique, étude sur les représentations collectives de l'histoire", *Annales ESC*, Paris, no. 4–5, July–October 1992: 963–87.

Kleinen, John. *Facing the Future, Reviving the Past: A Study of Social Change in a Northern Vietnamese Village*. Singapore: ISEAS, 1999.

Kolko, Gabriel. *Vietnam: Anatomy of a War, 1940–1975*. London: Allen & Unwin, 1986.

Kwon, Heonik. *After the Massacre: Commemoration and Consolation in Ha My and My Lai*. Berkeley: University of California Press, 2006.

Ky Thu. *Refermer le passé douloureux*. Hanoi: Editions Van Hoc, 1995.

La Motte (de), Dominique. *De l'autre côté de l'eau. Indochine 1950–1952*. Paris: Tallandier, 2009.

Lafont, Pierre-Bernard, ed. *Les frontières du Vietnam — histoire des frontières de la péninsule Indochinoise*. Paris: L'Harmattan, coll. Recherches asiatiques, 1989.

Langlet, Philippe. *L'ancienne historiographie d'Etat au Vietnam, tome I. Raisons d'être, conditions d'élaboration et caractères au siècle des Nguyên*. Paris: PEFEO, 1990.

Leys, Simon. *Ecrits sur la Chine*. Paris: Robert Laffont, 1998.

Lockhart, Greg. *Nations in Arms: The Origins of the People's Army of Vietnam*. Sydney: Allen and Unwin, 1991.

Lombard, Denys. *Le carrefour javanais, essai d'histoire globale*. Paris: Editions de l'EHESS, 1990.

Malarney, Shaun. "The Emerging Cult of Ho Chi Minh? A Report on Religious Innovation in Contemporary Northern Viet Nam", *Asian Cultural Studies*, no. 22, March 1996: 121–31.

_______. "The Limits of State Functionalism and the Reconstruction of Funerary Ritual in Contemporary Vietnam", *American Ethnologist*, vol. 23, no. 3, 1996: 540–60.

_______. *Culture, Ritual and Revolution in Vietnam*. New York: Routledge Curzon, 2002.

Marr, David G. *Vietnamese Anticolonialism, 1885–1925*. Berkeley: University of California Press, 1971.

_______. "The Vietnamese Language Revolution", in Wang, Guerrero, Marr, eds, *Society and the Writer: Essays on Literature in Modern Asia*. Canberra: Research of Pacific Studies, Australian National University, 1981, pp. 21–33.

_______. *Vietnamese Tradition on Trial, 1920–1945*. Berkeley: University of California Press, 1981.

_______. *Vietnam 1945: The Quest for Power*. Berkeley: University of California Press, 1995.

Martin, Helmut. *Cult and Canon: The Origins and Development of State Maoism*. New York: Sharpe, 1982.

McCargo, Duncan, ed. *Rethinking Vietnam*. London & New York: Routledge Curzon, 2004.

Michaud, Jean, ed. *Turbulent Times and Enduring Peoples: Mountain Minorities in the Southeast Asian Massif*. Richmond: Curzon, 2000.

Moise, Edwin. *Land Reform in China and North Vietnam: Consolidating the Revolution at the Village Level*. Chapel Hill: University of North Carolina Press, 1983.

Morris, Stephen J. *Why Vietnam Invaded Cambodia. Political Culture and the Causes of War*. Stanford: Stanford University Press, 1999.

Mus, Paul. *Viet-Nam, sociologie d'une guerre*. Paris, Seuil, 1952.

Népote, Jacques. "Quelle histoire? Pour quels Vietnamiens?", *Péninsule*, Paris, no. 11–2, 1985–86: 7–26.

Ngo Van. *Viêt Nam 1920–45 révolution et contre révolution sous la domination coloniale*. Paris: L'insomniaque, 1995.

Nguyên Thanh Hung. "Der Mythos von den Hung-Königen und das nationale Selbsversändnis der Vietnamesen", *Verfassung und Recht in Übersee*, Hamburg, no. 3, Fall 1979: 249–58.

Nguyên Thê Anh. "How did Hô Chi Minh become a Proletarian? Reality and Legend", *Asian Affairs*, London, 16, part 11, 1985: 163–70.

________. *Monarchie et fait colonial au Viêt-Nam (1875–1925). Le crépuscule d'un ordre traditionnel*. Paris: L'Harmattan, coll. Recherches asiatiques, Paris, 1992.

________. "La conception de la monarchie divine dans le Viêt Nam traditionnel", *BEFEO*, Paris, no. 84, 1997: 147–58.

Nguyên Thê Anh and Alain Forest, eds. *Guerre et paix en Asie du Sud-Est*. Paris: L'Harmattan, 1998.

Nguyên Thi Hiên. *Possessed by the Spirits: Mediumship in Contemporary Vietnamese Communities*. Ithaca: Cornell University Press Southeast Asia Program Publications, 2006.

Nguyên Tung, ed. *Mông Phu, un village du delta du fleuve Rouge*. Paris: L'Harmattan, 1999.

Nguyên Van Huyên. "Contribution à l'étude d'un génie tutélaire annamite Li Phuc Man", *BEFEO,* Paris, 1938: 1–110.

Nguyên Van Khoan. "Essai sur le Dinh et le culte du génie tutélaire de villages au Tonkin", *BEFEO,* Paris, v. XXX, 1930: 107–39.

Nguyên Van Ky. *La société vietnamienne face à la modernité. Le Tonkin de la fin du XIXe siècle à la seconde guerre mondiale*. Paris: L'Harmattan, 1995.

________. "Les enjeux des cultes villageois au Vietnam (1945–1997)", in John Kleinen, ed., *Vietnamese Society in Transition. The Daily Politics of Reform and Change*. Amsterdam: Het Spinhuis, 2001, pp. 183–201.

Nguyen Van Thang. *Ambiguity of Identity. The Mieu in North Vietnam*. Chiang Mai: Silkworm Books-Mekong Press, 2007.

Papin Philippe. "Sources, approches et premiers résultats pour une histoire du village vu d'en bas", *BEFEO*, Paris, no. 83, 1996: 89–114.

________. "Terres communales et pouvoirs villageois à la fin du XIXe siécle: le cas du village de Quynh Lôi", *Annales ESC*, Paris, no. 6, 10–11, 1996: 1303–23.

Pelley, Patricia. "The History of Resistance and the Resistance to History in Post-Colonial Constructions of the Past", in K.W. Taylor and J.K.Whitmore, eds, *Essays into Vietnamese Pasts*. Ithaca: Cornell University Press, 1995, pp. 232–45.

________. *Postcolonial Vietnam: New Histories of the National Past (Asia-Pacific)*. Durham: Duke University Press, 2002.

Pham Quynh Phuong. *Hero and Deity: Trân Hung Dao and the Resurgence of Popular Religion in Vietnam*. Chiang Mai: Silkworm Books-Mekong Press, 2009.

Pike, Douglas. *History of Vietnamese Communism, 1925–1976*. Stanford: Hoan Institution Press, 1978.

________. *PAVN: People's Army of Vietnam*. London: Brassey's Defence Publishers, 1986.

________. *Vietnam and the Soviet Union: Anatomy of an Alliance*. Boulder: Westview Press 1987.

Po Dharma and Mak Phoeum. *Du FLM au FULRO: Une lutte des minorités du sud indochinois, 1955–1975*. Paris: Les Indes savantes, 2006.

Porter, Gareth. "Vietnamese Communist Policy toward Kampuchea, 1930–1970", in David P. Chandler and Ben Kiernan, eds. *Revolution and Its Aftermath in Kampuchea: Eight Essays*, Monograph Series no. 25. New Haven: Yale University Southeast Asia Studies, 1983, pp. 57–98.

———. *Vietnam: The Politics of Bureaucratic Socialism*. Ithaca: Cornell University Press, 1993.

Post, Ken. "The Working Class in North Vietnam and the Launching of the Building of Socialism", *Journal of Asian and African Studies*, London, vol XXIII, no. 1–2, January–April 1988: 141–55.

———. *Revolution, Socialism and Nationalism in Vietnam*. Hants: Darmouth Publishing Company, 1989 (3 volumes).

Pye, Lucian W. *Asian Power and Politics: The Cultural Dimensions of Authority*. Cambridge: Harvard University Press, 1985.

Qiang Zhai. "Transplanting the Chinese Model: Chinese Military Advisors and the First Vietnam War, 1950–1954", *The Journal of Military History*, 57, October 1993: 689–715.

———. *China & the Vietnam Wars, 1950–1975*. Chapel Hill: The University of North Carolina Press, 2000.

Reid, Anthony and Nhung Tuyêt Trân, eds. *Viêt Nam: Borderless Histories*. Madison: University of Wisconsin Press, 2006.

Ruscio, Alain. *Les Communistes français et la guerre d'Indochine, 1944–1954*. Paris: L'Harmattan, 1985.

Salemink, Oscar. *The Ethnology of Vietnam's Central Highlanders: A Historical Contextualisation, 1850–1990*. London: Routledge Curzon, 2003.

Sardesai, D.R. *Vietnam: The Struggle for National Identity*. Boulder: Westview Press, 1988.

Shao, K. "Zhou Enlai's Diplomacy and the Neutralisation of Indo-China", *The China Quarterly*, London, no. 107, September 1986: 483–504.

Sheng, Michael. "The triumph of internationalism: CCP-Moscow relations before 1949", *Diplomatic History*, no. 1, vol. 21, Winter 1997: 95–104.

Sheridan, Mary. "The Emulation of Heroes", *The China Quarterly*, London, no. 33, January–March 1968: 47–72.

Shreiner, Klaus H. *Politischer Heldenkult in Indonesien*. Hamburg: Dietrich Reimer Verlag, 1995.

Smith, Ralph. *An International History of the Vietnam War: Revolution versus Containment 1955–61*. New York: St. Martin's Press, 1981.

———. "Ho Chi Minh's Last Decade, 1960–69: Between Moscow and Beijing", *Indonesia Report*, London, no. 27, April–June 1991: 1–19.

Sokolov, Anatoli. *Kommintern in Vietnam*. Moscow: Iv Ran, 1998.

Stowe, Judy. "Money and Mobilisation: The Difficulties of Building an Economy in Time of War", in C.E. Goscha and B. de Tréglodé, eds. *The Birth of a Party-State. Vietnam since 1945*. Paris: Les Indes savantes, Paris, 2004.

Stuart-Fox, M. *Buddhist Kingdom Marxist State: The Making of Modern Laos*. Bangkok: White Lotus, 1996.

Tavernier, Emilie. *Le culte des ancêtres*. Saigon: Editions Albert Portail, 1926.

Taylor, Keith. *The Birth of Vietnam*. Berkeley: University of California Press, 1982.

Taylor, Keith and John Whitmore, eds. *Essays into Vietnamese Pasts*. Ithaca: Cornell University Press, 1995.

Taylor, Philip. *Goddess on the Rise: Pilgrimage and Popular Religion in Vietnam*. Honolulu: University of Hawaii Press, 2004.

Taylor, Philip, ed. *Modernity and Re-enchantment: Religion in Post-revolutionary Vietnam*. Singapore: ISEAS, 2007.

Tertrais, Hugues. *La Piastre et le fusil — Le Coût de la guerre d'Indochine, 1945–1954*. Paris: Comité pour l'histoire économique et financière de la France, 2002.

Tessier, Olivier. "Aide (*giúp đỡ*) et réciprocité dans une société villageoise du Nord du Vietnam: entre solidarité et dépendance", *Moussons*, Aix-en-Provence, no. 13–4, IRSEA: 205–42.

Thai Quang Trung. "Hanoi-Pekin-Moscou: 30 ans d'amitiés illusoires", *Défense nationale*, Paris 36, no. 2, February 1980: 69–84.

________. *Collective Leadership and Factionalism, an Essay on Hô Chi Minh's Legacy*. Singapore: ISEAS, 1985.

Thaveepoorn, Vasavakul. *Schools and Politics in South and North Vietnam: A Comparative Study of State Apparatus, State Policy, and State Power (1945–1965)*. Unpublished dissertation, Cornell University, 1994.

Thayer, Carl. "Vietnam's Two Strategic Tasks: Building Socialism and Defending the Fatherland", *Southeast Asian Affairs*, Singapore, 1983: 299–324.

________. *War by Other Means: National Liberation and Revolution in Viet Nam 1954–1960*. Sydney: Allen & Unwin, 1989.

Tôn Thât Thien. *The Foreign Politics of the Communist Party of Vietnam. A Study of Communist Tactics*. London: Crane Russak, 1985.

Tønnesson, Stein. *Vietnam 1946: How the War Began*. University of California Press, 2009.

Tran Ngoc Them. *Recherche sur l'identité de la culture vietnamienne*. Hanoi: Editions Thê Gioi, 2008.

Trân Thi Liên. "Les Catholiques vietnamiens dans la république du Viêt Nam (1954–1973)", in Pierre Brocheux, ed., *Du conflit d'Indochine aux conflits indochinois*. Brussels: Complexe, 2000.

________. "The Catholic Question in North Viet Nam from Polish Sources (1954–56)" and "New Evidence on the Cold War History of Vietnam (1954–1975)", *Cold War History*, vol. 5, no. 4, November 2005: 431–52.

Tréglodé (de), Benoît. "Premiers contacts entre le Viêt Nam et l'Union Soviétique (1947–1948). Nouveaux documents des archives russes", *Approches-Asie*, no. 16, 1999: 125–35.

———. "Les relations entre le Viêt-Minh, Moscou et Pekin à travers les documents (1950–1954)", *Revue historique des armées*, Paris, no. 4, 2000: 55–62.

———. *Héros et Révolution au Viêt Nam*. Paris: L'Harmattan, 2001.

Tréglodé (de), Benoît and Christopher Goscha, eds. *The Birth of a Party-State. Vietnam since 1945*. Paris: Les Indes savantes, 2004.

Tréglodé (de), Benoît and Stéphane Dovert, eds. *Viêt Nam contemporain*. Paris: Les Indes Savantes, 2009.

Trinh Van Thao. *Viêt Nam, du confucianisme au communisme*. Paris: L'Harmattan, 1990.

Truong Chinh. "Marxisme et culture vietnamienne. Rapport de la 2e conférence nationale de la culture tenue en juillet 1948", *Écrits*, Hanoi, 1977: 225–311.

Turley, William S. *Vietnamese Communism in Comparative Perspective*. Boulder: Westview Press, 1980.

Ungar, Estar. "The Struggle over the Chinese Community in Vietnam 1946–1986", *Pacific Affairs*, no. 4 (Winter 1987–1988): 596–614.

Veyne, Paul. *Les Grecs ont-ils cru à leurs mythes?* (Did the Greeks believe their myths?). Paris: Seuil, 1983.

Vickermann, A. *The Fate of the Peasantry: Premature "Transition to Socialism" in the DRV*. New Haven: Yale University Press, 1986.

Vo Nguyên Giap. *Unforgettable Years and Months*. Cornell University, Southeast Asia Program, Data paper no. 99, Ithaca, 1975.

Walder, Andrew G. *Communist Neo-Traditionnalism: Work and Authority in Chinese Industry*. Berkeley: University of California Press, 1988.

White, Christine. "Mass Mobilisation and Ideological Transformation in the Vietnamese Land Reform Campaign", *Journal of Contemporary Asia*, Stockholm, 13, no. 1, 1983: 74–90.

Whitmore, John K. "Social Organisation and Confucian Thought in Vietnam", *Journal of Southeast Asian Studies*, Singapore, vol. XV, no. 2, September 1984: 296–306.

Whitmore, John K. and Pham Cao Duong. "The Vietnamese Sense of Past", *Vietnam Forum*, New Haven, 2, Winter–Spring 1983: 4–16.

Wiegersma, N. *Vietnam: Peasant Land, Peasant Revolution, Patriarchy and Collectivity in the Rural Economy*. New York: St. Martin's, 1988.

Woodside, Alexander. *Vietnam and the Chinese Model*. Cambridge: Harvard University Press, 1971.

———. "The Triumphs and Failures of Mass Education in Vietnam", *Pacific Affairs*, Vancouver, 56, no. 3, Fall 1983: 401–27.

Secondary Sources in Vietnamese

Bế Viết Đẳng dir. *50 năm các dân tộc thiểu số ở Việt Nam* (Fifty years of ethnic minority studies in Vietnam). Hanoi: nxb Khoa học Xã hội, 1995.

C.B. (Hồ Chí Minh). "Anh hùng giả và Anh hùng thật" (Real and false heroes), *Nhân dân*, no. 149, 21 November 1953.

Chiến Hữu. "Thi đua ái quốc" (Patriotic emulation), *Sinh hoạt nội bộ*, no. 8, May 1948: 16–7.

Đàm Ngọc Liên. "Chuyển sang cuộc thi đua mới" (Pass over to the new emulation), *Sự thật*, 1990: 5.

Đào Duy Ký. *Những người sống mãi* (Those who live forever). Hanoi: Vụ văn hoá đại chúng, 1956.

Đào Phiếu. *Nguyễn Văn Cừ, một Người lãnh đạo xuất sắc của Đảng* (Nguyễn Văn Cừ, an exceptional Party leader). Hanoi: nxb Sự thật, 1987.

Department of the National Assembly, *Lịch sử Quốc hội Việt Nam 1946–1960* (History of the National Assembly 1946–1960). Hanoi: nxb Chính trị Quốc gia, 1994.

Diệp Đình Hoa. "Vài vấn đề văn hóa người Việt Vùng Bắc Huyện Quỳnh Phụ, Thái Bình qua Tín ngưỡng thờ ở Định" (Some questions on North Vietnamese culture, Quỳnh Phụ district, Thái Bình on the rites and beliefs held in the community centre), *Tạp chí Dân tộc học*, Hanoi, no. 1, 1981: 37–46.

________. *Làng Nguyễn, Tìm hiểu làng Việt II* (The village of Nguyễn. Research on the Vietnamese village, II). Hanoi: nxb Khoa học xã hội, 1994.

Đinh Gia Khánh, Lê Hữu Tầng, dir. *Lễ hội truyền thống trong đời sống xã hội hiện đại* (Traditional festivals in contemporary society). Hanoi: nxb Khoa học xã hội, 1993.

Đoàn Giỏi. *Trần Văn Ơn*. Hanoi: nxb Thanh niên, 1963.

Đồng Thế. *Kể chuyện Lê Hồng Phong* (Telling the story of Lê Hồng Phong). Hanoi: nxb Kim Đồng, 1970.

Dương Đại Lâm. *Pắc Bó, quê tôi* (Pắc Bó, the land of my birth). Hồi ký, Hanoi: nxb Quân đội Nhân Dân, 1967.

Hải Như, Nguyễn Văn Thiện. *Người anh hùng Vàng Pè* (The hero of Vàng Pè). Hanoi: nxb Phổ thông, 1965.

Hồ Chí Minh. *Con người xã hội chủ nghĩa* (Socialist man). Hanoi: nxb Sự thật, 1961.

________. *Toàn tập* (Complete works). 7 volumes. Hanoi: nxb Chính trị Quốc gia, 1995.

________. *Về người xây dựng con người mới* (On building the new man). Hanoi: nxb Chính trị Quốc gia, 1995.

Hoàng Cầm. *Chặng đường mười nghìn ngày. Hồi Ký* (An eternal voice, memoir). Hanoi: nxb Quân đội Nhân Dân, 1995.

Hoàng Thị Ái. *Một lòng với Đảng* (My heart is with the Party). Hanoi: nxb Phụ Nữ, 1964.

Hoàng Tranh. *Hồ Chí Minh và Trung Quốc* (Hồ Chí Minh and China). Beijing: nxb Giải phóng quân, 1987.

Hoàng Văn Hoan. *Giọt nước trong biển cả* (A drop of water in the ocean). Beijing: nxb tin Việt Nam, 1986.

Lê Mậu Hàn. *Đảng cộng sản Việt Nam, các Đại hội và Hội nghị Trung ương* (The Vietnamese Communist Party, the congresses and plenums). Hanoi: nxb Chính trị Quốc gia, 1995.

Lê Minh Ngọc. "Tín ngưỡng Thành hoàng và ý thức tâm lý cộng đồng làng xã" (Belief in spirits and village psychology), in *Nông thôn Việt Nam trong lịch sử*, vol. I. Hanoi: nxb Khoa học Xã hội, 1977, p. 337.

Lê Quốc Sử. *Ngô Gia Tự*. Hanoi: nxb Kim Đồng, 1979.

Lê Văn Hiến. *Nhật ký của một Bộ trưởng* (Journal of a minister). Danang: nxb Đà Nẵng, 1995

Lê Văn Kỳ. *Mối quan hệ giữa truyền thuyết người Việt và hội lễ về anh hùng* (Relationship between Vietnamese tradition and festivals for new heroes). Hanoi: nxb Khoa học Xã hội, 1997.

Lưu Văn Lợi. *Năm Mười năm Ngoại giao Việt Nam 1945–1995* (Fifty years of Vietnamese diplomacy), Tap I. Ngoại giao Việt Nam 1945–1975. Hanoi: nxb Công an nhân dân, 1997.

Mai Văn Tạo. *Anh Tu Thạch* (Mister Thạch). Hanoi: nxb Y học, 1981.

Minh Huê. *Con gái người anh hùng, Truyện thiếu nhi* (A heroic girl, a story for children). Hanoi: nxb Kim Đồng, 1972.

Ngô Gia Khảm. *Một đảng viên, hồi ký cách mạng của anh hùng Ngô Gia Khảm* (Member of the Party. Revolutionary memoir of the hero Ngô Gia Khảm). Hanoi: nxb Kim Đồng, 1965.

Ngô Thông. *Chiến sỹ thi đua dân công Nguyễn Thị Cam* (Nguyễn Thị Cam, emulation fighter of the people's work). Phòng Chính trị Bộ Tư lệnh LK V xb, 1953.

Nguyễn Đức Thuận. *Bất khuất* (Invincible). Hanoi: nxb Thanh niên, 1967.

Nguyễn Khánh Toàn. "Việc xây dựng con người mới và trách nhiệm của khoa học xã hội" (On building the new man and the responsibiliy of the social sciences), *Học Tập*, Hanoi, no. 8, 1968: 51.

Nguyễn Kiến Giang. "Thờ cúng tổ tiên trong đời sống tâm linh người Việt" (Ancestor worship in the spiritual life of the Vietnamese), *Xưa và Nay*, Hanoi, no. 23, 1 January 1996: 16–8.

Nguyên Ngọc. *Đất nước đứng lên* (The nation arises). Hanoi: nxb Văn học, 1956.

Nguyễn Thị Thập. *Qua những chặng đường, hồi ký* (A crossroad of paths: A memoir). Hanoi: nxb Phụ Nữ, 1982.

Nguyễn Từ Chi. *Góp phần nghiên cứu văn hoá và tộc người* (Contribution to the study of culture and people). Hanoi: nxb Văn hoá thông tin-Tạp chí Văn hóa Nghệ thuật, 1996.

Nguyễn Tuân. *Ký* (Journal). Hanoi: nxb Văn học, 1976.

Phạm Công Minh and Nguyễn Quang Sáng. *Đầu tầu 109*! (At the head of train 109!), *Chuyện anh hùng Lao Động Lê Minh Đức*. Hanoi: nxb Lao Động, 1958.

Phạm Thị Kim. *Phạm Hồng Thái*. HCMC: nxb Văn nghệ, 1994.

Phan Bội Châu. *Việt Nam vong quốc sử* (History of the loss of the Vietnamese nation). Saigon: Tao Đàn, 1969.

________. *Việt Nam nghĩa liệt sĩ* (Hommage to Vietnamese martyrs). Saigon: Tao Đàn, 1969.

Phan Ngọc. *Bản sắc văn hoá Việt Nam* (Cultural identity in Vietnam). Hanoi: nxb Văn học, Hanoi, 2002.

Research Institute on Marxism-Leninism and Hồ Chí Minh Thought, *Hồ Chí Minh Biên Niên Tiểu Sử* (Hồ Chí Minh biographical account). Vol. I 1890–1930 published in 1992; vol. II 1930–1945 and vol. III 1945–46 published in 1993; vol. IV 1946–1950 published in 1994; vol. V 1951–1954, vol. VI 1955–1957 and vol. VII 1958–1960 published in 1995. Hanoi: nxb Chính trị Quốc gia.

Research Institute on Marxism-Leninism and Hồ Chí Minh Thought, *Lịch sử Đảng cộng sản Việt Nam* (History of the Vietnamese Communist Party), Vol II. 1954–1975. Hanoi: nxb Chính trị Quốc gia, 1995.

Tạ Thị Kiều, Nguyệt Tú. *Lớn lên với Thôn xóm* (Growing up in the village). Hanoi: nxb Phụ Nữ, 1966.

Tầm Nguyên. "Anh hùng chủ nghĩa" (Heroism), *Sinh hoạt nội bộ*, no. 4–5, 11–2, 1947.

Tân Sinh (Hồ Chí Minh). *Đời sống mới* (The new life). Việt Minh Nghệ An, 1948.

Thành Tín (Bùi Tín). *Hoa xuyên tuyết, hồi ký* (Novel of a water-lily, a memoir). Irvine: nxb Nhân quyền, 1991.

Thành Tín (Bùi Tín). *Mặt thật, hồi ký chính trị của Bùi Tín* (Face open. Political memoir of Bùi Tín). Irvine: Saigon press, 1993.

Thế Lệ. *Nguyên tắc khen thưởng và tiêu chuẩn Thi đua* (Principles of compensation and criteria in emulation). Hà Tĩnh, 1967.

Tô Hoài. *Vừ A Dính*. Hanoi: nxb Kim Đồng, 1962.

Tôn Quang Phiệt. *Phan Bội Châu và một giai đoạn Lịch sử chống Pháp của nhân dân Việt Nam* (Phan Bôi Châu, a historical period in the Vietnamese people's struggle against France). Hanoi: nxb Văn Hóa, 1958.

Tôn Thất Tùng. *Đường vào khoa học* (The road towards science). Hanoi: nxb Y học và Thể thao, 1974.

Trần Cần. *Mạc Thị Bưởi*. Hanoi: nxb Phổ thông, 1957.

________. Văn Huy. *Mẹ Suốt* (Mother Suốt). Hanoi: nxb Phổ Thông, 1967.

Trần Cần. Mai Lang. *Anh hùng Nguyễn Văn Trỗi* (The hero Nguyễn Văn Trỗi). Hanoi: nxb Phổ thông, 1967.

Trần Dân Tiên (aka Hồ Chí Minh). *Những mẩu chuyện về đời hoạt động của Hồ Chủ tịch* (Exemplary elements of the life of President Hồ). Hanoi: nxb Văn Học, 1960.

Trần Đăng Khoa. *Khúc hát người anh hùng* (Celebrating the hero). Hanoi: nxb Phụ Nữ, 1974.

Trần Đình Vân, Phan Thị Quyên. *Sống như anh* (To live like you). Hanoi: nxb Giáo Dục, 1965.

Trần Hoàng Môi, Lâm Sam. *Sáng tạo con người mới trong điện ảnh* (Creating the new man in the movies). Hanoi: nxb Văn hoá Nghệ thuật, 1962.

Trần Huy Liệu. "Anh hùng tạo thời thế hay thời thế tạo Anh hùng" (Does the hero create circumstances or do circumstances create the hero), *Nghiên cứu Lịch sử*, Hanoi, no. 96, March 1967: 1–3.

Trần văn Giàu. *Giá trị tinh thần truyền thống của dân tộc* (Value of the traditional spirit of the people). Hanoi: nxb Khoa học xã hội, 1980.

Trường Chinh. *Thi đua ái quốc và chủ nghĩa anh hùng mới* (Patriotic emulation and the new heroism). Nhà tuyên truyền và văn nghệ, 1953.

________. *Tăng cường tính Đảng đi sau vào cuộc sống mới của để phục vụ nhân dân, phục vụ Cách mạng tốt hơn nữa — Văn nghệ xây dựng chủ nghĩa xã hội và đấu tranh thống nhất nước nhà* (Strengthening the nature of the Party to better participate in the New Life in order to better serve the people and the revolution — The Arts build socialism and the struggle for national unification). Hanoi: nxb Văn hoá nghệ thuật, 1963, p.55.

TTKHXHNVQG, Institute of History, *Lịch sử Việt Nam 1954–1975* (History of Vietnam from 1954 to 1975). Hanoi: nxb Khoa học xã hội, 1995.

Văn Tạo. *Chủ nghĩa anh hùng cách mạng Việt Nam* (Revolutionary heroism in Vietnam). Hanoi: nxb Khoa học xã hội, 1972.

Văn Tạo and Nguyễn Quang Ân, eds. *Ban Văn Sử Địa 1953–1959* (The Culture-History-Geography Committee 1953–1959). Hanoi: Institut d'histoire, 1993.

Võ Nguyên Giáp. *Chiến đấu trong vòng vây* (The surrounded struggle). Hanoi: nxb Quân đội Nhân Dân, nxb Thanh niên, 1995.

Vũ Cao, Mai Văn Hiến. *Nguyễn Thị Chiên*. Việt Bắc: nxb Quân đội Nhân Dân, 1952.

Vũ Hồng. "*Sự ra đời của Đảng và bước ngoặt lịch sử của chủ nghĩa anh hùng*" (Birth of the party and the main stages of heroism), *Học tập*, Hanoi, no. 4, 1967: 75–81.

Vũ Khiêu. *Đạo đức mới* (A new morality). Hanoi: nxb Khoa học xã hội, 1974.

________. *Anh hùng và Nghệ sĩ* (Hero and artist). HCMC: nxb Văn học Giải phóng, 1975.

________. *Tư tưởng đạo đức Hồ Chí Minh* (Hồ Chí Minh's concept of virtue). Hanoi: nxb Khoa học xã hội, 1993.

Anh hùng lực lượng vũ trang nhân dân (Hero of the armed forces). Vol. I: 1978; vol. II: 1980; vol. III: 1981; vol. IV: 1982; vol. V: 1983. Hanoi: nxb Quân đội Nhân Dân.

Avoóc Hồ, Hồi ký cách mạng (Uncle Hồ, memoir of the revolution). Hanoi: nxb Kim Đồng, nxb Văn hóa-dân tộc, 1977.

Con Đường Cách Mạng — Hoàng Văn Thụ, Lê Thanh Nghị, Nguyễn Duy Trinh, Trần Độ (The revolutionary way. Hoàng Văn Thụ, Lê Thanh Nghị, Nguyễn Duy Trinh, Trần Độ). Hanoi: nxb Thanh niên, 1970.

Danh nhân đất Việt Nam (Famous people from Vietnam). 3 volumes. Hanoi: nxb Thanh Niên, 1989.

Danh nhân sự Việt Nam (Famous people from Vietnam). 2 volumes. Hanoi: nxb Giáo Dục, 1987.

Gương liệt sĩ (Exemplary martyrs). Hanoi: nxb Kim Đồng, 1984.

Hồ Chủ tịch dân chủ, kỷ luật và đạo đức cách mạng (President Hô, democracy, discipline, and revolutionary morality). Hanoi: nxb Sự thật, 1967.

Hồ chủ tịch nói về dân chủ, kỷ luật và Đạo đức cách mạng (President Hồ speaks about democracy, discipline and revolutionary morality). Hanoi: nxb Sự thật, 1967.

Những ngày kỷ niệm lớn trong nước (The important days of remembrance in the country). Hanoi: nxb Quân đội Nhân dân, 1972.

Sơ tuyển Văn Thơ yêu nước và cách mạng (Notebook of patriotic and revolutionary poems). Hanoi: nxb Giáo Dục, 1959.

Thế hệ anh hùng, đề cương giới thiệu cuốn sách Người tốt, việc tốt (Heroic generation, text presenting the book — the good man works well). Hanoi: nxb Thanh niên, 1969.

Truyện bảy anh hùng. Truyện anh hùng Chiến sĩ thi đua (History of seven heroes. History of heroes/emulation fighters). Hanoi: nxb Chính trị Quốc gia, 1954.

Tuổi Trẻ anh hùng (The hero's youth). Hanoi: nxb Thanh niên, 1969.

Vận động phong trào thi đua ái quốc (Activities of the patriotic emulation movement). Uỷ ban Vận động thi đua ái quốc Trung ương, Sở Thông tin Nam Bộ, 1949.

Việt Nam đất nước Anh hùng (Vietnam heroic land). Hanoi: nxb Sự thật, 1975.

INDEX